D1293878

"Teachers and school mental health consultants will find this book a major resource; it's eminently instructive and practical in guiding their work with students who have emotional and/or behavioral problems. The very experienced authors combine functional behavioral analysis with an in-depth understanding about four common types of challenging students, and provide a wealth of strategies for optimally changing, teaching, and interacting with such children."

—*Richard E. Mattison, MD, director of school consultation and professor of psychiatry, Stony Brook University School of Medicine*

"*The Behavior Code* presents a cogent, succinct, highly readable support system for teachers, behavior specialists, and site administrators. Authors Rappaport and Minahan employ the process of Antecedent/Behavior/ Consequence data collection coupled with case studies to illustrate its practicality and application. The manual is highly useful for staff professional development related to student behavior support plans and behavior intervention plans, both of which support improved student learning."

—*Leslie M. Codianne, associate superintendent of student support services, Monterey Peninsula Unified School District*

The Behavior Code

The Behavior Code

A Practical Guide to Understanding and Teaching the Most Challenging Students

JESSICA MINAHAN
NANCY RAPPAPORT, MD

Harvard Education Press
Cambridge, Massachusetts

Eighth Printing, 2020

Library of Congress Control Number 2011941943

Paperback ISBN: 978-1-61250-136-9
Library Edition ISBN: 978-1-61250-137-6

Published by Harvard Education Press,
an imprint of the Harvard Education Publishing Group

Harvard Education Press
8 Story Street
Cambridge, MA 02138

Cover Design: Sarah Henderson
Cover Photo: Jaime Monfort/Getty Images
The typefaces used in this book are Minion and Myriad Pro.

Contents

Introduction   **1**

CHAPTER 1   **Breaking the Code**   **7**
             What Teachers Need to Know About Behavior

CHAPTER 2   **The FAIR Plan**   **27**
             Putting the FAIR Plan into Practice

CHAPTER 3   **"Get Away from Me!"**   **43**
             The Student with Anxiety-Related Behavior

             FAIR Plan for the Student with Anxiety-Related
             Behaviors   **87**

CHAPTER 4   **"You're Not the Boss of Me!"**   **91**
             The Student with Oppositional Behavior

             FAIR Plan for the Student with Oppositional Behavior   **122**

CHAPTER 5   **"I Don't Care"**   **127**
             The Student with Withdrawn Behavior

             FAIR Plan for the Student with Withdrawn Behavior   **152**

CHAPTER 6   **"I Didn't Mean To . . ."**   **157**
             The Student with Sexualized Behavior

             FAIR Plan for the Student with Sexualized Behavior   **187**

CHAPTER 7   **Commonly Asked Questions**   **191**
             Some Answers, and a Challenge

APPENDIX A   **Sample Antecedent, Behavior, and Consequences (ABC) Data Sheet**   203

APPENDIX B   **Curriculum Resources**   205

APPENDIX C   **Lunch Buddies Permission Form**   210

APPENDIX D   **Technology Resources**   211

APPENDIX E   **Calming Activities**   219

APPENDIX F   **Self-Monitoring Sheet**   222

APPENDIX G   **Taking Responsibility for Choices Worksheet**   225

APPENDIX H   **FAIR Plan Implementation Worksheet**   227

Notes   229

Acknowledgments   243

About the Authors   245

Index   247

Introduction

About 10 percent of the school population—or 9 to 13 million children—struggle with mental health problems. In a typical classroom of twenty, chances are good that one or two students are dealing with serious psychosocial stressors relating to poverty, domestic violence, abuse and neglect, or a psychiatric disorder. There is also growing evidence that the number of children suffering the effects of trauma and those with autism-related social deficits is also on the rise.

These children represent the most challenging students in our classrooms today. Their mental health problems make it difficult for them to regulate their emotions and focus on learning. Most of the time, they lack basic skills necessary to regulate their behaviors and, sometimes, to even recognize their own actions. They can be inflexible and have outbursts for no apparent reason—disrupting the classroom routine daily. They can disengage socially or be clingy, sleepy, or irritable. They can defy school personnel repeatedly and argue incessantly. Sometimes—although more rarely—they make sexual gestures and exhibit other forms of sexually inappropriate behavior. They are the students who keep administrators up at night and the ones teachers fear and even dread having in their classes. Many of their stories are heartbreaking.

Despite their best efforts, school providers do not always do a good job with these students. Children with behavioral challenges often fail in school, waste too much time in detentions and suspensions, fall years behind in academics, and never master the skills they need to make adequate progress. Although schools have become a major site for students to receive mental health interventions over the past thirty years, school programs are still relatively fragmented. Counselors and teachers lack adequate time and resources to provide evidence-based curricula and classroom strategies that, when consistently delivered, can change students' behavior. School psychologists are often relegated to testing students, creating individual education programs (IEPs), and dealing with bureaucratic demands of students in special education. School counselors have a high caseload and must devote the majority of their time to students categorized with the most severe emotional and behavioral disturbances. One result is that disruptive students are frequently referred for psychiatric medication before comprehensive and effective behavioral plans have been attempted.

Teachers are often ill equipped to respond to students' challenging behaviors. These educators receive minimal training in child and adolescent mental health issues or to develop interventions that can help reduce behavioral incidents and increase access to the curriculum.[1] The usual methods, such as sticker charts with an emphasis on students' performance to gain rewards, or sending the students to the principal's office, usually fall flat with these students.

School staff today are under enormous pressure to show progress for every student every year. Yet they are in a bind. One disruptive child can effectively derail an entire lesson. Teachers recognize their own problems in dealing with disruptive students and often have little confidence in how to change the trajectory of the student. Surveys show that coping with disruptive students is teachers' number one problem.[2]

Without effective behavior intervention plans, staff often feel they must choose between the risky route of putting academic demands on these students and the path of least resistance, that is, minimizing academic demands to avoid the students' becoming more disruptive.

Teachers do not need to make this choice. For thirty years combined, we have worked as consultants helping teachers and other school personnel to work with the most disruptive and difficult-to-reach students. We have helped administrators, teachers, and other school staff in many schools to create behavior intervention plans that combine an understanding of child psychological disorders with research-based behavior modification strategies. We share a common philosophy that these hard-to-reach students are not meeting their potential, and that it is crucial to support schools and teachers in their efforts to productively and successfully engage these students. Based on consultation experience, we apply both clinical and behavioral theory into practical strategies that, in many cases, keep students from being placed out of district or in self-contained classrooms and that reduce or eliminate their inappropriate behaviors.

In this book, we provide the conceptual background for breaking the code of what we believe are the four most challenging students in the classroom: students with *anxiety-related, oppositional, withdrawn,* and *sexualized* behaviors. We focus on students in K–6 for several important reasons. First, elementary teachers are working in more inclusive environments than teachers of older students. Consequently, K–6 teachers particularly need support. Second, early intervention and school success is essential for these younger students: the longer students exhibit inappropriate behavior, the less likely they are to improve. Third, older students are often identified as having a diagnosis that then allows them to access to specialized support services.

Our experience in schools has taught us that to be effective and help each student reach his or her potential, teachers need a new approach to clearly understand what drives student behavior. Teachers also need a variety of strategies that allow them to intervene effectively before the behavior is entrenched.

We include possible causes for these behaviors to help teachers understand the students' behavior and decipher patterns—on the part of both students and staff—that will help these educators choose strategies that can often change students' behavior dramatically. We have included some of the students' stories in this book because it is important to maintain hope for these children when it can seem as if their problems will never get better.

Building on an understanding of what drives behavior, we provide a framework for a different kind of behavioral intervention plan that we call the FAIR Plan (for functional hypothesis, accommodations, interaction strategies, and response strategies). Unlike typical behavior intervention plans, FAIR takes our deep clinical understanding and knowledge of multidisciplinary research and best practices for these students and applies them within a behavioral construct. Traditional approaches don't take into account an understanding of mental health and the student's skill deficits contributing to the behavior. Through the FAIR Plan, we spell out the best ways to intervene and support students with the four types of challenging behaviors.

The letters in FAIR represent the four components of a behavior intervention plan. With a *functional hypothesis and antecedent analysis,* teachers document behaviors and make a hypothesis about what the student is communicating through his or her behavior and what in the environment could be a catalyst for the behavior. *Accommodations* need to be in place to help the student function better. *Interaction strategies* will promote desired behavior, and *response strategies* may be considered if prevention efforts fail.

As may be obvious, we use the acronym FAIR for a philosophical reason as well. We believe strongly that without more effective behavioral support like the FAIR Plan, these most challenging students don't have—and won't have—a chance to learn to their potentials in our schools.

The FAIR Plan is a flexible, empathetic, and practical approach that puts a primary emphasis on preventing inappropriate, disruptive, or uncooperative behaviors before they occur. It also emphasizes strategies for teaching the skills that students need in order to behave appropriately in school. Our method also requires school staff to consider how their responses may unintentionally encourage students to continue their inappropriate, unproductive behaviors.

FAIR Plans are best used and adapted for students in consultation or collaboration with school and outside personnel. Appropriate professionals may include psychologists, social workers, inclusion specialists, behavior analysts, and child psychiatrists. Mental health evaluation is a necessary component for many of these students with behavioral problems in the classroom. However, many teachers work in schools without adequate professional support. Indeed, this lack of support is a major reason why we decided to write this book. We wanted teachers who may not have access to child psychiatrists and behavioral analysts to benefit from the lessons we have learned about what makes a difference with these students. We have constructed the FAIR Plan so that it can be used as a behavior intervention plan for students both in special education and in regular education.

The early chapters in this book are meant to lay a foundation for understanding the remainder of the book. In chapter 1, we discuss the fundamental concepts that drive behavior in general, as well as inappropriate behavior in children. In chapter 2, we introduce the conceptual steps that teachers will use to construct a FAIR Plan and a simple, concrete way of documenting patterns needed to begin to put together a plan for each child. We also explain the individual components of a FAIR Plan. We dedicate chapters 3 through 6 for each of the four challenging behaviors and examine the various ways these types of students present in schools. In each of these chapters, we offer a brief overview of relevant psychiatric diagnoses. We then provide strategies to intervene within each category of behavior. Because some of these strategies can be used for several of the behaviors we discuss, we have located particular strategies in the chapter where they are most pertinent. For example, we discuss how to manage transitions and how to encourage self-monitoring in the chapter on students with anxiety-related behaviors, as they can particularly benefit from these strategies. These practices can be helpful for other students, too. At the end of each of these chapters, we provide a template of a FAIR Plan tailored for each behavior addressed in the chapter. Teachers can use these templates to construct FAIR Plans for their own students.

Chapter 7 answers some commonly asked questions that school staff have posed to us over the years as we have worked with them to implement this approach. At the end of the book, we have included numerous appendices devoted to resources that teachers can also customize to implement some of the strategies in the FAIR Plans.

Finally, a few words about terminology. Although much of this book is addressed to teachers, this book can be used by anyone in the classroom, no matter what his or her position (e.g., inclusion aides, classroom assistants, interns). This book is also aimed at general education teachers in inclusive settings, special education teachers in self-contained classrooms, and educational and clinical specialists and administrators consulting to teachers. *Everyone* can learn to change behavior—you do not have to be a seasoned therapist or be able to prescribe medication. The behavioral approach is an incredibly effective, research-based methodology that school staff can do and can do well.[3]

We also use the terms *school counselor, school mental health clinician,* and *school social worker* interchangeably throughout the book, recognizing that schools have a variety of mental health clinicians who provide therapeutic support for students. When we refer to the student's *team* throughout the book, we are referring to both the IEP team in the case of a student receiving special education services and the larger school team (e.g., mental health staff and administrators) for students not receiving special education. Parents are a member of both types of teams.

We use the pronoun *we* throughout the book for ease of reading, even though we sometimes may be describing the clinical experiences of only one of us—either Jessica or Nancy alone. As a convenience, we use the pronouns *he* and *she* interchangeably throughout this book when referring to a generic student. The students who are named in this book represent composites of students from our practice, and while many of the patterns of behavior are real, any resemblance to a particular student we have treated is purely coincidental. We are excited to offer the practical strategies outlined in the FAIR Plans. These strategies are a product of our years of working with the most challenging students *in the moment*, even in schools cramped for space, classrooms with large student-to-teacher ratios, and with students who have burned bridges with the school.

Every day, we are amazed by how much effort it can require to see improvement in a child who is struggling with challenging behavior. Even as seasoned clinicians, we find that having a systematic approach helps ground us and give us momentum. As we constructed and distilled these FAIR Plans from what we hope is our cumulative wisdom, we had a fierce desire that teachers not be left alone. Without an effective plan to change these challenging behaviors, the students and the teachers will ultimately pay a substantial cost.

CHAPTER 1

Breaking the Code

What Teachers Need to Know About Behavior

Students with emotional and behavioral challenges are performing poorly both academically and behaviorally in our schools.[1] One recent study found that these students made no significant progress in reading, math, or behavior over the course of a full school year, whether they were in a special education or full inclusion classroom.[2] They are more likely than students with other disabilities to be suspended for a long period and more likely to change teachers, classes, and schools than their disabled and non-disabled peers.[3] Not surprisingly, the outcomes for these students are bleak. In 2006–2007, only 20 percent of students with emotional and behavioral disturbance (E/BD) ages 14 to 21 who exited the school system received a high school diploma.[4] Of students with E/BD, 48 percent drop out of grades 9–12, as opposed to 30 percent of all students with disabilities and 24 percent of all high school students.[5] After high school, only 30 percent of students with E/BD were employed, and what's worse, 58 percent had been arrested.[6]

However, if the classroom is set up to promote their success, these students and other challenging students who have similar behaviors but may not have individual education programs (IEPs) can improve their performance in school and succeed. We have seen many students who were discouraged and considered lost causes turn around and thrive in the classroom with the strategies described in this book. It is our responsibility as educators to reach these students and provide the support and opportunity they need to successfully learn and achieve.

In this chapter, we will lay out the fundamental concepts that will help teachers to understand the behavior of even their most challenging students. In the next chapter, we will show teachers how to construct a FAIR Plan that will put students on a more productive path. In doing so, we hope to demystify behavior and give teachers a concrete framework they can use to solve problems productively and intervene effectively. Our perspective is that all teachers who are willing to be behavior detectives can learn to identify why challenging students behave a certain way, what school factors contribute to the behavior, and what strategies will lead to more appropriate, constructive behavior for school and for life.

WHY CHALLENGING STUDENTS ARE SO CHALLENGING

When intervening with students during a busy school day, teachers often make instantaneous assessments of why a student acted a certain way, and the educators then respond according to their assumptions. When a student acts inappropriately, it is also common for teachers to pull that student aside to explain or to coach the child on how to behave better next time. These quick responses work with most students because their behavior seems logical and fits with common patterns that are easy to recognize and anticipate. Most students have the fundamental skills that are required to act appropriately, so with help and support, they are capable of self-correcting.

With challenging students, however, the intent of the behavior can be unclear and confusing to teachers and does not necessarily fit into known patterns. Teachers can also overestimate a student's ability to behave in a given moment. After many years of consulting with school personnel, we have learned that students who are anxious, oppositional, or withdrawn or who demonstrate sexualized behavior can be especially baffling to even the most experienced teachers and specialists. The difficult reality is that teachers are often called upon to react quickly to a behavior, even when they do not understand it. If a student is racing out of the school building or screaming in the cafeteria, teachers need to respond immediately to control the situation. However, making an incorrect assumption—which is so easy to do with our most challenging students—can lead to an inadequate response and repetition of the behavior.

For example, one day, Jimmy, a second-grade student, pushed Devan off the computer. When the teacher saw this, she assumed Jimmy pushed Devan to get a turn on the computer faster. Her logical response, based on this assessment, was to ban Jimmy from using the computer for the remainder of the day. Although it wasn't obvious at that moment, after she looked at patterns of Jimmy's behavior over time (his pattern of aggressiveness toward Devan during social times and picking him as his partner during science and physical education time), the teacher realized that rather than pushing Devan to get a turn on the computer, as she had assumed, Jimmy was trying to engage Devan socially. Banning Jimmy from the computer was not a response that encouraged Jimmy to learn more appropriate ways of interacting with peers. Instead, it punished him for his failed attempt to interact with the other students. The teacher's response and the reason for Jimmy's behavior were mismatched, and therefore the intervention was ineffective.

Interpreting behavior and understanding the motivation behind it can be difficult. We find it helpful to tell teachers that challenging behavior can often be *counterintuitive*. For example, a child wants to make a friend, but does so by pushing a classmate off a chair. Or, as we discuss later on, some children seek any kind of attention, even if it means provoking teachers to yell at them.

In addition to the counterintuitive nature of students' challenging behavior, it is also often unexpected. Teachers tell us that the most frustrating aspect is that such behavior seems to come out of the blue or for no clear reason. Take the case of Susan, a kindergartner with Asperger's syndrome. Susan was beginning to line up for chorus with her class, when she rushed over to the reading nook area, where Brendan was asleep on the beanbag chair. Susan yelled, "Why is he sleeping? Wake him up, wake him *up!*" and then lunged toward Brendan. The surprised teacher, Ms. Rogers, separated them so that Brendan wouldn't be hurt. As a response, Ms. Rogers revoked Susan's reward time on the computer and took her to the principal's office to call her mother.

Ms. Rogers explained to Susan that it's OK if sometimes, students are tired and sleep in school. The teacher's assumption was that a student doing something out of the norm disturbed Susan, who, like many students with Asperger's syndrome, is very rule-oriented. However, when questioned about the incident hours later, Susan remarked, "He can't sleep there; I need it after chorus." As it turns out, Susan was afraid that Brendan would sleep too long in the beanbag and that it would not be available for her after chorus, when she would use it for a calming break. Once Ms. Rogers had this information, she was able to appropriately develop a plan B with Susan: if the reading nook area wasn't available for her calming breaks, Susan could use a nearby office. This plan was written on the bottom of Susan's daily schedule posted on her desk, helping to relieve her anxiety. Ms. Rogers's initial response to the behavior (explaining why some students sleep at school) was based on the incorrect assumption that Susan was upset that a student was doing something out of the norm. Therefore, Ms. Rogers's response might not have prevented Susan's behavior from recurring the next time the child saw another student resting on the beanbag chair. Understanding the reason for Susan's behavior and offering the appropriate intervention helped to relieve Susan's anxiety and potentially eliminated a future outburst.

In addition to the students' behavior being counterintuitive because of confusing and unpredictable reasons for the behavior, some challenging students may have inconsistent or underrecognized difficulty in performing a skill. Even when teachers do correctly assess the intent of a student's behavior, their instincts can still fail them when teaching the student a more appropriate, alternative behavior. When students act inappropriately, it is the job of the teachers to teach them a suitable replacement behavior—for example, "Instead of pushing, you need to ask for a turn."[7] If the replacement strategy being taught is too difficult for the student to master, these interventions fail. Teachers never knowingly ask or expect a student to do something that he or she cannot do. However, at a given moment, what the student is able to do or understand can be unclear or inconsistent to the teacher. Students with trauma histories, impulsivity, oppositional or inflexible behavior, depression, or anxiety can fluctuate in performance and ability according to their *current internal state*.[8] Teachers can believe that students are more capable than they actually are at a given moment, thinking, "I don't know why he's flipping out while playing the recorder. He wasn't bothered by the noise yesterday." Or, "She wrote three pages last week, and now she isn't even writing a sentence—she's just being lazy." These complicated students can also have an uneven profile, where sometimes they are sophisticated and age-appropriate, yet at other times they can't complete simple tasks that a much younger child can do.[9] For example, a student may be very socially savvy and charming in conversations with teachers, but have a tantrum over not getting the blue marker during art class. This inconsistency can lead a teacher to have unrealistic expectations for the student.

Ms. Lombardi, a seasoned physical education teacher, accidentally picked an intervention that was too difficult for her fifth-grade student. Ms. Lombardi had been teaching Goran since he was in kindergarten, so she was confident she "got him." Even though he had trouble in the classroom because of his frequent interruptions and impulsivity, he was doing well in P.E. On the first day of the ropes unit, Ms. Lombardi had the students buddy up and take turns on each of the stations. She paired Goran with Julia. Usually, partners alternated between going first and second at each station. At the first station, Goran was excited to be able to climb the ropes before Julia. When it was time for Goran and Julia to go to the second station, where they would swing with a rope over an obstacle, Goran started yelling and punching the floor mat. Ms. Lombardi rushed over to ask what was happening. Julia shrugged her shoulders, saying, "I didn't do anything." Ms. Lombardi asked, "Was it your turn to go first, Julia?" Julia nodded. Ms. Lombardi knew that Goran had trouble taking turns. She guessed correctly that Goran had an outburst because he couldn't go first at this station. Ms. Lombardi explained to Goran that he had gone first on the last station and that it was Julia's turn. She told him he could wait right next to the rope for his turn. As Julia was about to grab the rope, Goran stole it and swung it away from her, hitting a nearby student in the head. Ms. Lombardi sent him to the office for the first time all year.

Ms. Lombardi assessed the reason for Goran's outburst correctly, but her intervention was unsuccessful. She knew that Goran had trouble taking turns and that usually reminding him to take turns did the trick. Because Goran was so excited about the ropes course and was so revved up, he was not able to wait near the rope without touching it. Reminding him to wait was unsuccessful because at that moment, he was especially impulsive and could not control his behavior as he had done in previous classes. In our consultation with Ms. Lombardi, she realized that Goran needed an accommodation to help him be patient during such a motivating activity, because of his limited impulse control in that situation. After consulting with us, she had a plan that when it was his partner's turn to go first for a highly motivating activity, she had him do push-up and sit-up contests with other students who were waiting in the corner of the gym. This was successful because he was busy and far from the rope station, a situation that decreased his chances of acting impulsively. Table 1.1 shows how the intuitive process that teachers often use for responding to behavior does not work with hard-to-reach students like Goran.

TABLE 1.1

Teachers' interpretation of the behavior of typical and hard-to-reach students

Steps of a teacher's response to a behavior	*How the intuitive process works for typical students*	*How the intuitive process does not work for hard-to-reach students*
1. Teacher assesses why the student behaved a certain way.	The intent of the behavior is transparent and logical. The teacher can come to the correct assessment quickly. Example: Jimmy pushes Devan off the computer so he can have a turn.	The intent of behavior can be deceiving. It's not logical or transparent. The teacher can get it wrong when making a quick assessment. Example: Jimmy pushes Devan off the computer to engage him socially.
2. Teacher responds to student according to his or her assessment of why the student behaved that way.	Since the assessment is correct, the teacher's response will most likely deter or reinforce the behavior, as desired. This response will help the student learn appropriate behavior. Example: Teacher does not allow Jimmy access to the computer.	Since the teacher's assessment was incorrect, the teacher will assign a response that does not successfully deter or reinforce the behavior. This will not help the student learn appropriate behavior. Example: Teacher does not allow Jimmy access to the computer, a consequence that does not address Jimmy's inability to interact with a peer appropriately.
3. Teacher teaches the student a replacement behavior that the student is capable of doing.	The teacher communicates to the student some alternative, more appropriate ways of behaving that will get the student what he or she wants. The student can implement the replacement strategy with minimal coaching and intervention from the teacher. Example: The teacher reminds Jimmy that in the future, he needs to wait nicely for his turn on the computer.	This step can fail because of one of the following reasons: 1. The teacher has incorrectly assessed the behavior and incorrectly responded to the behavior. The teacher will then teach a student an irrelevant replacement behavior that the student will not implement, because it does not match the reason the student behaved that way. Example: Reminding Jimmy how to appropriately wait for the computer doesn't teach him appropriate ways to get Devan's attention. 2. The student doesn't have the prerequisite skills to demonstrate the replacement behavior. Example: Asking Goran to wait inches away from the extremely motivating ropes station is not something he is capable of at that moment, because of his severe impulsivity.

ESSENTIAL CONCEPTS FOR UNDERSTANDING BEHAVIOR

Why did a student punch a classmate in the face? Why won't the kindergartner perform simple requests? Why does another student growl at morning meeting time? Why does a fourth-grader sob and try to bolt from the playground? Understanding the following critical concepts helps teachers choose how to intervene better with students' problematic behavior: [10]

- Misbehavior is a symptom of an underlying cause.
- Behavior is communication.
- Behavior has a function.
- Behavior occurs in patterns.
- The only behavior teachers can control is their own.
- Behavior can be changed.

Misbehavior Is a Symptom of an Underlying Cause

A student would behave if he or she could. If the student is displaying problematic, maladaptive behavior, it is a symptom of an *underdeveloped skill*.[11] When students blow up or act out, it is a sign that they are stuck and can't cope with the situation. The problem many teachers face is that most of the behavior demonstrated by students with emotional and behavioral challenges looks purposeful. For example, after being asked to clean up after a snack, a student says to the teacher, "Why don't you [expletive] pick it up yourself?" with a smile on his face. Teachers may describe a student like this as manipulative, bratty, spoiled, controlling, or obnoxious. It is hard to like a student who repeatedly behaves in such an oppositional way.

For this reason, it's helpful to be reminded that students with extreme behavior challenges like those described in this book may be impaired by an emotional, behavioral disability or disadvantaged life situation—even though they don't look impaired. Teachers have a high tolerance for a student who uses a wheelchair and who needs extra help in P.E. class, because this student has a visible disability. However, since the nature of an emotional and behavioral disability can manifest itself in difficult, disruptive, aggressive behavior, most people do not react sympathetically. But it is vital to understand that the student *is* disabled. This student's brain is wired in a way that results in maladaptive, irrational behavior in moments of anger, frustration, and anxiety.

Some students are born with this brain wiring, but others have developed these brain changes from damaging life events. Some challenging students may be oversensitive to stress and have an overactive *fight-or-flight response*. During this response, a part of the brain (the *locus coeruleus*) sends signals to other parts of the brain and body to get help responding to a situation that is perceived as stressful.[12] Other students may lack basic social skills that are needed to navigate an interaction with a peer, the flexibility to follow a nonpreferred demand like "clean up after your snack," or the self-regulation to withstand an anxiety-producing task.

In one school, we were called in the wake of an incident with Alyssa, a third-grader. One day, out of the blue, Alyssa began to scream at her classmate Peter in the cafeteria, saying that she was going to kill him. Her teacher, Ms. Rose, intervened to separate her from a frightened Peter. After interviewing Alyssa, Ms. Rose thought she understood what provoked the incident. As it turned out, Alyssa had decided several hours before lunch that she was going to sit next to her classmate Leah at lunch. When Alyssa walked into the cafeteria, she saw Peter sitting next to Leah at the table. Alyssa flew into a rage and screamed that Peter was stupid and she was going to kill him. Ms. Rose was baffled by such a blatant overreaction to such a small setback. Ms. Rose kept asking Alyssa why she didn't problem-solve or act differently. But Ms. Rose neglected to understand that Alyssa's underlying problem was that she lacked some basic social skills that would have enabled her to negotiate a solution with Peter. In table 1.2, we outline some typical questions teachers

TABLE 1.2

Teachers' common reactive questions: the case of Alyssa

Ms. Rose's questions for Alyssa after the incident with Peter	*Skills needed to do what the teacher asked*
Why didn't Alyssa just sit in a different seat or ask Peter to switch seats?	Ability to self-calm, self-regulate, think flexibly
How does Alyssa think Peter felt when she flew off the handle and called him stupid?	Ability to understand another person's point of view
Doesn't Alyssa know she won't be able to sit in the cafeteria tomorrow, because she was unsafe today?	Ability to think about the consequences of one's actions

ask students after observing an incident, and the reasons why these questions don't work with our most challenging students.

What we want to emphasize is that some students in our classrooms *can't* behave optimally.[13] It is not these students' fault, and they should be thought of in an empathic way. With effective, comprehensive behavior intervention plans tailored to their unique circumstances, these students can change, even if they have a low threshold for anger, frustration, and anxiety.

Behavior Is Communication

All behavior is a form of communication. This is a key principle that helps when teachers are mystified by students' behavior. Even though students' behavior can look bizarre or disruptive, *their actions are purposeful and are their attempt to solve a problem.* Even if the behavior is not productive or is inappropriate, it is critical to step back and try to decipher what the student is trying to communicate and what the function (or intent) of the behavior is. Instead of asking, "Where did that come from?" ask, "What is the student communicating?" With practice, teachers can learn to stop and "listen" to the message the behavior is conveying. Rather than assume they know the reason for a behavior, teachers can ask these critical questions and, by answering them, begin to break the behavior code and respond in more productive ways.

Behavior is the primary way that babies communicate. Most people are able to imagine an infant's intent. If the baby is crying, the caretaker makes a best guess as to what the baby needs. Over time, ideally, the caretaker and the baby build an exquisitely attuned way of responding to each other, adapting as the toddler begins to babble and point and then gradually uses words to communicate. People understand that behavior is communicative with babies, but it becomes less apparent with older children once they can speak. However, just because a person is able to communicate in conventional ways such as speaking, writing, or drawing doesn't mean the person stops communicating through behavior. The more escalated the student is, inwardly as well as outwardly, the more likely he is to use behavior rather than words to show how he feels. When a student becomes agitated or explosive, he is irrational and less able to demonstrate the higher-level brain processing needed for achieving perspective and thinking about the future consequences of his behavior. This leaves a child more likely to growl or to kick the wall than to speak. Hiding under the table may be one way of avoiding an overwhelming task. The behavior exhibited is the student's most efficient way of communicating in that moment.

Behavior Has Function

Once teachers begin to see that behavior is communication, the next logical step is to ask, "Why is this message being relayed?" In his book *Severe Behavior Problems*, prominent behavior analyst Mark Durand categorizes all human behaviors as being motivated by four functions: to get attention, to escape or avoid something, to gain something tangible like an object, or to get some sensory (smell, taste, feel) satisfaction.[14] These functions are directly relevant to how teachers interact with students.

While it's normal for everyone's behavior to be motivated by one or more of these functions, behavior becomes problematic when it is unsafe, stigmatizing (produces negative attention from peers or teachers), interferes with learning, prevents access to other environments (gym, art, cafeteria, recess), or is not age appropriate.

Behavior is never random or aimless. Individuals would not repeat a behavior unless they were getting something out of it. The behavior, even when counterproductive, may be the most efficient alternative for the student.[15] Usually, it is a certain response from other people that fuels inappropriate behavior. This may be whining to get a teacher's attention, faking an illness to get out of class, or swearing to convey "I want your attention now." People are not usually conscious of seeking a certain response, especially if they have been acting this way over and over again. If a student repeatedly has tantrums and then gets to leave a classroom, she has learned that tantrums work for her in her desire to escape. To address this poor learning history, teachers first need to figure out what the student is getting from inappropriate behavior. If teachers find different ways to respond to the student's behavior so as not to inadvertently reinforce the behavior, they can shift the student's learned expectations. Once the behavior message is translated (e.g., "I want more attention!"), picking an effective intervention is easier.

Attention function

Most people at least occasionally exhibit attention-seeking behavior. A child works hard to read so that his teacher will praise him. A sixth-grade girl dresses up for the first day of school so a certain boy will notice her. Most of us want attention, and behavior can elicit many types of attention: notice from peers, teachers, a group, or an individual; nonverbal (e.g., smiling, nodding) or verbal attention; and positive (affirming) or negative (e.g., criticism, insults) attention. However, attention-seeking behavior becomes abnormal or problematic when students demand too much attention, seek negative attention, or resort to disruptive or aberrant behavior to get attention. Educators often unintentionally reinforce the behavior of students who are seeking negative attention. School systems are usually structured to punish students' undesired behavior. Common practices are to lecture a student, call a student's name when the child is misbehaving, or have the principal talk to the student. These responses all provide negative attention, which make them the wrong approach for students who are seeking it.

Rita was a fourth-grade student who interrupted repeatedly during class. Her teacher, Mr. O'Brien, was at his wit's end. He had tried to reward Rita if she didn't interrupt, by giving her extra computer time when she succeeded, and he had tried to deter her by pulling her out of class for a three-minute lecture after each interruption. None of these responses solved the problem.

For many students, this negative attention would prevent them from repeating the behavior. However, Rita was not like most students, because she lacked social skills: any kind of attention encouraged her to continue her behavior.[16] When Mr. O'Brien lectured her, he was unintentionally reinforcing her behavior by providing one-on-one negative attention.

Most students do not seek out or provoke others to get negative attention. The students who do behave in a way that elicits negative responses usually do so because negative attention is more efficient (faster and perhaps easier to obtain), intense, dramatic, and obvious and can verify the student's existing poor self-image. Students are not usually conscious of seeking attention.

If a student taps his pencil repeatedly on the desk, a teacher may attend to the student in a few seconds. If that same student sits quietly working, it could take a long time for him to be praised. Inappropriate behavior is, unfortunately, not only a fast way to get attention, but often also predictable and consistent. A student can predict that if he taps his pencil on his desk, the teacher will consistently attend to him within seconds. If he demonstrated appropriate, on-task behavior, it would be very difficult to predict when, if ever, the teacher would praise him. Teachers who successfully address the behavior of challenging students who desire attention have learned to make positive attention as fast, consistent, and predictable as negative attention.

Some other students may act inappropriately because they crave intense, dramatic responses from teachers and peers. Negative attention can be a rush for the student. For example, if a student screams and throws a ceramic pencil holder on the floor, shattering it, a typical teacher reaction would be to rush over and remove the student or remove the other students from the area. The movement, proximity, speed, and maybe even the tone and volume of the teacher is intense. Often following such an incident, the teacher and parents have a dramatic, heated meeting. In light of her prior experience, the student can predict that if she acts in a certain way, she will get this sort of intense response.

Appropriate behavior, on the other hand, does not often gain such intense attention. As ridiculous as it sounds, to match the intensity of the pencil-holder-throwing scenario, the teacher would need to run (not walk) to a student the second she raised her hand nicely. The teacher would have to move the furniture, stand within an inch of the student, and involve other teachers to surround her. A big meeting with her parents about how she raised her hand nicely would follow all this commotion.

Students with social deficits often seek intense forms of negative attention because they cannot "read" or ascertain more subtle, nonverbal types of attention such as a teacher's smile or a wink. Thus, they may not even realize they were receiving attention. Typically, negative attention is more obvious than positive attention. If a student says "hi" to a peer and misses the student's smile in return, the first student may provoke a more obvious response by screaming "Hi!" He may even repeatedly scream "Hi!" until the peer responds more obviously, even if the peer has become irritated. Depending on the severity of the student's social disability, he may not even be able to recognize the peer's negative response.

For students with low self-esteem, seeking negative attention can become a self-fulfilling prophecy that is explained by the self-verification theory. This theory posits that a child may feel she doesn't like herself so, therefore, she is only comfortable with negative attention, which mirrors the negative feelings she harbors about herself.[17] One notable characteristic of children who seek negative attention because of a poor self-concept is that they may also reject positive attention. A student who crumples her paper and averts her gaze when the teacher says, "Great work!" may not be able to tolerate being praised, because she doesn't feel deserving.

Negative attention is desirable for some students for the following key reasons:

- Negative attention is predictable and consistent.
- It is efficient (easier).
- It is intense and dramatic.
- It is obvious.
- Negative attention verifies a child's poor self-image.

Escape function

Most people try at times to escape or avoid people, things, events, or places. For them, not answering the phone when an unpleasant relative calls and surfing the Net rather than finishing a work report are examples of escape strategies. A student asking to go to the nurse's office to avoid a quiz is also a form of escape.

Escape-motivated behavior is normal, but it becomes problematic if students avoid all or most social interactions, academics, or demands or demonstrate disruptive or aberrant behavior to avoid something. Because escape-motivated behavior is not always easy to identify, a teacher can inadvertently reinforce it by allowing the student to avoid something for a short time or entirely. Some students can find an activity so aversive that they feel they have to avoid the task, even for a few moments. People who repeatedly use the alarm clock snooze button can relate. The student might whine, try to negotiate, or ask to go to the bathroom to temporarily avoid a task. The student may eventually start the work, but has successfully delayed it for a while.

For example, during independent work time, Reggie shouts at his peer, "Stop looking at me!" The teacher sends him to the office. When he returns to the classroom, the teacher encourages him to get back to work. For most students, this is a perfectly reasonable intervention, and the student will then complete his work. However, Reggie successfully escaped from the work demand for a short time, and if this desire was what motivated his behavior, he was successful. Other common school discipline procedures that unintentionally reinforce escape behavior are removing work materials after a child destroys them or removing the student from the classroom. Even if the student brings the work along, this allows a delay.

Tangible function

Tangibly motivated behavior takes place when a person hopes to be rewarded with something concrete—perhaps money, shelter, or a particular object. Most adults would stop working if they didn't get a paycheck. Many students would not line up nicely in the cafeteria if they weren't expecting food. This is normal. However, when a student demonstrates disruptive, unsafe, or other inappropriate behavior to get something, this becomes problematic or abnormal. When a student has difficulty sharing, this is often an example of tangibly motivated behavior. If a student steals another student's iPod or fights over a ball during recess, this could be tangibly motivated because she is trying to get a specific object.

Students who act inappropriately to get a tangible item often have difficulty with delayed gratification; they want the item *now*. These students can often be rigid and inflexible. "I want what I want, when I want it" is another way to express how tangibly motivated students think. Keeping to his or her own agenda, no matter what, becomes the thing that is motivating this student. It is common for any student to get frustrated when the computer breaks while she is playing or to get upset when she spills juice on herself. However, most students would not have a meltdown, but would try and solve the problem rationally. For example, if a child arrived at the corner store and discovered it was closed, she might make a quick new plan to go to a twenty-four-hour store down the street. On the other hand, a child with tangibly motivated behavior would bang on the store window and yell, "Let me in!" She is too "stuck" in what she wants to generate a new plan.

This behavior is atypical when it interferes with learning (e.g., there is only *one* way to solve a certain math problem) or social interactions (e.g., someone cheats to win a game) or involves explosive, unsafe, or other inappropriate behavior as a result of getting stuck or as a means to get what they want. For example, a third-grader may scream and throw herself to the floor after the teacher announces that recess will be indoors, having an outburst instead of being flexible and adjusting to the situation. Students who are stuck can be bossy (even bullying), can insist everything go their way, may not take turns well, and can be easily frustrated, hard to negotiate with, or demanding.

Sensory function

Humming loudly while writing, chewing on the end of a pencil, or standing rather than sitting while working: these are all behaviors that fall into the last category, sensory function. A student engages in these behaviors because they feel good, taste good, sound good, or are visually soothing or calming. This is a normal behavior function in many people. The behavior becomes a problem when it interferes with learning or social interactions (e.g., humming instead of interacting with peers at snack time), when it is stigmatizing (e.g., peers think the student looks weird), or if a student engages in inappropriate, disruptive behavior to gain access to a desired sensory experience. Sensory-seeking behavior is common with students with sensory processing dysfunction and students on the autism spectrum.[18]

Some students with sensory difficulties have trouble with the sensory input from the environment and can find it overwhelming. They try to mask the uncomfortable input through a different, more pleasing sensory-seeking behavior (e.g., humming to themselves to block out the noise of the loud cafeteria), but this can interfere with learning. Some other students find certain behaviors like rocking back and forth very soothing. It is their way of coping or regulating themselves. Students with sensory processing dysfunction may underreact (be hyposensitive) or overreact (be hypersensitive) to situations. People seek sensory input from all of the five senses: auditory, visual, olfactory (smell), taste, and tactile (touch). When a student yells when he gets glue on his hands or a peer gets too close, or acts distressed by the tag on the back of his shirt, he may have tactile hypersensitivity. Students who are hypersensitive to noise may cover their ears when in the noisy cafeteria.

In addition to gaining sensory input through the commonly known five senses, there are two additional senses: proprioceptive and vestibular.[19] *Proprioceptive* sense refers to sensory feedback that is received through muscles and joints about the body's position in space. Proprioceptive input-seeking behaviors would include crashing movements—slamming books on the desk, walking heavy-footed, or leaning on other peers during circle time. The vestibular sense involves the input received through the inner ear which helps with balance. A student who is seeking vestibular input may spin in a chair repeatedly, twirl down the hallway, or hang upside down on the monkey bars. A clue for determining whether a behavior has a sensory function is if the behavior occurs over and over, even if the student is by himself. Students are often unaware of these types of behavior, and this can make the behavior difficult to change. Table 1.3 reviews these four functions of behavior.

Multiple functions

It is important to recognize that behaviors can serve more than one function at the same time.[20] For example, a student bolts from the classroom to escape cleaning up

TABLE 1.3

Four functions of behavior

Attention function	Escape function	Tangible function	Sensory function
Peer attention	Avoid a task	Want an item	Tactile
Adult attention	Avoid a demand	Want to follow his own specific agenda	Olfactory
Group or individual attention	Avoid an activity		Taste
Negative attention	Avoid a person		Visual
Positive attention	Avoid an environment		Auditory
Nonverbal and verbal attention			Proprioceptive
			Vestibular

Sources: adapted from Vincent Mark Durand, *Severe Behavior Problems: A Functional Communication Training Approach* (New York: Guilford Press, 1990); and Carol Stock Kranowitz, *The Out-of-Sync Child: Recognizing and Coping with Sensory Integration Dysfunction* (New York: Perigee Books, 2005).

and is chased by four adults. In this situation, teachers have unintentionally provided attention for the behavior. This bolting episode has both an escape function and an attention function.

The same behavior can also have different functions in different environments. A child may scream for attention in math class, but may scream to escape from P.E. class. Teachers need to respond flexibly depending on the intent of the student's behavior. The response needs to take into consideration the function of the behavior in each student. If teachers give a student a time-out, that could work in math class if it removes the attention the student is seeking, but it will not work in P.E. class if the student is looking for an escape.

Behavior Occurs in Patterns

Teachers often tell us that a student's behavior came out of nowhere or was totally unpredictable: "She started yelling for no reason!" However, not only is there a reason, but these reasons can become apparent because human behaviors occur in patterns.

When teachers feel they have tried everything with a student but the student is still acting inappropriately, the next step is to investigate in a systematic way. The key to breaking the behavior code is to *look for patterns*. These patterns can be based on time of day (she always yawns in the morning before snack), activity (he always asks to go to the nurse when math starts), people (she participates more in class when Ms. Irving is there), and many other factors. Patterns are the clues that teachers need to determine the intent or function of the student's behavior. Once the pattern is discovered, the function or intent of the behavior will often reveal itself: "Aha! He is swearing because he wants the teacher's one-on-one attention," or "Oh! He refuses to speak every time an unfamiliar adult enters the room."

In addition to coming in patterns, every behavior has bookends: the environmental variables that occur *prior* to the students engaging in an unwanted behavior (the antecedents) and the response of the teacher and peers *after* the student engages in a behavior. When trying to understand behavior, teachers need to notice these bookends. This is what fuels the behavior and allows it to persist.

By looking for patterns in antecedents and analyzing patterns in the responses, you can better guess the function of a refusal or outburst. If over time, a teacher notes that his or her response to the student's behavior is consistently a one-on-one lecture by the assistant principal and the behavior remains unchanged, the teacher might hypothesize that this type of attention is reinforcing the behavior. If the student displays disruptive behavior after any writing task is assigned, the teacher could hypothesize that the student is engaging in the behavior to escape writing. Simple documentation and note taking is key to uncovering these behavior patterns. In the next chapter, we will explain how to uncover patterns of behavior to determine the underlying causes, or functions, and to look for ways that teachers may be inadvertently reinforcing negative behavior in their responses.

In addition to noting the patterns and bookends of behavior, it's important to understand and document the impact of the student's family, life events, community, peers, and other variables on a child's behavior, whenever this information comes to the teachers' attention (e.g., student tells teacher, parent reports information to teacher, peers relay conversations they had with student, student discloses to counselor). Behavior analysts call these factors *setting events.*[21] Setting events are environmental events or conditions (e.g., lack of sleep, change in routine, noisy environment, crowds, allergies, illness) that increase the likelihood that challenging behavior may occur.[22] Teachers should also consider the setting events when ana-lyzing students' behaviors.

The Only Behavior Teachers Can Control Is Their Own

Often by the time we're asked to consult with school staff about a particularly chal-lenging student, teachers feel the student is frequently calling the shots. They may desperately wish they could get a student "under control" and may be so frustrated that they're just holding on until the end of the school year. However, the emphasis should not be on controlling the student, but rather should be on how to change the dynamic between the student and teacher.

Teachers need to feel empowered to improve students' behavior. Over time, we have discovered that one of the most powerful ways to help teachers is to show them how changing their *own behavior* can help guide students toward behavior change. Although behavior plans are typically thought of as a way to improve students' behavior, good behavior plans, such as the FAIR Plan, are really a guide for help-ing teachers develop new behaviors so the educators can interact with challenging students in a more productive and preemptive way.

To avoid a student's shutting down during spelling activities, the teacher can change the way he or she introduces the activity and responds to the behavior. Instead of saying, "Time for a spelling quiz—I made it tough this time," the teacher could say, "We are going to only do five at a time, and I will help you if you're stuck." The teacher can change his or her own response to the shutdown behavior. A ques-tion like "Do you want me to help you with spelling now or during choice time?" prevents escape from task, rather than allowing the student to miss the quiz.

Behavior Can Be Changed

When administrators, teachers, parents, or other school staff report that they are "managing" a student's behavior, this often points to a problem. In our experience, managing disruptive behavior means trying to minimize the impact on others or keeping the student from having an outburst by removing any provoking elements in the environment until he or she can be placed in a specialized classroom or school. When a second-grader starts to bang his fist on the desk, the teacher, to allow the class to function, might ask him to sit in the other second-grade classroom. For the short term, this plan often manages the student's behavior and restores order in the class. Unfortunately, this will not provide long-term change. Typical behavior management plans offer an immediate action to diminish the impact of a given behavior on surrounding people and things. We don't want to minimize the need for a short-term plan, but we encourage teachers not to stop there. If the ultimate goal is to reduce or change the inappropriate behavior, merely managing the behavior won't cut it: the student has to learn a new way to behave.

Behavior change can be quick, or it can be incremental and take time. For some students, when the interventions are spot-on in understanding the function of the student's behavior and teaching underdeveloped skills, the student can show change quickly. We've had students stop behaving inappropriately in only three weeks, whereas other students have tapered off a behavior over a three-year period. If the student has been demonstrating an inappropriate behavior for years and lacks the necessary skills, it may take longer for her to change. Behavior will not change much at all if it continues to be reinforced by teachers' responses.[23] The more intensely the student is taught the underdeveloped skills and the more the environment is changed to encourage appropriate behavior, the faster the student's behavior is likely to change.

Chapter Summary

- Challenging behavior is a disability: a student would behave if he or she could.

- Challenging behavior is often counterintuitive:
    - The intent of the student's behavior can be hard to decipher.
    - Because of the incorrect assessment, the teacher's response doesn't match.
    - Because of the incorrect assessment, the teacher teaches a replacement behavior that the student cannot replicate.

- There are several essential concepts for understanding behavior and intervening effectively:
    - Misbehavior is a symptom of an underlying cause or undeveloped skills.
    - Behavior is communication.
    - Behavior can serve four functions: attention, escape, tangible motivation, and sensory satisfaction. Some behaviors can serve multiple functions.
    - Behavior occurs in patterns and has bookends made up of antecedents and responses.
    - The only behavior teachers can control is their own.
    - Behavior can be changed.

CHAPTER 2

The FAIR Plan

Putting the FAIR Plan into Practice

There is no question that working with challenging students is difficult and sometimes exhausting. It requires strategizing and patience. In our consultation with teachers to optimize classroom environments for students, we have found that it helps to have a structure for this work. That is why we devised the FAIR Plan, which we mentioned briefly in the introduction. We have also customized the FAIR Plan for the four types of challenging behavior we cover in this book.

The FAIR Plan is different from traditional behavior intervention plans used in schools today in several important ways: First, it helps teachers consider the psychological profile of the student in addition to the underlying functions of the student's behavior for a more comprehensive understanding and a more accurate tailoring of interventions. Second, it emphasizes preemptive strategies, with reaction strategies as a last resort. Third, it translates complex, research-based psychological and behavioral knowledge into doable and effective interventions for teachers. Finally, the FAIR Plan rewards students for their ability to use these prevention strategies rather than simply "being good"—a more realistic approach, given that for many reasons, these students need explicit instruction with skills before they can manage their behavior more consistently. The plan is a practical, empathetic, and ultimately more successful way of interacting with and teaching these students.

Most important, the goal of the FAIR Plan is to change inappropriate behavior to appropriate behavior for the long term rather than, for example, simply "managing the behavior" until the end of the year (or school career). Achieving this type of change requires teachers to take five basic steps that use the fundamental concepts of behavior outlined in chapter 1:

1. Manage antecedents (what occurs in the environment immediately prior to the behavior) with necessary accommodations or modifications, and change the way you interact with a challenging student.
2. Reinforce desired behavior.
3. Teach a replacement behavior.
4. Address underdeveloped skills that are at the root of a child's inability to behave appropriately.
5. Respond to a student's inappropriate behavior in a way that deters it.[1]

That's it. We have constructed the framework of the FAIR Plan to incorporate these steps in ways that are easy to implement and to remember.

MANAGING ANTECEDENTS

The major emphasis of FAIR is antecedent management. This means minimizing or accommodating antecedents that are troubling to a student and therefore tend to set off an incident of inappropriate behavior. If George screams repeatedly during transitions, this is a clue to the teacher that he may need accommodation support during transitions until he learns the prerequisite skills to make transitions independently. By understanding what antecedents are problematic for the student, such as being close to students or reading aloud, the teacher can intervene effectively and create a classroom environment that is supportive and proactive.

Note that the FAIR Plan requires teachers to be flexible and understand the underlying factors in the student's behavior. A challenging student's ability to perform can be inconsistent—until new skills are taught. Depending on the day's events and the student's tolerance level and skill level, a student may be able to do only five minutes of math one day, and thirty-five minutes the next. The teacher will learn to "read" the student in the moment and react accordingly to promote appropriate behavior and success. The FAIR Plans in the next four chapters include many strategies to give teachers a choice in the types of interventions that the most challenging students need. Above all, flexibility on the part of the teacher is key.

REINFORCING A DESIRED BEHAVIOR

Successful use of the FAIR Plan means meeting students where they are and encouraging them to do better. If a student can't tolerate academic demands without an outburst, the teacher may start by asking her to do only ten minutes of work, reinforce her, and over time build up the student's tolerance. As the student demonstrates small attempts at self-regulating or the use of prosocial skills, the teacher will reinforce and reward her. Reinforcing the student's use of strategies and practice of skills is an essential factor in a student's journey of learning appropriate behavior.

TEACHING A REPLACEMENT BEHAVIOR

For the student to be willing to replace the old behavior with a new one, the alternative behavior must meet three conditions:

- The replacement behavior must *achieve the same results* as the inappropriate behavior (e.g., escape from a demand).
- The replacement behavior should be *as efficient* at getting the desired outcome as the inappropriate behavior.
- The replacement behavior needs to be *within the student's ability.* [2]

Teaching replacement strategies is frequently overlooked in schools. However, the student needs to be taught a replacement behavior to be used while he is building the skills needed to behave appropriately without accommodations. A replacement behavior is an appropriate behavior that serves the same function as the inappropriate behavior. For example, instead of disrespectfully refusing to read out loud during reading group, a student can learn a replacement behavior, such as asking to read quietly—a behavior that gets him what he wants in an appropriate way. This might be saying, "I pass," or holding up a card that says, "I pass." Many people would argue that this is giving in to the student and allowing him to avoid the task. But the truth is, he wasn't reading out loud before, either. The purpose of the replacement strategy is to eliminate the inappropriate behavior (rudely speaking to the teacher) while he learns to overcome his difficulty with reading aloud.

In short, the replacement behavior needs to get the student the same desired response as the inappropriate behavior, or she won't use it. A student could be taught that instead of banging her fists on the desk, she could ask politely, "Can I have a break, please?" This will get her the desired break from the task, but through appropriate behavior. If the replacement behavior is not equally efficient, the student may regress to poor behavior, again getting an immediate response if she bangs her fists on the desk. This behavior is nonverbal and simple for the student to execute. If a teacher tried to have the student replace this behavior by quietly raising her hand, waiting five minutes for the teacher to call on her, and then asking, "Can I have a break please?" it would require too much effort from the student. Fist banging is much more efficient. A better replacement strategy for fist banging would need to be easy, nonverbal, and immediate, such as a student grabbing an "I want a break" icon that allows her to take a break quietly in the corner of the room. This replacement is within the child's ability to perform since it is nonverbal and she has difficulty speaking in sentences when frustrated.

TEACHING UNDERDEVELOPED SKILLS

After implementing accommodations and teaching a replacement behavior, the tough work begins. Teaching the student underdeveloped skills eventually eliminates the need for the replacement behavior. For example, the fist-banging student who does not want to read aloud needs to work on reading skills, perhaps with additional support, and may need to be referred for an evaluation, if she hasn't been already. Or perhaps the student can read but has anxiety around performance (e.g., reading in front of people). In this case, anxiety management and self-regulation skills need to be taught. Figure 2.1 shows how replacement behavior works as a placeholder until the desired behavior is taught.

RESPONDING TO INAPPROPRIATE BEHAVIOR

It is important for teachers to respond in ways that are consistent with the function of the student's behavior, as discussed earlier. When prevention goes awry and

FIGURE 2.1

Replacement behavior as a first step toward desired behavior

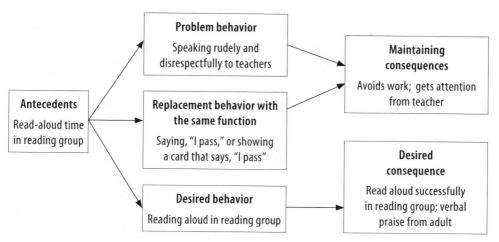

Source: adapted with permission from O'Neill et al., *Functional Assessment and Program Development for Problem Behavior: A Practical Handbook* (Pacific Grove, Calif.: Brooks/Cole Pub., 1997).

incidents do occur, the teachers' response needs to reinforce the student's desired behavior and avoid accidentally reinforcing the undesired behavior. Preventing the student's inappropriate behavior, however, needs to be the emphasis, not the response.[3]

PUTTING THE FAIR PLAN INTO PRACTICE

Challenging students require the support of a well-designed behavior intervention plan—a proactive action plan to address behaviors that are impeding learning for these students or others.[4] As we have described above, the FAIR Plan, a behavior intervention plan that builds on the fundamental principles of behavior discussed in chapter 1, includes an understanding of a student's underlying mental health profile and the five steps for preventing inappropriate behavior.

The four components of the FAIR Plan (functional hypotheses of behavior and antecedent analysis, accommodations, interaction strategies, and response strategies), already mentioned in the book's introduction, must be included in behavior intervention plans for students with anxiety-related, oppositional, sexualized, or withdrawn behavior. Students exhibiting these behaviors, we believe, are the most challenging in the classroom today. If developed for a student with an IEP or a 504 plan (an education plan under Section 504 of the Rehabilitation Act of 1973), the FAIR Plan becomes part of those documents. But it is also designed to be user-friendly for any teacher, regardless of whether the student has been identified for special education services or not. Now we'll delve into each of the essential steps of building the FAIR Plan.

Functional Hypothesis of Behavior and Antecedent Analysis

Why might the child be exhibiting a given behavior? What is the child communicating, and why? As discussed previously, this is one of the first questions teachers need to ask themselves prior to moving forward and picking interventions or a consistent response to the student. Without understanding the function, picking an intervention is like throwing darts in the dark.

Before you begin each plan, create a list of the targeted behaviors, prioritizing the most unsafe or concerning behaviors first. We encourage teachers to be as explicit as possible—what does the behavior look like? Avoid words, such as *tantrum*, that could be interpreted different ways. Instead, use a more observable description such as *screaming, kicking furniture, swiping materials off the desk*, or *stomping feet*. Having an observable and measurable definition of the problem will help as a reminder of the types of behaviors you are trying to track and analyze.

In order to decipher the function of a student's inappropriate behavior, we encourage the teachers to take notes in a particular way that will make it easier to determine patterns of behavior. A simple three-column ABC format takes only a few minutes and is a thorough way to document behavior incidents.[5] This ABC method breaks a behavioral incident down into three parts: the *antecedent*, or what happened immediately prior to the behavior; a description of the *behavior* itself; and the *consequence*, or teacher's or peers' response immediately following the behavior. The ABC format is an invaluable tool to discover what is fueling students' behavior. Table 2.1 shows how one teacher used this format to document each incident over a month with Neal, a student with oppositional behavior.

TABLE 2.1

ABC data sheet for Neal, a student with oppositional behavior

Date, time, duration	Setting event(s)	Activity	Antecedent (what happens immediately before behavior)	Behavior (description of behavior)	Consequence (what happens immediately after behavior)
12/20, 9:15 a.m., 2 min	Substitute teacher for art	Art class	Teacher says to group, "Make sure to write a title on your work."	Neal yells, "Fat idiot!" at the teacher and storms to his place in line.	The teacher tells him to push in his chair before lining up.
1/7, 10:30 a.m., 15 sec		Language arts	Teacher tells Neal he needs to add more details to his story.	Neal throws his pencil, which hits a peer's head.	The teacher sends him to the principal's office.
1/11, 1:45 p.m., 4 min	Mom reported he didn't sleep at all last night	Phonics	Assistant says, "OK, now turn the paper over and continue."	Neal puts his head down and says, "I hate you!"	The teacher tells him he can have a break in the reading corner.
1/13, 12:15 p.m., 2 min		Language arts quiz	Teacher says, "Make sure to mirror the question in your responses."	Neal scribbles on the paper and rips it up.	The teacher tells him to sit at the back table and put his head down.

Note: adapted from Sidney W. Bijou, Robert F. Peterson, and Marion H. Ault, "A Method to Integrate Descriptive and Experimental Field Studies at the Level of Data and Empirical Concepts," *Journal of Applied Behavior Analysis* 1, no. 2 (1968); Beth Sulzer-Azaroff and G. Roy Mayer, *Applying Behavior-Analysis Procedures with Children and Youth* (New York: Holt, Rinehart and Winston, 1977).

It is important to look for patterns in both the antecedent column and the consequence column. The antecedents to Neal's behaviors appear to be related to writing. Now teachers can try to figure out why he is finding writing difficult or stressful. The antecedent column will help determine where and how the student may need support. The consequence column will highlight the teacher's responses to Neal's behavior. These responses show that he is successfully avoiding writing demands, which implies that the function of his behavior is to escape writing tasks. By taking notes in this format, teachers can make the patterns pop out and can become more analytical and reflective—and empowered.

Teachers need to organize these notes in a way that works best for them. Typically, a teacher only needs to collect ABC data on one student in the class, so organization of the documentation is not so cumbersome. In classrooms where ABC data is collected for multiple children, though, teachers might keep a separate notebook for each student or have one binder of ABC data with separate sections for each student or an ABC sheet stapled into their planning book (see appendix A for a sample ABC sheet).

ABC documentation may provide insight into the reason for the student's behavior and have the added advantage of improving communication with other staff (e.g., if the principal asks specific questions after a behavior incident). In the case where a teacher needs additional resources (as we recommend in some situations), a teacher who has clear and thorough documentation is better positioned to demonstrate the student's behavior and choose interventions. ABC data can sometimes also be useful when teachers need to ask for a more comprehensive and more formal functional behavior assessment. While only trained professionals such as a board-certified behavior analyst can complete such an assessment, ABC notes and observations from teachers and other school personnel can be invaluable in the process. ABC notes are not a substitute for a functional behavior assessment, as they don't decipher function thoroughly, but they are an easy and effective tool for teachers to see patterns, hypothesize the function of the student's behavior, and reflect on their responses.

To analyze the behavior accurately, teachers need to complete all columns in the ABC form consistently. Here's where the role of detective kicks in. We realize that teachers have a lot to manage in the aftermath of a student's behavioral outburst. They need to refocus the class and possibly debrief with other teachers. After such a packed and stressful day, documentation can seem like one more overwhelming, extra demand.[6] Critical information is left out when teachers document only the fine points of the student's behavior *during* the incident by taking anecdotal notes. As mentioned earlier, what occurred right before the behavior and what happened right after are as important to consider as the particulars of the incident. As

Sherlock Holmes said in Conan Doyle's *Study in Scarlet*, "It is a capital mistake to theorize before one has data. Insensibly one begins to twist facts to suit theories, instead of theories to suit facts."

When we work with teachers of challenging students, we suggest documenting a minimum of five incidents. The time it takes to collect notes can vary from student to student. Usually, if the teacher is concerned enough to start ABC note taking, the behavior is occurring frequently and five behavior incidents can be documented over a period of one to three weeks. ABC notes should be used initially to decipher behavior, but they can also be used to monitor progress and to see if interventions are working throughout the year.

On our sample ABC sheet, we have also included a column for recording setting events. It is important to share any known setting events with parents and mental health staff. For example, parents might be unaware that at school, their child says he hates his babysitter. When setting events are shared, larger home and school interventions can be brainstormed and implemented, such as getting the student outside counseling or helping the family get resources and support services.

Accommodations

After the teacher looks at the ABC data and identifies a pattern of antecedents and potential underdeveloped skills, the next step is to select accommodations to support the student in these areas. For ease of reading, we are going to include modifications under the category of accommodations, even though there is a difference. Accommodations are adaptations to the students' academics or schedule that do not change or lower standards, such as providing test questions in a multiple-choice format instead of an open-ended, written response. Modifications are adaptations that *do* change or lower expectations, such as giving a fifth-grade student a first-grade level math quiz.[7]

All decisions about interventions have long-term effects that need to be considered. For example, if a teacher stops asking Joe to write and decides to scribe for him, will Joe ever learn to write? When accommodations and modifications seem to be helping a student, such as when an alternative recess eliminates all problematic behavior, many teachers don't know when to discontinue the intervention. We advise a gradual reduction in a successful accommodation or modification after a significant period of success. For example, after six weeks of appropriate behavior during alternative recess, a teacher may want to slowly begin to have the student join one recess per week. The teacher should not start this process during times of change such as right before winter vacation or during a change in the student's life (e.g., grandma is living with family for a month).

When choosing accommodations, teachers need to think about the whole range of possibilities. In our FAIR Plan, we ask teachers to consider accommodations in four categories that address every aspect of the student's school day: *environment* (the larger context in which the child lives and studies); *executive functioning* (aspects of the child's thought process); *curriculum* (the learning challenge before the student); and *skill development* (the explicit instruction needed to address underdeveloped skills that are at the root of inappropriate behavior). It is important that teachers consider accommodations in all these categories, so we briefly explain each one.

Environment

For each type of presenting behavior in the chapters to follow, we suggest possible environmental modifications that are helpful to maintain the student's appropriate behavior. These typically include daily and weekly schedule changes as well as the physical classroom setup. Depending on the student and the intensity of the behavior, these accommodations can include providing movement breaks throughout the day for an active student or providing a separate lunch outside the cafeteria for a student with significant anxiety. Often, if these strategies are used preventatively or as part of the response to behavior, they can help students make it through the day and avoid inappropriate behavior.

Executive functioning

Executive functioning, an umbrella term referring to future planning skills, includes such cognitive processes as planning, organizational skills, selective attention and inhibitory control, and flexible thinking.[8] In our combined experience, most students who demonstrate inappropriate behavior (especially extreme behavior) have some deficit in executive functioning. Students with emotional and behavioral challenges do worse on executive functioning tasks than comparison groups, according to some studies.[9] Accommodations for students with executive functioning skill deficits include techniques to help students prepare for transitions, organize their ideas, and complete written assignments. For example, if a teacher gives a transition warning that math is ending in five minutes, this is only helpful if the child has an internal sense of the length of five minutes and can shift from one activity to another (cognitive shifting). If a student has poor executive functioning, this verbal warning does not help the child stop an activity at the correct time. Providing the student with a visual representation of a five-minute duration, coupled with the verbal warning, is useful because the student may find the warning abrupt and then forget about it five minutes later—by the end of class—and thus may be surprised all over again. This technique also makes passage of time concrete and visual.

Curriculum

A teacher's primary goal in school is to teach students academics and give them access to the curriculum. In this book, we will not be recommending specific curricula. Rather, we will provide some simple, practical tips on delivery and supplemental activities.[10] These can include supplementing pencil-and-paper tasks with word processing for students with low frustration tolerances or anxiety; alternating easy and hard work for students with oppositional behavior; incorporating choice in how a student will demonstrate knowledge (e.g., instead of writing a report, allow the student to write a rap song); and avoiding open-ended writing assignments for students with anxiety. A flexible, child-centered approach toward instruction is a good match for the students in this book, as they are at risk for demonstrating escape-motivated behavior toward academics and developing subsequent achievement gaps.

Skill development

Inappropriate behaviors are frequently the result of underdeveloped skills. Students' underdeveloped skills need to be improved to decrease inappropriate behavior. Many challenging children have underdeveloped skills in the areas of flexible thinking, self-regulation, and the ability to self-calm. In each chapter, we address potential deficits and identify some curricula that teachers and others can use to teach—and to allow the student to practice—underdeveloped skills. The explicit instruction of skills, however, will most likely be implemented by a special educator (a self-contained classroom teacher or an inclusion specialist), a social worker, or a school psychologist, as classroom teachers usually do not have the time or materials for this level of instruction. In appendix B, we provide a list of suggested resources and curricula that school personnel will find helpful in designing instruction.

Interaction Strategies

Interaction strategies are the third component of the FAIR Plan. We devote a section of every chapter to this important activity because it is typically left out of traditional behavior intervention plans and yet it is one of the most important components for changing behavior. Relationship building with challenging students is an art, especially with those who are defensive, such as some students with withdrawn behavior or trauma histories. Building relationships with students is also a *must*! Positive relationships between teachers and students have a significant impact on the behavior of the student. Studies have shown that kindergarten and first-grade students with chronic conflict relationships with their teachers were less compliant and liked school less than other students and were at increased risk for poor academic achievement.[11] These students' challenging behavior can push teachers away, making conflict more likely. Sadly, a conflict-ridden relationship with their teacher can become yet another rejection for the students, and the cycle continues.[12] In our experience, teachers are not well prepared to interact with the students we write about in this book. In response to a student's frequent inappropriate behavior, teachers can find themselves repeating a student's name twenty times per day, arguing with her, or ignoring her to avoid a possible bad interaction. Traditional ways teachers interact with noncompliant students, such as being directive or authoritative, usually backfire.

We recommend that teachers make an extra effort to connect with the student throughout the day. Before any intervention will work, students need to know the teacher likes them and wants what's best for them. When students don't trust a teacher or feel that the teacher has low expectations of them, their behavior mirrors this.[13] This relationship-building should be done during times of calm (i.e., not immediately after the child acts out, as it may reinforce the behavior) and throughout the year. Relationship-building should be done intensively in the beginning of the year and after disruptions in schedule such as vacations. As part of the FAIR Plan, teachers can identify a range of relationship-building activities, from having a special lunch to going for a quick one-on-one walk or bringing in an item for the student to use because she mentioned she liked it. The box "Relationship-Building Ideas" lists some activities to consider.

Critical junctures for adding interaction strategies include the day following a behavioral incident, when the student may be feeling remorse or shame and may

Relationship-Building Ideas

BASIC ACTIVITIES:

- Go for a walk with the student.
- Take the student along to do errands like making copies.
- Have the student help organize a bookshelf or other materials in the classroom.
- Have lunch with the student.
- Bring in small items the student likes.
- Listen to the student's favorite music with him, and talk about it.
- Bring in magazine or newspaper stories on the student's favorite sports team or another favorite interest.

MORE-INVOLVED ACTIVITIES:

- Have food delivered for a special lunch with the student.
- Watch the student's favorite movie with her over a few sessions.

feel the adults are angry with or disappointed in her. At the end of the school year, many of our students have difficulty with the anticipated transition. They know they are leaving the particular teacher and may react by acting badly toward the teacher, as a way of relationship sabotage. Teachers need to invest more to strengthen the relationship at this point, even though they may be exhausted and want to withdraw.

In addition to offering longer-term relationship-building strategies (where, when, how) in the following chapters, we will share practical, preventative strategies for interacting with students *in the moment*. Such strategies reduce the likelihood that the student will demonstrate inappropriate behavior. These in-the-moment interaction strategies include suggestions on how to respond to "I'm stupid" from a student with withdrawn behavior or the best way to handle a student with a trauma history who asks for a hug. We suggest ways to tell argumentative kids to do something they don't like in a way that will make them less likely to argue. Teachers can interact with students to promote cooperation and reduce stress. This doesn't mean teachers should be permissive or unnatural. In fact, strictness, in the sense of being consistent in your approach, is better and more comfortable for some students. We find, and research supports, that sometimes it really is not what you say, but how you say it, that makes the difference.[14]

Response Strategies

The first three components of the FAIR Plan emphasize gathering information and preventative strategies. The last component outlines what the teacher does *after* the student behaves inappropriately. As a teacher, you respond to your students' behavior throughout the day. Your responses are an opportunity to either escalate or deescalate a student's behavior. These responses also will either reinforce the behavior (i.e., increase the likelihood it will reoccur) or help to diminish it.

Teachers' responses need to match the function of the behavior. You can assess what this function is by looking at consequence patterns from ABC notes. Function-matched responses are a must to reduce or eliminate problem behavior. As we've discussed, if your hypothesis as a teacher is that the student is crying to get your attention, then you need to give the child attention for not crying (e.g., give a token for every class in which the student uses a strategy other than crying). This response breaks the cycle of the student's getting attention for crying. In the four chapters that follow, we give teachers common function-matched responses to implement with students.

Having the FAIR Plan can be empowering to teachers. After consulting with us for a month, one teacher, Ms. Martinez, began to incorporate the behavioral concepts into her approach to intervene with Ross, a particularly tough student. He was often explosive and was suspended the second week of third grade for breaking a window with a microphone stand. In October, Ross developed a new behavior. He refused to work, instead arguing with his teacher. Ms. Martinez e-mailed us in November, relaying how excited she was about Ross's progress:

> I wanted you to know that instead of calling the principal and going home and crying as I did before your consult, I realized that I could figure out why Ross was arguing and I could make a plan. It's only his way of communicating. Right away, I took out the ABC sheet you gave me, and I realized he had a pattern of arguing during writing assignments and that he was successfully getting out of them. I had been telling him to draw quietly if he wasn't going to do work. Once I realized his pattern and how I was reinforcing his escape, I was so energized I stayed up all night making a plan to change the cycle. The next day, I gave Ross more support and options

during writing and told him to ask for a break or for help if he was feeling frustrated. Knowing that he was only arguing because he was afraid of writing made the whole problem seem less overwhelming. I can happily report Ross has only argued once in three weeks, and I am no longer scared of what he might do next!

DECIDING WHICH FAIR PLAN TO USE

The next four chapters are devoted to helping teachers understand the underlying causes of students' anxiety-related, oppositional, withdrawn, or sexualized behavior and develop strategies for understanding and teaching students whose learning—and that of others—is being impeded by these behaviors. We recommend that before teachers choose which FAIR Plan to use, they and the rest of the team members read this whole book, as there is some overlap in behaviors in students. A student with withdrawn behavior, for example, can sometimes be oppositional, so interventions in both the withdrawn and the oppositional chapters can apply. Teachers should feel free to borrow from the different types of plans where appropriate. A common conundrum is how to know when oppositional behavior is due to underlying anxiety: should the FAIR Plan for students with anxiety-related behavior or oppositional behavior be used? The chapter on students with anxiety-related behavior will outline eight behavior clues to help guide this decision. We have chosen the strategies listed on all the FAIR Plans because they are behaviorally sound, they take into account the psychological profile of the student, and they work. Teachers should not feel concerned about choosing interventions incorrectly but focus on choosing the best fit for the student.

The FAIR Plans are meant to be live documents that should also be assessed and tweaked as needed all year. The student's behavior will guide this process. If the student is doing well, a teacher may want to pick more challenging interventions such as teaching a more difficult social skill; conversely, if a student starts to slip into old patterns, the teacher and team should revise the FAIR Plan.

At the end of each of the next four chapters, we provide a FAIR Plan worksheet. This document outlines the components of an effective behavior intervention plan and provides all the intervention choices discussed in the chapter, in an easy-to-use, bulleted worksheet. The template should guide the development of the FAIR Plan for the individual student. Since there are more suggested interventions than the student may need on each FAIR Plan worksheet, you and your team need to select the interventions that you think will help the student the most. Once you complete this careful process, it's time to put the plan into action.

We have defined some essential concepts. Now we are ready to provide more detail about how to help each of the most challenging students!

Chapter Summary

- ABC note-taking is an invaluable tool to discover patterns in antecedents and consequences and to hypothesize the function of behavior.
- Long-term behavior change has four steps:
  - Antecedent management
  - Reinforcing the desired behavior
  - Teaching a replacement behavior
  - Teaching the underdeveloped skill or skills
- Replacement behaviors must meet the following requirements:
  - Achieve the same desired outcome as the inappropriate behavior
  - Be within student's ability
- The FAIR Plan is a behavior intervention plan that includes four elements:
  - *Functional* hypothesis of behavior
  - *Accommodations*
  - *Interaction* strategies
  - *Response* strategies

CHAPTER 3

"Get Away from Me!"

The Student with Anxiety-Related Behavior

Nelli was late for school again. The teachers didn't typically expect her before 9 a.m. (half an hour after the start time of second grade), but today she arrived even later, at 9:15. When Nelli arrived, Ms. Tucker made an extra effort to welcome her. After Nelli unpacked her belongings, she was asked to line up with the other students. Ms. Tucker was relieved that Nelli had arrived at school in time for P.E. (Nelli's favorite activity), although the teacher could never be sure how Nelli was going to react to anything. Ms. Tucker was about to lead her students down the hall when Nelli's classmate Becky screamed. The teaching assistant, Mr. Chen, shouted, "Nelli, stop!" and rushed over to the line of kids. Nelli was holding Becky's arm. In a matter of seconds, Mr. Chen physically escorted Nelli toward the far corner of the classroom and separated her from the other students. Becky held her arm and yelped, "She squeezed me!"

Ms. Tucker called a neighboring teacher to walk her students to P.E. so that she could assist Mr. Chen. Nelli screamed, "Get the hell away from me!" and started to swing at Mr. Chen. Ms. Tucker and Mr. Chen quickly moved away from her. They stood in front of the door to block the exit because Nelli had bolted from the classroom before. Nelli started to throw books off the shelves, Ms. Tucker's belongings off her desk. Then the girl picked up a globe, threatening to throw it at Ms. Tucker. Within three seconds, Nelli smashed the globe on the floor next to Ms. Tucker's feet.

After an experience like Ms. Tucker's, most teachers are left feeling perplexed and defeated and may resign themselves to the mistaken belief that there is no way to prevent this kind of unexpected outburst. In this example, Ms. Tucker anticipated that Nelli would make a transition smoothly because she was heading to her favorite activity. When there is no obvious reason for the student's behavior, as was the case with Nelli, adults are left feeling uneasy, as they don't know when another such outburst might occur.

We are addressing in this chapter a subset of students with anxiety and who have avoidant or inappropriate behavior or responses. There has been little guidance for teachers about how to support this population of students. Anxiety can be tricky, in that it is sometimes hidden until the student reaches a breaking point. It can be difficult for teachers to recognize if their students are anxious, especially since children have difficulty identifying when they are anxious and are wary of telling someone if they do realize it. Teachers can feel betrayed when a student acts out repeatedly after they have worked hard to develop an incentive plan, spent money on the student's favorite snacks, and ordered several books about a favorite subject for reading group in a desperate effort to get the student to behave. The teachers can become exhausted, and the student can become discouraged. At this point, the teacher, principal, and counselor might start the conversation about whether the student should remain in the class.

In this chapter, we explain how anxiety affects some students in school. We give specific strategies to keep ahead of the student's anxiety and to focus interventions on the anxiety instead of the student's varying behaviors that are a result of the anxiety. By using the FAIR Plan to understand the student with anxiety, teachers can create a classroom environment that is reassuring, mediates the student's anxiety level throughout the day, and teaches the student coping skills.

The anxiety a student feels can be hard to detect because there aren't always consistent outward signs. Anxiety is an invisible disability—teachers can't look at a student and know what is going on internally. Think of a student's high level of anxiety as similar to a can of soda that has been shaken: the can looks the same on the outside, whether the contents have been shaken or not. The only way to find out if a can has been shaken is to open it. If the soda explodes, you know. Sometimes, a teacher discovers the student's high anxiety when the student erupts after the teacher makes a small demand. If Roberta has a fight with her father in the morning and comes to school without much reserve, a simple demand such as "Please get in line" can ignite a huge reaction. Teachers might be completely surprised or irritated: "All I asked her to do was to line up for her favorite activity!" Or they may constantly walk on eggshells watching for signs of the student's distress to avoid a meltdown. "Why did you react that way?" is unlikely to get a clear response, as an anxious child usually does not make the connection between her anxiety and her volatile behavior. She may just reply, "I was mad," or be equally baffled by her own response.

WHEN IS ANXIETY PROBLEMATIC?

Because fears and worries are common in all children, it is important to differentiate these normal feelings from anxiety that interferes with how a child functions. Anxiety is defined as an abnormal and overwhelming sense of apprehension and fear marked by physiological signs, by exaggerated assessment concerning the reality and nature of the threat, and by self-doubt about one's capacity to cope with it.[1] Anxiety symptoms may be disproportionate to actual events; interfere with a child's daily ability to function (which may be seen as difficulty with peers, low self-esteem, academic failure, or stress in family relationships); and be present for a substantial period.[2]

A BRIEF OVERVIEW OF THE DIFFERENT ANXIETY DISORDERS

There are different types of anxiety disorders, but they all share some common features. These include a subjective feeling of discomfort or fear, overt behaviors of avoidance or escape, and physiological arousal such as sweating, nausea, and dizziness.[3]

Generalized anxiety disorder (GAD) is present in children who tend to have multiple pervasive worries that occur most of the time, nearly every day. Symptoms may include feelings of tension, negative self-image, restlessness, and irritability. Children with GAD can be preoccupied about peer relationships, school performance, health, personal attacks, and natural disasters.[4] In school, they may be excessively worried about upcoming assignments, ask for more help, and need extra reassurance with changes in routines or new experiences. One study found rates of GAD in a sample of eight- to thirteen-year-olds to be 3.8 percent of males and 9 percent of females.[5]

Other anxiety disorders are more specific. Separation anxiety disorder is focused on distress about separating from the child's primary caregiver. Although it is normal for younger children to have some anxiety when separating from their caretakers, separation anxiety disorder may be present when the child experiences excessive and continued stress when anticipating even a brief separation from the caregiver or when an actual separation occurs. These students may try to prevent a separation by having a tantrum or clinging to the parent, they may display physical symptoms such as nausea or headache in hopes they can stay home, or they may make repeated attempts to call home when at school.

Social anxiety disorder (also known as social phobia) can be present when children avoid interacting with peers, teachers, or both; have performance anxiety when sharing in front of a class (e.g., reading aloud, giving a presentation); and have accompanying physical symptoms such as flushing, trembling, or stomachache.[6] Moderate social anxiety can be developmentally appropriate, but social anxiety disorder causes intense distress and impairment because of fear of a social situation.

Post-traumatic stress disorder (PTSD) is another common childhood anxiety disorder. A third of the U.S. population has had exposure to trauma such as natural disaster or loss of a family member or abuse, and more than 6 percent of American children meet criteria for a lifetime diagnosis of PTSD.[7] Children with PTSD have been exposed to a life-threatening event and may continue to reexperience the event. This reexperiencing of the event is manifested by intrusive thoughts or memories, dreams, or (less commonly in children) flashbacks. Children may be reminded of traumatic events by triggers in the environment (e.g., sights, smells, sounds) or internal triggers (e.g., intrusive thoughts and physiological arousal such as increased heartbeat). They may show traumatic play, that is, repetitive play that lacks spontaneity and flexibility of themes. Reenactment refers to repeating some aspect of the traumatic experience either consciously or unconsciously.[8] Children with PTSD can exhibit avoidance behavior and emotional numbing, avoiding people, places, or situations that remind them of the traumatic event; can have a foreshortened sense of the future; and can be emotionally distant.[9] These children can use a lot of emotional energy to avoid traumatic reminders that may make them feel terrified and helpless. This can decrease their capacity to function in school, where they may stare into space, appear shut down, isolate themselves, show markedly decreased interest in activities, and have trouble focusing on classroom activities.

Hyperarousal—extreme anxiety—can manifest in children with PTSD as irritability, angry outbursts, and difficulty with concentration. In school-age children, hyperarousal can also manifest as somatic complaints such as headaches.[10] Children's symptoms must occur for at least a month and cause significant distress or impairment to be diagnosed as PTSD.

Panic disorder is very rare before adolescence.[11] Around puberty, children may begin to have panic attacks, which can present as shortness of breath, dizziness, trembling, and intense fearfulness. Some children who have separation anxiety disorder go on to have panic disorder as adults.[12]

Children with obsessive-compulsive disorder (OCD) have recurrent obsessions or compulsions that occur for at least one hour per day and cause significant distress or have an impact on function.[13] Obsessions are thoughts, and compulsions are actions. Obsessions are involuntary, intrusive thoughts or pictures that keep repeating themselves. When students are thinking obsessively, it is often accompanied by an uncomfortable feeling of dread. Common obsessions are contamination, worry of harm to self or others, symmetry urges (discomfort with the way objects are arranged), and doubting.[14] Compulsions (repetitive behaviors) temporarily relieve the obsessions. These can include washing or cleaning, checking behaviors such as making sure doors are locked, counting, ordering, or hoarding. In school, students with OCD can exhibit perfectionism and be excessively slow in generating work because they are too preoccupied with their compulsions. They may avoid bathrooms or contact with other peers because of fears of contamination. Table 3.1 summarizes the features of these various anxiety disorders.

In addition to students with diagnosed anxiety disorders, students with depression, Asperger's syndrome, nonverbal learning disability (also called nonverbal learning disorder), and any social deficits often have co-occurring anxiety. Not surprisingly, these children may also be particularly likely to be victims of bullying, which can increase anxiety levels.[15]

The strategies presented in this chapter are helpful in managing anxiety in most students. For students with OCD, PTSD, or separation anxiety, the strategies in this chapter will need to be supplemented, as OCD requires very specialized interventions and separation anxiety involves working with the parents intensely, which goes beyond the scope of a classroom behavior intervention plan.[16]

TABLE 3.1

Anxiety diagnoses

Disorder	Features
Generalized anxiety disorder (GAD)	Excessive anxiety and worry about a number of events or activities
Phobias	Persistent, unreasonable fear of a specific object or situation (e.g., flying, dogs, blood)
Social phobia	Marked, persistent fear of one or more social or performance situations
Separation anxiety disorder (SAD)	Excessive anxiety about separation from the home or people to whom the child is attached
Panic disorder	Recurrent panic attacks with persistent concern or worry about having another attack
Obsessive-compulsive disorder (OCD)	Recurrent, excessive, unreasonable obsessions (persistent, intrusive thoughts) and/or compulsions (repetitive behaviors) that cause distress or impairment
Post-traumatic stress disorder (PTSD)	Following exposure to an extreme traumatic stressor, re-experiencing the event, avoiding related stimuli, and increased arousal, irritability, hyper-vigilance, nightmares, dissociating, and emotional numbness

Source: adapted from American Psychiatric Association, *Diagnostic and Statistical Manual of Mental Disorders*, 4th ed., text revision (*DSM-IV-TR*) (Washington, D.C.: American Psychiatric Association, 2000).

THE IMPORTANCE OF INTERVENTION

Anxiety can be a highly disabling disorder, with lifetime prevalence rates estimated at between 8 and 27 percent in adolescents.[17] It can, if untreated, lead to chronic mental health problems, substance abuse, self-harming behaviors, and suicide attempts.

Anxiety can severely affect students' functioning. High levels of anxiety interfere with verbal working memory and impede students' academic performance.[18] We've all experienced losing basic skills in time of stress: forgetting your address when asked during an interview, blanking out when asked your sibling's age on a first date. Children who are anxious often have to exert more effort to perform well, as they drain resources to manage their emotions.[19] One study showed that children who were the most anxious in the autumn of first grade were almost 8 times more likely to be in the lowest quartile of reading achievement and almost 2½ times more likely to be in the lowest quartile in math achievement in the spring of first grade.[20] If their anxiety is left unrecognized and untreated in the school setting, such children are often soon at risk for academic difficulties, poor social relationships, and behavior problems and are likely to maintain anxiety for years to come.[21] This unacceptable fate can be averted.

BEHAVIORAL ATTRIBUTES OF STUDENTS WITH ANXIETY DISORDERS

Some students with anxiety can show consistent and recognizable signs that they are anxious. Examples include flushed cheeks and tense muscles (see the box "Some Clues for Identifying Student Anxiety"). Often, however, we don't know that a student is feeling anxious until we see behavioral signs. Understanding and tuning in to these signs can be useful for teachers to know when a student is feeling anxious.

Some students with anxiety can be hard for teachers to identify. Their behavior can be similar to other students with low frustration tolerance or chronically oppositional profiles.[22] Yelling, kicking, punching, insisting on things going their way, crying, leaving the classroom, and being irritable or easily frustrated are behaviors most people would associate with oppositional students, but these behaviors are also seen in students with anxiety.

Some students with anxiety can have an overreactive response to stress, which causes them to demonstrate inflexible, irrational, impulsive, shutting down, and emotionally intense behavior when they are in the classroom. Because of this, they can have a harder time regulating their mood and social interactions and acting and thinking rationally when under pressure.[23] While these behaviors may look like oppositional behavior rather than anxiety, what sets students with anxiety apart is the underlying cause of their oppositional behavior. A useful analogy is a person who has a heart attack. Several factors (e.g., diabetes, high blood pressure, smoking, obesity, stress) could have caused the crisis, and determining and addressing the underlying cause is critical to preventing future problems.

Some Clues for Identifying Student Anxiety

How do you know behavior is caused by underlying anxiety? Here are eight clues that anxiety is the culprit:

1. Student has a diagnosis of an anxiety-related disorder or a social deficit (at risk for social anxiety).

2. Student is inflexible, irrational, impulsive, or emotionally intense or seems to overreact.

3. Student shows a sudden change in behavior.

4. Student displays inconsistent behavior.

5. Student has a pattern of difficulty during certain times:
   - Unstructured times
   - Transitions
   - Writing demands
   - Social demands
   - Novel events
   - Unexpected changes in routine

6. Student shows avoidance.

7. Student shows desire for control and predictability.

8. Student has perfectionistic tendencies.

EXAMPLE OF A CHILD WITH ANXIETY AND OPPOSITIONAL BEHAVIOR

In preparation for a fourth-grade science experiment, Ms. Reynolds asked Ty to pass out the paper towels. He wanted to pass out the petri dishes instead. Ms. Reynolds encouraged him: "Ty, please pass out the paper towels, and maybe next time, you can pass out the petri dishes." Ty exclaimed, "Pass them out yourself!" and put his head on his desk.

Ty's teacher and a school administrator interpreted his behavior as oppositional. Teachers expect anxious students to appear meek, quiet, shaking, fragile, and frightened. Ty's reaction of talking back to the Ms. Reynolds and refusing to follow a direction is far from the expected behavior of an anxious student. His reaction was loud, powerful, and defiant. Teachers might respond as if the student were merely oppositional and might not address the underlying anxiety.

AN OBSERVABLE DEFINITION OF ANXIETY IN THE CLASSROOM

For children with anxiety, we typically observe the student to determine which signals might indicate that the student is going to lose control. These signals can be subtle, seemingly insignificant changes in behavior, such as a shift from sitting calmly to fidgeting in a chair, from talking normally to getting snappy, or from working hard to laying his or her head down on the desk. Once the teacher recognizes these changes in behavior as possible symptoms of anxiety, the teacher's responses will be better matched to the situation. The observable definition we use for anxiety is "any sudden change in behavior."[24] Like all students, students with anxiety can have other reasons for a change in behavior besides anxiety (e.g., hunger, fatigue, having to go to the bathroom). Checking in with them will help you sort it out.

Let's use Peggy as an example of how recognizing these changes in behavior and intervening early can make a big difference. Peggy was a fourth-grader who had witnessed domestic violence and was seeing the school counselor for support. Peggy had been quietly working when suddenly, she started to argue with the teacher about whether she could use a pen to do her worksheet. This type of sudden change in behavior should be a signal to the teacher that she may be anxious. Knowing this, the teacher can observe this change and say to himself, "Peggy is getting anxious." Using this type of self-talk will help the teacher to adopt a more sophisticated way of thinking about the behavior and to approach the student empathically, which will help a student like Peggy feel safer and calmer.

The teacher's instinctive response to Peggy's arguing may be to tell her to stop, have her lose points, or remove her from the class. However, since the teacher is aware that the real problem is anxiety and not what Peggy is arguing about (the pen), he can instead check in with Peggy. We recommend checking in with students when they show behavior change, with the assumption that it is anxiety if they are known to be anxious or if they occasionally have explosive behavior: "Anything bothering you?" or "You seem anxious; do you want to take a break?" or "What's the thought in your head?" Since Peggy can have trouble expressing herself, the teacher can also offer a choice of strategies, such as, "Do you want to get a drink of water or use putty at your desk?" These supportive responses can reduce anxiety and encourage self-regulation.

INCONSISTENT BEHAVIOR

Inconsistent, unpredictable patterns of behavior can be another clue that a student suffers from anxiety. It can be incredibly challenging to develop a consistent program for these anxious students, since their ability to manage a given situation fluctuates with their level of anxiety. As we discussed in chapter 2, analyzing the antecedents (what happened immediately before a behavior occurred) is usually a helpful way to see patterns, predict future behavior problems, and intervene to prevent reoccurrence. However, the antecedents of behavior in students with anxiety can be extremely variable. One day, asking Stephen to read aloud can go well, and another day, he may storm out of the classroom when he is asked to do the same task. Asking him to read did not cause the outburst, but asking him to do it when he had a high level of anxiety did. He couldn't cope with the demand at that particular moment. Professionals who don't understand this can make the mistake of overemphasizing the antecedent (assuming Stephen has a problem with reading) and creating interventions to address that. It's hard to detect the student's underlying anxiety that also needs to be addressed to reduce the behavior. Taking ABC notes is necessary to see what patterns or inconsistencies emerge in the antecedents, to allow appropriate interventions.

Another reason for inconsistent behavior patterns is internal or external triggers that provoke some students' behavior. Many students with anxiety experience internal triggers in the form of intrusive thoughts and physiological reactions. One student may be short of breath at P.E. and overreact, thinking that he or she is in danger, and run out of the gym. If another student thinks over and over again, "I'm going to fail the test," this student may start to cry hysterically when the teacher passes out the test. To the teacher, it appears that each student is overreacting. Different daily events, objects, people, smells, and noises can all trigger an anxious response. Students with PTSD are particularly susceptible to these external triggers, which can serve as reminders of a traumatic event and result in dysregulation and inappropriate behavior. Since teachers usually can't spot or anticipate a trigger, which can be either internal or external, they can only see the triggered behavior, which seems to have come from nowhere.

PREDICTABLE BEHAVIOR PATTERNS OF SOME STUDENTS WITH ANXIETY

Even though inconsistent behavior patterns are common in students with anxiety, there are some exceptions. Students with anxiety who have phobias, exhibit perfectionism, or avoid certain activities, people, or places can actually show consistent patterns of behavior. For example, it can be pretty obvious that a child who has a stomachache before every math test is apprehensive. A child who runs out of the room every time she sees a spider shows patterns that a teacher can figure out.

Activities that can be consistently difficult for students who suffer from anxiety

- Unstructured times
- Transitions
- Writing demands
- Social demands
- Novel events
- Unexpected changes in routine

The times of the school day that have the least amount of structure are particularly stressful for these students with anxiety. Unstructured times, such as transitions, lunch, snack, and recess are less predictable because there is no teacher to spell out exactly where a student needs to be and what he needs to be doing. Unstructured time requires much skill in the areas of the student's executive functioning, self-regulation, flexible thinking, problem solving, and social skills. Novel events or unexpected changes, such as a substitute teacher or a fire drill, can also be stressful, as predictable routines are disrupted. There is a lot of skill involved in navigating unstructured time well, and many students find it anxiety-producing. During lunch, the student can sit wherever he wants, which requires social navigation. He has to rely on his own skills and problem solving to fill the time. He could talk to a peer, eat lunch, go to the bathroom five times, or stare at the wall. Unstructured times of the day also typically have a social component, such as choosing whom to talk to, initiating conversation, reciprocating conversation, enduring possible rejection (e.g., when a favorite peer doesn't sit next to the student), keeping appropriate body space, staying regulated—not moving too much, not talking too loudly.

Since students with anxiety like predictability, structure is very calming and reduces anxiety for them. These students do better in a structured classroom, where there is explicit instruction about the schedule and what students are expected to do. There are often designated seats and clear expectations and plans (e.g., first use your graphic organizer, and then write your rough draft). When the teacher asks questions about the content and there are structured discussions, there are less spontaneous social demands. It's comforting for the student to know what is expected of him, for how long, and what is coming next.

EXAMPLE OF A STUDENT WITH ANXIETY IN AN UNSTRUCTURED CLASSROOM

Carol had frequent outbursts in class, calling her teacher stupid, making crow sounds, and at times standing up to dance during class. We later discovered, after observing the classroom, that the teacher emphasized cooperative learning groups (two or more students working together on a miniproject during class). The student's behavior only occurred during these cooperative learning activities. These activities were unstructured and had a high social demand. Students were asked to pick their own groups, and Carol was expected to navigate a small group of students working together without the support of an adult. Carol suffered from social anxiety, poor self-regulation and executive functioning difficulties. Her fear of not being picked by her favorite peers and her difficulty in navigating the group were catalysts for her inappropriate behavior.

AVOIDANCE BEHAVIORS

Students with anxiety about specific events or activities are likely to avoid or escape them. If a student has social anxiety, he may want to walk into the cafeteria and sit with his friends, but when he sees the group of chatting, giggling students, he feels anxious and instead isolates himself. Once he sits by himself, the student feels relief from the anxiety of joining the students. His avoidance creates an immediate reduction in anxiety, which is a powerful negative reinforcement.[25]

Removal of an aversive event (e.g., an approaching social situation) through avoidance behavior means the avoidance behavior worked: it terminated the anxiety-producing event. As a result, the student is likely to continue to avoid social situations in the future. Avoidance behavior can be obvious, such as when a student runs out of the room or hides under furniture, or it can be subtle, such as when a student temporarily avoids starting work by engaging the teacher in conversation.

Increased rigidity and the desire for control and predictability are attributes of students with anxiety as well. When a child is experiencing a clinically significant level of anxiety, she may insist that her belongings are arranged in a certain way (markers lined up, folders stacked perfectly), or she may need to be first or get her way (wanting the teacher to read a certain book or expecting to be called on immediately). Table 3.2 shows some classic ways that anxiety may present in school, as well as some less obvious symptoms. Schedules and previewing are strategies that help to create an environment that is more predictable for students with anxiety. Embedding choice in interventions allows the student to have some control throughout the day.

TRANSITIONS

Transitions happen multiple times throughout the school day. As we mentioned, transitions are some of the most difficult times of the day for some students with anxiety, because they require flexibility and executive functioning skills. Teachers can help these students with anxiety handle transitions more successfully so that students don't become uncooperative (e.g., refuse to get off the computer or start the next activity). There are big transitions, such as going from math class to lunch. Small transitions include getting off the computer to go to the next math center.

TABLE 3.2

Behavioral attributes of anxiety in schools

Classic attributes	Less obvious attributes
Is easily frustrated	Has difficulty completing work
Has somatic complaints such as stomachaches and headaches; has trouble breathing	Acts irritable
	Acts angry
Exhibits fear	Does not follow school rules
Seems on the lookout for danger	Has inconsistent patterns in antecedents
Easily upset by mistakes (perfectionism)	Exhibits ritualistic or repetitive behavior
Cries	Is inflexible
Startles easily	Acts out of the blue; seems overreactive
Blushes, trembles	
Frequently expresses worry	

Assigning one approach to all transitions is a mistake. A typical transition warning used by teachers is the countdown approach: "Five more minutes until cleanup." This strategy, however, is effective for only one aspect of a transition.

Particularly for students with anxiety-related behavior, it is important that teachers understand that there are four components of a transition:

- The cessation of the first activity
- Making the cognitive shift to the next activity
- Starting the next activity
- Lack of structure and specific expectations during the transition time

Let's look at these four components, using the example of Dalia's transition from playing a computer game to returning to her desk to work on a math paper. The first component, the cessation of the first activity, means that Dalia has to stop playing on the computer. The second component, making the cognitive shift, means that Dalia needs to change gears in her mind, moving from thinking about her computer activity to thinking about her math assignment. For the third component, she needs to sit down at her desk, pick up a pencil, and begin working on the math paper. A fourth component to most transitions, the lack of inherent structure and specific expectations during transition time, presents more challenges. Playing a computer game is a structured activity with clear expectations and physical parameters, as is doing a math worksheet at a desk. The transition between the activities has a less defined duration, fewer physical parameters, and less clear expectations. Many elementary school classrooms have long, whole-class transitions. Asking a group of twenty second-grade students to clean up and line up for lunch can take much longer than anticipated. These transitions can last up to five minutes. Some children can self-regulate during this time by talking quietly with their friends or doing an independent activity such as reading or daydreaming. Students with anxiety cannot always regulate themselves during this low-structure time.

It's important to choose an appropriate warning for each component of the transition (summarized in table 3.3). The most useful way to help a student stop an activity (especially a preferred activity) is to give a transition warning with a natural close. It is very unsettling for some students to be asked to stop midstream. Instead of saying five more minutes for independent reading, find the end of the chapter or thought (a natural stopping place), and place a sticky note with the words "stop

TABLE 3.3

Components of a transition and appropriate warnings

Component of a transition	Appropriate transition warning
The cessation of the first activity	Find a stopping point (a natural close), and use a concrete warning for that point (five more pages, read until the sticky note, one more YouTube video, etc.).
Making the cognitive shift to the next activity	Use visual schedules, photographs of what "being ready" for the next activity looks like.
Starting the next activity	Use traditional countdown type of warnings (five more minutes, use of timers).
Lack of structure and specific expectations during the transition time	Suggest tasks or activities that "absorb" the downtime (push in chairs, pass out papers, sharpen pencils).

reading" on that page. This will prevent the student from resisting the termination of an activity as much, leading to fewer instances where the student calls out, "Wait!" or ignores the transition, continuing to read. Other concrete transition warnings, for example, are "Five more bites, and then you can be finished," "Finish drawing that person, and then clean up," or "At the end of this inning, you need to stop playing computer baseball."

Most students visualize a future picture of the next event prior to making a transition. For an anxious student who is not able to visualize the transition, the shift may be more difficult. One strategy to help a younger student with this component of the transition is to take a photograph of the child at the next activity. With older students, a teacher can give them a visual schedule containing a list of activities in sequence and discuss with them where the next activity starts.

To add structure to transitions that have a lot of waiting or downtime, which often occurs during whole-class transitions, ask the student to engage in structured concrete tasks during transitions. Think of these structured tasks or activities as sponges absorbing the downtime.[26] Teachers should create a list of these tasks—the box "Sponges" provides some suggestions. Structured tasks also provide students some distraction from their worried thoughts. The transition task should include clear expectations such as where the student should be, what materials are needed,

> ## "Sponges"
>
> *Here are some activities that a student can do when there is wait time or other down time during the day:*
>
> - Put notices in students' mailboxes
> - Fold notices or papers
> - Clean white boards or chalkboards
> - Push in chairs
> - Organize books
> - Take attendance or lunch orders
> - Sharpen pencils
> - Sort colored pencils and crayons
> - Other classroom jobs
> - Simon Says or other nonverbal imitation games (for whole class)

and how long it should take; these expectations can prevent the student's behavior from escalating.

SUCCESSFUL EXAMPLE OF A STUDENT WITH PRESCRIBED TRANSITION SUPPORT

Teachers we've worked with have been amazed at the difference a prescribed transition can make. Here is an example of a student's response: Ablah was explosive and disruptive in the fall term of fourth grade. She suffered from PTSD and had difficulty returning to school after the weekends. After observing Ablah and collecting ABC data, we realized that she was having great difficulty during transitions, particularly when moving from a favorite activity to a less preferred activity. Upon analyzing the transitions more closely, we found that Ablah was having difficulty stopping the first activity. When her teacher simply changed the transition warnings to allow for a more natural close to the activity, Ablah's explosive behavior was eliminated. She even learned to stop an activity herself with the cue "Find a stopping place."

SETTING STUDENTS UP FOR SUCCESS

Considering the unpredictable nature of children with anxiety, teachers are often walking on eggshells to avoid upsetting the student, not knowing how the child will behave in any given situation. Teachers feel powerless in this situation: "He's totally unpredictable!" They can be at a loss on how or when to intervene. Over time, teachers may decrease demands on students so as to avoid an outburst (e.g., let a child play a favorite game on the computer all day). Although this may be important in the short term to reorganize the school environment and develop a behavior intervention plan, having low or no demands often means that structure from the child's day is removed and routines are no longer in place. This sort of unstructured day can be very stressful for students with anxiety and thus can be counterproductive in the long term.

Many schools, however, are not aware of what the antecedents to the student's behavior are, or the antecedents are very inconsistent, a common situation with anxious students. Overgeneralizing that all demands constitute possible problems for the student, the schools remove all demands. This should be a last resort. Once a no- or low-demand situation is put in place, it's difficult for the student to tolerate demands when they are reintroduced. The longer the child has low or no demands, the harder it will be to reintroduce higher expectations for behavior.

We have seen students play on the computer and with Legos for most of the year, a practice that has dire implications for their academic and social development. Another example of a low-demand response to an anxious, aggressive student is Andrea, a twelve-year-old girl with a mood disorder and anxiety. Andrea explained her own anxiety-related behavior: "When the teacher tells me what to do, I get overheated and usually blow up." The school counselor said that Andrea was unwilling to follow her class schedule or self-evaluate her behavior and showed no response to consequences. As a result, the school was in a holding pattern. Andrea sat in the office most of the day drawing, her preferred activity.

By removing demands, teachers are missing great teachable moments for students to learn to cope and self-regulate their anxiety. In our experience, many of the strategies we illustrate in the FAIR Plan can prevent the need for a no-demand situation. Another difficult side effect of implementing a low- or no-demand program for students is that if their behavior improves in this situation, people in schools can think that the students are stable. However, they are only acting out less because they are doing their preferred activities. As their inherent anxiety has not been reduced, reintroducing demands because the students seem ready will not be successful.

When we met Ang, she had been out of her third-grade classroom for four months, doing preferred activities such as making beaded bracelets, playing on the equipment in the occupational therapy room, and listening to music with the counselor. She spent most of her day in the special education teacher's office. During this time, her behavior had improved: she stopped bolting from teachers and had shown no aggressive behavior in the past month. Teachers were nervous about how and when to reintroduce demands. By having demands gradually and thoughtfully added, Ang was able to tolerate doing work for two hours a day within three weeks. This gradual process is a key behavioral technique referred to as *exposure*, the gradual and regular confrontation of anxiety-provoking stimuli. Exposure results in *habituation*, a decrease in the anxious response to the stimuli. When the task is adapted to the child's readiness to confront the task, the child habituates or has decreased anxiety because of the repeated exposure. A school mental health provider can help teachers implement this type of intervention in the classroom.[27] In Ang's case, her teachers started by allowing her to choose which of four math activities to do and gave her the choice to work for five, ten, or fifteen minutes before a ten-minute break. This type of choice making within activities and duration provided embedded control. Eventually, Ang was able to increase the work periods to twenty-five minutes with a five-minute break at the end.

Deciding when to push a student with anxiety and when not to is incredibly difficult. Finding the highest level of exposure or demand that is tolerable to the student is a good starting place, and then it can be increased gradually and safely from there. The FAIR Plan strategies can help you avoid the need to default to a no-demand plan.

ANXIETY-REDUCING BREAKS: A KEY PART OF THE MANAGEMENT PLAN

All anxiety management plans need to consider including anxiety-reducing breaks throughout the day. When breaks are given throughout the day noncontingently, it can alleviate the students' need to engage in escape-motivated behavior (see the box "Why Gold Stars Don't Always Work"). Give them the break *before* they "ask" for one through inappropriate behavior. Breaks need to be administered regularly during the day to prevent the students from being overcome with anxiety over time. For some students, breaking down the day into smaller parts helps them persevere, as they only have to think about getting through one segment of the day at a time.[28]

Why Gold Stars Don't Always Work

In traditional behavior plans, there is a focus on rewarding the absence of students' inappropriate behavior or rewarding appropriate behavior. For example, "If you have a quiet voice, you can earn a sticker, and after ten stickers, you can earn a prize." The student is rewarded for not screaming. For anxious students, however, this approach falls short, typically because the criteria for rewarding behavior is constant, despite the child's fluctuating level of anxiety. A goal such as "If you don't interrupt, you will earn five points every class period" may be achievable for the child during most class periods, but not when he is anxious. It's incredibly challenging to set daily or hourly behavior criteria for such students, since teachers know that anxiety can change a student's performance day-to-day and even moment-to-moment. In math class, the student may easily earn five points, but ten minutes later, after a small, problematic social interaction with a peer in science class, he may be totally dysregulated, unable to sit in his seat or to stop talking. After this difficult class, he may be discouraged that he was not able to earn his reward. Over time, this cycle can lead to low self-esteem and a feeling of failure. Students' inconsistent ability to perform must be taken into account when you are creating an incentive program. Otherwise, you might fuel the student's anxiety and unwittingly set the student up for failure and a poor self-image.

It is important to prevent unintentionally punishing the student for having an elevated level of anxiety and subsequent poor performance at any given moment. Remember, the student *cannot* act appropriately, because of anxiety; it's not that she won't. Instead, target specific strategies that the student needs to practice implementing, and make earning rewards *contingent on the student's use of these strategies* when she is frustrated. These may include taking five deep breaths, squeezing a "fidget toy," tensing and relaxing muscles, and using words (e.g., "I'm frustrated!"). This response encourages the student to use strategies and prevents her frustration at failing to meet an unfair criteria.

We recommend a set schedule, such as when the students first arrive, halfway through the day, and at the end of the day. A set schedule will keep their anxiety at a minimum and prevent inappropriate behavior. Setting these regular breaks is particularly helpful for students with explosiveness and who have a pattern of more outbursts or other inappropriate behaviors in the afternoon.

Breaks should also be used for specific anxiety-provoking activities. If writing is often an area of stress for a student, plan on giving the student a break before, during, or after the activity. The timing of the break should be what works best for the student—many students need a break after an anxiety-provoking task, but for others, a break during or before the activity is more effective (e.g., using relaxation techniques before reading aloud in class), so that they are regulated for the activity. Because anxiety can affect performance, relieving anxiety prior to the task is helpful with many students. The teacher needs to determine whether to have students take a break before, during, or after an anxiety-provoking activity to best alleviate anxiety. Students will be able to cope better with the demand and have a larger threshold for frustration and stress, if the break is properly timed. On the other hand, for students with escape-motivated behavior, if the break occurs *after* the student gets anxious and exhibits inappropriate behavior, the child has successfully avoided the task and the behavior will be reinforced.

Anxiety-reducing breaks can be as short as five minutes and can occur in or out of the classroom. Take the child's lead, being careful not to impose an idea about what's calming. "Sit on the beanbag, and we can talk for a minute" may sound relaxing to some, but it may not be for all students. When in doubt, don't talk—wait and see if the student engages in conversation. When interacting one-on-one with a student, adults often chat to fill the silence, but the child may need quiet time to process.

Think about what the student needs. If he is overwhelmed by too much language, talking during his break can make him more anxious. If she has social anxiety, it may be more appropriate to have a break that does not require her to interact with anyone—don't ask her to bring a friend. If he doesn't like loud noise, don't situate the break in the noisy cafeteria. If the student tends to have negative thoughts obsessively (ruminate), the break for the student should include a distraction from the student's own thinking. This may include watching a clip of a video or playing a game that takes a lot of concentration rather than listening to music, drawing, or other passive activities. The break has to be as free as possible from anything the student finds stressful. As long as the student doesn't resist, incorporate positive practice of self-calming strategies during a break. Of course, such strategies should not be forced which can cause a battle, producing more anxiety. Having a student become more frustrated and anxious because the teacher asked her to do yoga is counterproductive.

Teachers have expressed concern that students may abuse the use of breaks and may ask for them too frequently. This may occur, but is usually only a short-term problem. Students will test the limits, but usually after a week or two, this behavior subsides. If the student continues to test the limits of break time to the point where it is disruptive, then set parameters, such as a maximum number of breaks per day. For example, give the student five break coupons, and tell her she can use them whenever she needs to throughout the day. At first, she may use up all five breaks within the first two hours of the day, but she will gradually learn to budget her breaks for times of need.

A positive side-effect of the use or overuse of breaks is that each time the student asks for a break, he is role-playing an appropriate way of asking. Role-play is an important learning tool for students who need to learn how to identify their internal state and figure out how to ask for what they need. When a student practices these skills, they may become more automatic, even when the student is stressed.

Sometimes, students may be concerned that if they take a break, they will get behind. This is often the worry with students who are already behind. In these situations, it is helpful to schedule breaks during extended academic blocks. For example, stealing ten minutes for a break during a one-hour reading class is less disruptive than during a short academic activity. "Drop everything and read" is an academic period during which students and teachers often feel comfortable introducing a break. Teachers can make the mistake of stopping preventative strategies like breaks when a student starts to improve. When the student hasn't had an outburst in two weeks, it's easy to forget to provide anxiety-reducing breaks and strategies, or to think the student doesn't need them anymore. However, the student needs the breaks every day to prevent outbursts, and teachers need to be disciplined and consistent with the strategies. If the student's behavior improves to the point where the teacher no longer feels breaks are needed, reducing breaks should be done thoughtfully. After six weeks or more of desirable behavior from the student, the team could consider a gradual reduction in breaks. We don't recommend reducing breaks during a period of transition or a life event for the student (e.g., before or after school vacation or when student's mother is ill). As with everything, this should be a data-based decision: if problematic behavior recurs, breaks should be reinstituted.

Helping Students Manage Social Demands: Lunch and Recess

If social demands are thought to be the primary cause of the student's anxiety, and if the student's behavior is very disruptive, the team may consider providing the student with an alternative lunch setting. The cafeteria is a noisy and overwhelming place in which negotiating social interactions that are difficult in the first place becomes even more paralyzing. Where do I sit? Who do I talk to? What if no one wants to trade food with me? What if I spill? This is a prime setting for social exclusion and cliques. Some students can navigate the situation, especially with staff support, but others are not so successful. Even if the student manages to get through lunch without an incident, she might be overwhelmed. For some students, a quiet, structured lunch in the classroom with one or two peers and an adult may be better. If the teacher designs the lunch group (sometimes referred to as "lunch buddies") around a common activity such as cartooning or board games, it's much easier to have peers volunteer to join, reducing the stigma of a separate lunch. Teachers are often surprised at the popularity of such lunch groups, which indicates that the cafeteria may be stressful for some students without anxiety as well. We have also used lunch groups as a way to concretely demonstrate that students have friends who want to spend time with them: "See how many kids want to be in lunch group with you?"

In elementary schools, recess after lunch can have as many as eighty students on the playground at a time. This can be stressful for anyone, but especially for students with anxiety. Whenever possible, alternative recess with a small group is ideal, such as playing later, when the gym is free, or going to a different yard on the side of the school instead of the overcrowded playground.

Teachers will be amazed at the behavior change they'll see in some students by modifying lunch or recess. The children will often be calmer and less anxious later in the day and less likely to explode. They may also feel less anxious earlier in the day, because they are not anticipating the stress of the cafeteria.

EXAMPLE OF A STUDENT WHO RESPONDED WELL TO ALTERNATIVE RECESS AND ALTERNATIVE LUNCH

Mark was suspended eight or nine times each year he was in school until his mother moved him to a different school system in fifth grade. Mark demonstrated some tough behaviors. He punched a student in the face during a game of basketball at recess, and during chorus, he tipped over fourteen chairs while yelling that the teacher sounded like a goose. He was constantly disruptive in class as well—calling out, falling out of his chair on purpose, and making silly noises.

After seeing no consistent pattern in his ABC data and noticing some escape behavior, such as his going to the nurse several times per day, we wondered whether anxiety was the culprit. In October, we instituted two mandatory breaks during Mark's day. The first was in the morning, prior to writing, when he often called out in class. The second took place right after lunch. The breaks allowed him to think about getting through only half of the day at a time and pace himself. We tried different activities with him during the breaks and suggested he bring peers. We quickly realized that exercising alone on a trampoline, with minimal adult conversation, was the most calming type of break for him, and he had less inappropriate behaviors after this type of break.

We also noticed that while he was taking exercise breaks, Mark talked incessantly. We instructed the adult with him to listen and encourage him to talk. Mark would often blurt out a piece of information revealing his sense of rejection and isolation, such as, "I didn't want to go to the birthday party anyway."

After realizing that Mark had social anxiety and thought he had no friends, we instituted a modified lunch. He picked two kids to eat with him in a separate room away from the cafeteria. We asked the teacher about his interests and found that the kids that he talked with the most loved to draw cartoons. We invited the students to a cartoon lunch group. Mark was always a member, and the group got so popular that we had to rotate the other peers on a schedule. Mark gained confidence that other kids liked him, saying things like, "Wow, Michelle said she would come." With the implementation of just two breaks per day and the lunch group, Mark became compliant 90 percent of the day, extinguished disruptive outbursts, and was working on using his words instead of whining when upset (whining now occurred at a rate of only twice per week). By the end of the year, after the implementation of the FAIR Plan, he was totally compliant in school, was able to focus better on academics, and even had regular play date invitations from other students.

THE FAIR PLAN FOR THE STUDENT WITH ANXIETY-RELATED BEHAVIORS

Let's now tailor the FAIR Plan for the student with anxiety who exhibits escape-motivated and inappropriate behavior.

Functional Hypothesis and Antecedent Analysis

Every time a student acts in a way that is inappropriate and is interfering with her learning (socially or academically), the teachers' ability to teach, or others' ability to learn, it is important to record the behavior on an ABC data sheet. A minimum of ten incidents is necessary to observe a pattern. Students with anxiety don't always fall into a pattern, so sometimes even ten to fifteen incidents may be required to see trends. Table 3.4 shows an example of an ABC data sheet for a third-grade student with anxiety. The hallmark characteristic of students with anxiety is their inconsistency in performance and behavior. This becomes evident when you look at the antecedents in table 3.4's ABC data.

Remember that setting events are incredibly important to record and to be aware of. Students are very affected by life events and changes, and their level of anxiety is directly related to these factors. Students with anxiety are often motivated by escape. When you are looking at the consequence column, it's important to see if teacher and staff responses reinforce escape. If not, what other function is emerging?

It is also important to record and monitor the duration of the behavioral episode. A reduction in the frequency of behavior incidents is an easy way to determine improvement, but reduction in the duration of the incidents over time is another way. Duration reduction is a sign that the student is learning and applying self-calming strategies, as the student is able to get back in control faster.

Students with anxiety may have many incidents that seem like random incidents, but the first things to look for are patterns. Some patterns in antecedents to look for are unstructured times, transitions, writing demands, social demands, novel events, or unexpected changes in routine. As you see these antecedents, keeping a tally will help you review the information later.

In figure 3.1, you can see that three incidents occurred during unstructured time (recess, lunch, and science observation), and four occurred during transitions (end of reading, art, author study, and writing). Seeing these patterns in the antecedents will help you narrow down some interventions. Obviously, Kevin needs support around transitions (specifically, stopping an activity) and unstructured times, as well as overall anxiety-management strategies.

In the consequence column, Kevin is successfully avoiding or escaping demands.

TABLE 3.4

ABC data sheet for Kevin, a third-grade student with anxiety

Date, time, duration	Setting event(s)	Activity	Antecedent (what happens immediately before behavior)	Behavior (description of behavior)	Consequence (what happens immediately after behavior)
1/10, 11:15 a.m., 3 sec	Mom's boyfriend moved out last night	Independent reading	Teacher tells class to put away books and line up for recess.	Kevin exclaims, "You're an idiot—I'm not finished!"	Teacher ignores him, and Kevin goes back to reading.
1/14, 10:45 a.m., 5 sec		Math	Kevin is told to wait to go to the bathroom until his classmate returns.	Kevin screams, "Screw you!" and goes to the bathroom, anyway.	Teacher tells him to ask nicely next time.
1/17, 11:45 a.m., 3 min		Recess	Kevin is playing with woodchips on the playground by himself, and two students run by laughing.	Kevin throws woodchips at them and yells, "I heard that! Don't laugh at me!"	Students tell the recess monitor, who tells Kevin to sit on the bench.
1/17, 1:00 p.m., 15 min	Forgot his permission slip so teacher had to call home before he could come	Science observation	Kevin is walking near the river with a buddy.	Kevin starts running down the side of the river off school property.	Buddy yells for teacher, who runs after Kevin, shouting for him to stop; Kevin is sent to the office.
1/18, 2:15 p.m., 5 min		Art	Teacher tells Kevin to stop working and put painting materials away for the second time.	Kevin says, "In a minute," and then tips paint jar over—paint spills all over the floor.	Kevin continues painting as art teacher scolds him.
1/21, 12:15 p.m., 3 min		Lunch	Kevin is sitting with three other boys.	Kevin squirts ketchup across table all over boy's shirt.	Lunch monitor sends Kevin to the office.

(continued)

TABLE 3.4 *(continued)*

ABC data sheet for Kevin, a third-grade student with anxiety

Date, time, duration	Setting event(s)	Activity	Antecedent (what happens immediately before behavior)	Behavior (description of behavior)	Consequence (what happens immediately after behavior)
1/24, 10:15 a.m., 1 min		Social studies	Kevin asks a peer if he can use the map book; the peer says no.	Kevin grabs the map book and throws it against the wall.	Teacher sends him to the desk in the hallway.
1/25, 9:30 a.m., 2 min	Dad dropped him off this morning; Kevin was at Dad's last night	Reading	Kevin is told to switch seats with Bob so Bob can work with a different partner.	Kevin exclaims, "Why do I have to move? Why can't Bob move? It's his problem!" and then kicks his desk.	The teacher asks Bob to move with his buddy to a back table.
1/25, 12:45 p.m., 12 min		Writing	Teacher starts collecting rough drafts of small-moment stories.	Kevin growls and makes a biting motion to the teacher, refuses to give the teacher his paper, and continues writing.	Teacher ignores Kevin and collects the papers of the rest of the class.
1/28, 2:00 p.m., 4 min		Author study	Teacher pauses the movie and tells the class to get coats on for recess.	Kevin walks up to the DVD player, shoves the teacher out of the way, and puts the movie back on.	Teacher asks teaching assistant to take the class out as she explains to Kevin why the movie needs to be turned off.

Note: adapted from Sidney W. Bijou, et al. *Journal of Applied Behavior Analysis* 1, no. 2 (1968); Beth Sulzer-Azaroff and G. Roy Mayer, *Applying Behavior-Analysis Procedures with Children and Youth.*

FIGURE 3.1

Tallying the antecedents and consequences in Kevin's ABC chart

Antecedents		Consequences	
Unstructured times (recess, lunch, science observation):	///	Removed to office, hallway, or bench (science observation, lunch, social studies, recess):	////
Transitions (reading, art, author study, writing) :	////	Class removed (movie):	/
Asked to wait (math):	/	Teacher does not persist with demand (independent reading, bathroom, art, reading, writing):	////
Peer said no (social studies):	/		
Asked to move (reading):	/		

He is removed from the class on five occasions. He is able to keep doing what he is doing and avoid demands in five situations, including when the teacher does not persist with demands in independent reading, art, and writing. These observations show that the function of his behavior is probably escape or avoidance.

Accommodations

The most important aspect of reducing anxiety is to create an environment that is as structured, predictable, and calming as possible. Antecedent management is 90 percent of the FAIR Plan for children with anxiety-related behaviors. Teachers will need to use the list of antecedents from the student's ABC chart to help accommodate the child's specific areas of need. For example, if there appears to be a pattern of inappropriate behavior during transitions, then specific transition warnings need to be implemented. Teachers will need to make accommodations and modifications throughout the school day in the following four areas introduced in chapter 2: the school environment, executive functioning, curriculum, and training in underdeveloped skills.

Environment

For students with anxiety, it is important to have scheduled, preventative breaks. You will need to find a space in the classroom for small breaks (this is usually more acceptable for younger students in grades K–2). In the classroom, try to have the space visibly separate from the other students. We've used partitions, file cabinets, or bookcases as walls for the space. Making it comfortable with beanbags or mats is helpful. Space outside the classroom is useful for all ages so that there is adequate space to exercise and practice self-calming.

If a student has significant social anxiety, alternative lunch should be considered. We recommend advocating for this space as early in the school year as possible, ideally in the summer prior to the start of school. The custodian and principal will need to be part of this discussion. A permission slip allowing classmates to leave the cafeteria and participate in small lunch groups needs to be sent home (see appendix C for an example). When selecting classmates to join a lunch group or any other social group, choose students who are likely to foster a friendship with the student, and always bring at least two students in addition to the student with anxiety. A small group is best because sometimes being one-on-one with another child is too intimate for the student with anxiety, and sometimes it can be too unappealing for the peer (particularly if the student with anxiety has exhibited some stigmatizing behavior in the past). Having the peers come together makes it easier, as they are more likely to go with a friend.

Executive functioning

Students with anxiety often have associated executive functioning deficits. They struggle with observing and being aware of their environment and how to monitor and change behavior as needed. They can also be inflexible in their thinking and often have tunnel vision. If a student walks into his classroom, worried about the upcoming spelling quiz, he may practically plow over peers on the way to his desk. He is too fixated on the upcoming task to observe his surroundings. Even if this student isn't anxious about something specific, his overall dysregulation in conjunction with inflexible thinking can lead to this seemingly oblivious behavior as well.

A useful strategy for these students in K–6 is for them to learn to read the room as a tool for awareness.[29] If you stop the student from entering the classroom and cue him to read the room, he can learn to walk in and observe his surroundings and manage his behavior appropriately. For example, if all the students are sitting quietly independently reading, he won't barge in yelling, "What time does the quiz start?" He will hopefully notice the behavior of the other students and quietly sit at his desk. Whether you say, "Read the room," or use another cue, it's important to teach the concept of scanning and observing the environment.

Time management strategies also need to be taught to students with anxiety. Many anxious students are perfectionists (particularly with OCD and generalized anxiety disorder) and become stressed about finishing a task. Having a skewed sense of time passing exacerbates these situations. If the student doesn't have an inherent understanding that five minutes is a small amount of time, the teacher may get an explosive, teary reaction from the student ("What? No way!") when a teacher says, "Don't worry; we'll be done in five minutes." Time can also feel interminable for students enduring an anxiety-provoking task. Most people can relate to looking at their watch over and over while in the dentist's office or how long fifteen minutes feels when you are waiting for blood test results. Making time visual and concrete is essential. Visual timers are very helpful tools, but they are not all created equal. Timers that have digital numbers that rapidly change (showing the seconds) or make a ticking sound, or that do both, can be stressful for students. Many people use Time Timers, which are visual timers that show the passage of time on the clock with a colored wedge that gets smaller and smaller as time elapses (figure 3.2).[30] This type of device is helpful for K–6 students who are desperate for the end of an activity or for students who struggle with transitions. We recommend using timers during anxiety-provoking, nonpreferred tasks. This helps students persevere and see that there is an end in sight. While using timers and discussing time with students, you may find it very helpful to narrate what you want students to extrapolate:

FIGURE 3.2

The Time Timer

Source: Photo from Time Timer, LLC, used with permission.

"Wow, five minutes went by really fast!" or " I can't believe it's already been ten minutes—that went quickly!" Eventually, the students will ideally internalize this and have a more realistic sense of how long five minutes is.

To help older students with the big picture, use an ordinary wall clock, and color in the segments or wedges of time for different parts in the sequence of an activity. This way, the student can watch the clock in real time as the minute hand passes through the colored overlay segments (figure 3.3). "It's nine forty-five; you should be starting your final draft now." This has the advantage of helping students with pacing as well.

Timed tests and games are to be avoided with students who suffer from anxiety. Untimed tests are familiar accommodations in most schools and are accepted for standardized tests if written in the student's IEP or 504 plan.

Visual schedules are essential for K–6 students with anxiety. Since novel change and transitions are difficult for these students, visual schedules give you an opportunity to preview their day with them. Knowing what's happening right now and what will be happening next relieves anxiety for the student. Whenever possible, preview a change in the student's routine as far ahead of time as possible. If the student is going to have prescribed anxiety management breaks, put those in the schedule as well, to help alleviate possible transition problems.

Organization is another huge challenge for older students with anxiety, and they need to be explicitly taught organization skills. They often have trouble with

FIGURE 3.3

Example of clock segments

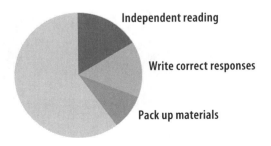

initiating tasks, and knowing how and when to start can often be a big challenge for these students. Since lateness can be a source of stress, many students will resist taking the time to organize before moving to the next activity, or they may lack the skills to do so. Adding time for organizing materials in the student's schedule within the last five minutes of each period can help alleviate their hesitation and can explicitly teach them how to organize. If the student has a chronically disorganized desk or locker, once per day the teacher might encourage her to organize this, writing this time into her visual schedule as well. Scheduling this immediately prior to a preferred activity is a good strategy, so the student does it quickly and with less resistance.

Curriculum

Writing is often an area of increased stress for students with anxiety. This includes open-ended writing assignments; personal narratives or topics involving self-reflection; composition; and smaller writing tasks such as explaining an answer in math and, sometimes, any pencil-and-paper task. Anxious students often have difficulty coming up with an idea to write about and have problems with organization, editing, spelling (especially for perfectionistic students), grammar, and punctuation. Handing a student a blank piece of paper and asking her to write a personal essay could cause the student to shut down or act out.

Although many teachers use graphic organizers and brainstorming exercises to prevent avoidance behavior and to help the student initiate a writing topic as seamlessly as possible, certain additional visuals can be helpful. A common dynamic that occurs in these situations is that the teacher ends up working one-on-one with the student, asking a lot of questions and making writing topic suggestions: "What do you like to do for fun?" or "I'm going to list some current events, and you tell me which one sounds interesting." Even if the teacher does get the student started writing, the child may have a hard time continuing the flow of ideas, which puts a big demand on the teacher. Using visuals may foster more independence and perseverance on the part of the student.[31] For older students, having some magazines with pictures or books, or even quickly printing out some Google images and placing them in front of the student may help her to not only come up with the initial sentence, but also to continue to compose a piece of writing. Photos of life at home sent in by parents or pictures of school are very helpful to use for younger students.

Word processing is a must for many students with anxiety. For a student who has perfectionistic tendencies (e.g., a student with OCD), handwriting, spelling, and making word choice mistakes can be debilitating. With pencil and paper, the student will have to erase and rewrite to fix mistakes. When the paper is too full of erase marks and vigorous crossing out, the student may have to rewrite or start again. Using a computer removes these obstacles to writing. In the older grades, most long writing assignments are already done on a computer, but whenever possible, use a computer for shorter assignments as well. Even if the student is not perfectionistic, editing is no small task for any student who is inflexible in her thinking—she may say, "I already wrote it!" Previewing a sequence of the steps of writing prior to starting an activity (i.e., first draft, read, edit, final draft) can prevent the student from being shocked at the idea of editing and creating a finished piece. Other technology should be considered for students with anxiety. For these students, "paper is the disability."[32] See appendix D for other ideas for technology resources.

In the area of spelling, students with anxiety can be nervous about making mistakes. We have seen students try to copy from a peer's spelling quiz or have meltdowns when they are unsure of how to spell a word. Usually, students who are perfectionistic are the most adamant about spelling correctly. The teacher may tell them how to spell a word or allow them to use spell check if it helps them to create a piece of written work with few interruptions. However, students may be embarrassed to ask for help with spelling, especially in the older grades. A respectful, subtle way to provide the correct spelling for the student is to write it on a sticky note and place it on his desk. Eventually, the student should be required to ask for this sticky-note help. If the student whines or avoids, but, when given a strategy such as "sound it out," can apply it and continue working, teachers may choose to stick it out. All this depends on the objective of the lesson. If the objective is to create a well-written document, then spelling might be less of a priority and accommodations make sense. If the focus of the lesson is accurate spelling, such as a spelling quiz or vocabulary lesson, accommodations may not make sense.

Creating a checklist for students that includes their specific area of weakness on the left and the strategies they need on the right can also be very helpful (see table 3.5 for an example). This checklist can be created by the teacher or by a consultant. By pointing out to the student the exact components of writing that are difficult for her, a teacher may prevent the student from having generalized anxiety about

TABLE 3.5

"My writing strategies": a checklist for students

Parts of writing	Strategies	Used?
Thinking of an idea	Look in a book Look at my writing idea list Computer picture help "Ms. _____, will you help me get a computer picture of _____?"	
Drawing	How-to-draw cards Sticky-note help "Ms. _____, will you help me draw a _____?"	
Sentences	Underline the number of words in the sentence. _____ _____ __ _____ "Ms. _____, will you help me plan a sentence?"	
Spelling	Frequently-used-words card Tap out the word Sticky-note help "Ms. _____, will you help me spell_____?"	

Source: Pics for PECS™ images are used and adapted with permission from Pyramid Educational Consultants, Inc. (www.pecs.com). Pyramid Educational Consultants, Inc. reserves all rights to the Pics for PECS™ images.

writing. We prefer to hear students say, "Spelling is hard for me" rather than "I am the worst writer" or "I hate writing." This identification of their own specific area of weakness is more proactive and conducive to initiating help and implementing strategies. For older students (grades 3–5), make the checklist without the pictures.

In all academic areas, including writing, presenting small amounts of work at a time can prevent a student with anxiety from feeling completely overwhelmed. We are not suggesting you reduce expectations; just put as few items as possible on the student's desk at once. Instead of handing a student a packet of math problems, hand her one sheet at a time. If looking at a whole sheet of math problems causes a student to overreact, covering half the paper until she's finished with the first half may prevent a shutdown. Over time, the amount of work presented to the student should gradually increase. Whenever possible, embed choice in academic demands (e.g., let them choose the order of math assignments). Choice will help students have some control, which will help them comply and feel calmer.

Previewing is another strategy that can help the day go more smoothly for a student with anxiety. Teachers often worry about the amount of time previewing takes and when they are going to fit it into their schedule. However, we have found that by sacrificing no more than five minutes first thing in the morning to preview the schedule, teachers can prevent a meltdown or avoidance behaviors later in the day—behaviors that will often take more than five minutes to manage. In addition to previewing the daily schedule, it is also helpful to show the student the actual assignment that he will face later in a nonpreferred subject. Do the first example together, or begin to initiate ideas: "This is the worksheet we're going to do in math today. Let's do the first problem together." Hopefully, having already seen the assignment, the student will not have an adverse reaction when he sees the same work later that day.

Homework is anxiety-provoking for many students, and some professionals argue against assigning homework to students with extreme anxiety.[33] Since navigating school is so effortful for students with anxiety, by the time they get home, many students can't engage in any other school-related activities. The team should consider reducing, accommodating, or eliminating homework for some students. One school we consult to had its second-graders only do their homework online. Students and parents reported high motivation and low avoidance to a previously onerous task.

Training in underdeveloped skills

Teaching a replacement behavior is crucial. A common function of inappropriate behavior for students with anxiety is escape. Functional communication strategies are essential replacement behaviors for escape-motivated behavior, giving the students a way to communicate their need for escape or help.[34] Replacement behaviors are taught while the students learn skills that ultimately lead to the elimination of the need for escape—first teach the students to escape through appropriate instead of inappropriate behavior, and then build their skills and strategies so that they no longer seek or desire escape.

For example, if a student is yelling in class when anxious to escape a demand, a typical response would be to remove her from the room, essentially allowing her a break from a demand because of her inappropriate behavior. To change this dynamic, she needs to be taught to escape a demand or situation through appropriate behavior, such as asking for a break or pointing to a break card, and be allowed to leave the room. Once the student has an appropriate way to escape, she can be taught the skills she needs to eliminate the need for escape.

Teaching skills that are underdeveloped in a child is an important part of changing behavior. Appendix B lists resources for more information about teaching these skills. Students with anxiety commonly have difficulty with flexible thinking, executive functioning, frustration tolerance, social skills, self-advocacy, positive thinking, motivation, self-regulation, and self-monitoring (a system to help students notice and rate their own behavior throughout an activity).[35] In a student's FAIR Plan, the explicit strategies on how to teach these skills need to be highlighted. This is an essential part of the FAIR Plan. Students won't move forward and change their behavior unless new skills are taught.

Self-regulation should be taught preventatively and then coached in the moment. Unfortunately, many students are so overwhelmed with anxiety or are so hyperfocused on the details of the problem that they are unable to identify how they feel or are aware of the gradual building of their frustration. Students with anxiety need to learn to identify when they feel anxious and recognize the physical symptoms (e.g., increased heart rate). Once they can identify that they are anxious, it will be easier for them to know when they need to use a self-calming strategy. The key to self-regulation is to catch yourself feeling a bit frustrated and to self-calm at that point, before getting furious. When anyone is intensely angry, self-calming is much more difficult.

Cognitive behavioral therapy is based on the idea that emotional disorders come from maladaptive or distorted thinking, which interferes with everyday living. Students (older than ten years old) can learn to recognize and monitor their emotions, identify patterns of thinking and their automatic thoughts, and develop appropriate functional responses by actively examining these thoughts.

Sources: Athena A. Drewes, *Blending Play Therapy with Cognitive Behavioral Therapy: Evidence-Based and Other Effective Treatments and Techniques* (Hoboken, N.J.: John Wiley & Sons, 2009); Patricia Romanowski Bashe and Barbara L. Kirby, *The Oasis Guide to Asperger Syndrome: Advice, Support, Insight, and Inspiration* (New York: Crown Publishers, 2005).

Throughout the day, teachers can implement tools that come from cognitive behavioral therapy. These include scales to help students identify their emotion or level of agitation (e.g., Five-Point Scale, emotional thermometer [see table 3.6], Alert Program).[36] In the first stage of teaching the student to use these tools, the teacher labels the student's emotion for him: "You are frustrated." It's great if the teacher also pairs this by pointing to the correlating visual. School counselors may teach specific lessons to help students learn to become aware of body reactions to feelings and to identify the physical reactions that may signal anxiety.[37] Teachers may reinforce the student's awareness of his emotions by narrating and labeling these cues in the moment (i.e., helping the student do body checks): "You look frustrated, your shoulders are up, your face is scrunched, your hands are clenched." Another helpful way to give students feedback on their internal state is for the teacher to do frequent "body checks" with the student.

In addition to teaching the student to recognize her emotions and how they may vary over time and across different situations, teaching specific self-calming strategies is equally important. These may include taking a break, yoga, exercise, reading, progressive muscle relaxation or breathing exercises.[38] See appendix E for more suggestions of calming activities. If the student has explosive behavior and is often removed to a smaller space (time-out room or safe space) when upset, that space should be used to practice self-calming once or twice a day. This positive practice of self-calming, whether in a separate space or not, will eventually help the student to use self-calming strategies automatically when she is upset. Have her practice self-calming strategies when her heart rate increases. To simulate the increased heart rate associated with an anxious feeling, ask the student to exercise (e.g., do

TABLE 3.6

Emotional thermometer

Feeling		Strategies
Angry		Take a break; take deep breaths
Frustrated		Get a drink; use my calming box
Excited		Take deep breaths
Anxious		Use my calming box
Sad		Use my words; use my calming box
Content		Use my words
Happy		Use my words; smile or laugh

Sources: Pics for PECS™ images are used and adapted with permission from Pyramid Educational Consultants, Inc. (www.pecs.com). Pyramid Educational Consultants, Inc. reserves all rights to the Pics for PECS™ images.
Adapted from Kenneth W. Merrell, *Helping Students Overcome Depression and Anxiety: A Practical Guide* (New York: Guilford Press, 2008).

jumping jacks or run in place) and then to use a self-calming strategy. This allows the child to experience how self-calming can decrease the heart rate and make her feel better.[39] We have seen students be escorted to a safe room and, while furiously swearing, independently engage in yoga poses and push-ups until they calm down, avoiding the need for adult intervention.

Providing a calming box for a student with anxiety is another very effective way to teach a student to self-calm in times of stress, especially if a separate room is unavailable. The box can contain calming sensory items such as a weighted blanket or pillow, putty, noise-reducing headphones, stuffed animals (for younger students), scented lotion, or music with headphones (see "Items for the Calming Box" for more suggestions). It is important to tailor the contents to the individual—for example, students with obsessive thoughts may not benefit from listening to music or using headphones, as it disengages them from people and they tend to focus more on their intrusive thoughts.

Having the student rate themselves, using one of the scales mentioned previously, prior to using the sensory or calming item and then after using the item can help the teacher decide what is helpful for the student. The student should have access to his box throughout the day.

Items for the Calming Box

These items, among others, can help children with anxiety calm themselves.

- Weighted blanket
- Weighted lap pillows
- Weighted ball
- Weighted vest
- Noise reduction headphones
- Portable music player with music
- Theraputty

- Heated neck warmer (if microwave is available)
- Yoga cards
- Stuffed animal
- Small action figure
- Small, soft blanket
- Portable study carrel (can be kept near the box)

Sources for these items include:

- FlagHouse: www.flaghouse.com
- Amazon.com

- School Outfitters: www.schooloutfitters.com

Once the teacher has taught the student to label his emotion, practice self-calming, and choose a helpful calming strategy when he's calm, he needs coaching to help him to put it all together when he is upset or anxious. Use minimal, concise language when a student is anxious—too much language can escalate his anxiety-based behavior. Having visuals or a list of strategies can be effective (e.g., "When I'm anxious, I can . . ."), as illustrated in table 3.6.

Students with anxiety often suffer from self-defeating thoughts. Cognitive behavioral therapy is based on recognizing the common thinking traps that lead to anxiety and evaluating the evidence to see if these thoughts are accurate (see table 3.7 for examples).[40] Thought-stopping instruction is also an important intervention that school counselors can teach students with anxiety and can be reinforced in the classroom. The technique helps to show these students that they have control over uncomfortable thoughts and can redirect them to focus on other things. If a child is upset about a mistake on a test and can't stop criticizing herself, thought stopping is useful as the student learns to stop thinking about the upsetting event or idea and pair thought stopping (which sometimes includes visualizing a stop sign) with a positive self-statement or calming image.[41]

Power cards are another intervention that can help students with anxiety.[42] These are the size of baseball cards and fit into a student's pocket. Often, a motivational or "cool" character is portrayed on the card with a self-talk message under it, such as "I am OK," "It's going to be OK," or "I can take a deep breath." This helps students feel empowered and can promote positive self-talk, which is an underdeveloped

TABLE 3.7

Common thinking traps

Trap	Definition
The walking-with-blinders trap	Only seeing the negative and overlooking the good in a situation
The avoider trap	Staying away from situations that seem frightening without trying them first
The should-be trap	Berating themselves because they should be perfect

Sources: Philip C. Kendall, *Cognitive-Behavioral Therapy for Anxious Children: Therapist Manual* (Ardmore, Pa.: Workbook Pub., 2006); Kenneth W. Merrell, *Helping Students Overcome Depression and Anxiety: A Practical Guide* (New York: Guilford Press, 2008).

skill for some students. These cards can be purchased, or teachers or therapists can make them on the computer.

Please refer to chapter 4, which discusses students with oppositional behavior, for more information on self-monitoring strategies.

Interaction Strategies

The teacher needs to explicitly spend time building a relationship with the student with anxiety. Some easy ways to fit this into a busy day are to bring the student with you when you are making copies, and to eat lunch with the student occasionally. These small moments of being together help develop a basis for the student to trust and feel safe with you, which is integral in a student's ability to manage anxiety.

Since anxiety is so difficult to recognize, it is important to have a working, observable definition of anxiety so that the teacher can catch the student before his behavior escalates. Consequently, any sudden change in behavior from the student should elicit a supportive response from the adult. The teacher will check in with the student: "Hey, buddy, how are you?" when he or she sees a change in the child's behavior (e.g., when he changes from quietly sitting to talking loudly). In addition to gaining information, a check-in can be a time to prompt the student to use a regulation strategy such as taking a break or taking deep breaths.

In the moment that a student is acting inappropriately, several interactive strategies are helpful. Make sure to use concise language: "Computer is all done" as opposed to "You've already been on the computer for fifteen minutes, and Janet didn't get a turn at all yesterday, so you need to get off." Too much language may escalate the situation and overwhelm the student, particularly if he has processing difficulties. Make empowering statements, such as reminding him that he has had success in a similar situation before and that he is capable of coping with the current situation: "I know it's hard, but you were able to take three slow, deep breaths and finish writing yesterday."

Students with anxiety can engage in behaviors that are stigmatizing such as yelling, exploding, or crying, which can make them self-conscious. They get discouraged at not being able consistently to perform. Self-esteem building is essential for these students. One of the most effective ways to build self-esteem is to implement noncontingent reinforcement.[43] All teachers are great at giving reinforcement after a student does something appropriate; this practice is called positive reinforcement.

The student learns from this that he can earn praise or attention by behaving in a certain way. Noncontingent reinforcement is different and not often implemented in school. It consists of random acts of kindness by the teacher toward the student: "Here's a sticker, just because I thought you would like it!" or "Hey, buddy, why don't you have an extra ten minutes of computer time." This is a powerful way to build the student's self-esteem, because over time, the student associates positive reinforcement not with something he did, but with who he is.

Providing opportunities for students to have leadership roles and take responsibility during the school day also increases their self-esteem. Some examples of responsibilities are running school errands, mentoring a younger student (e.g., reading to a kindergartener), or giving a new student a tour of the school.

Response Strategies

Preventative antecedent management is the major emphasis of the FAIR Plan for students with anxiety. We will discuss consequences and teacher responses, but it is important to know that antecedent management and teaching underdeveloped skills is the heavy lifting to change behavior in these students.

Responses to inappropriate behavior such as time-outs, removing the student from the room, giving her a long break, and allowing her to avoid a demand are not helpful consequences for escape-motivated behavior. These responses will reinforce the behavior. Instead, teach the replacement behavior of asking for breaks appropriately; allow the student an opportunity to work toward extra breaks by having her engage in a nonpreferred activity and use her newly acquired strategies. Start by having the student engage in a nonpreferred activity for five minutes, followed by a break for twenty minutes. Over time, build up the duration of the nonpreferred activity.

It's important to veer from traditional student behavior plans when delivering reinforcement for individuals with anxiety. Rather than giving rewards or points when a student gets through a period without acting inappropriately, use rewards to reinforce the student for using a self-calming strategy. This will avoid using set criteria for behavior expectations for a student who has fluctuating ability to perform.

For example, when Raul screams unexpectedly while doing his math sheet, instead of giving him a break (which would reinforce escape) or penalizing him (have him lose points), remind him that he is anxious and that he should try to use a strategy. It's usually helpful to do verbal coaching in this moment: "You can do it. Try some deep breaths." Reminding students they will earn rewards for using a strategy can be motivating in this moment as well. When students are first learning strategies, reinforce any approximation of the appropriate behavior (e.g., if the student raises his hand an inch, reinforce him: "Oh, you're raising your hand to ask for help! Nice use of a strategy.").[44]

Appendix F shows an example of a sheet that students with anxiety can use throughout the day to self-monitor and keep track of points earned for using a strategy. For students who have difficulty accurately evaluating their own behavior, we recommend that the teacher rate the student's behavior as well, telling the student why that rating was chosen. There should be at least three rating options, to avoid promoting all-or-nothing thinking (good or bad). Remember, the students are not earning points for their behavior; they are just rating themselves. Points are earned only by using a strategy. It is best to use the numerical scale of 1 through 3, as we've done in appendix F. Using emotional words or symbols in the rating criteria (e.g., the phrases "great effort" and "poor effort," or smiley faces and sad faces) can make the child feel overly criticized. If there is conflict when the teacher and student are rating the student's behavior, then we recommend not using the numbered rating system but merely recording a check after the teacher and student have had a reflective conversation.

A FAIR PLAN FOR NELLI

In the course of observing Nelli, the little girl whose story began this chapter, her teacher documented many random incidents in ABC notes, but observed a pattern of disruptive behaviors during transitions and unstructured times. Nelli seemed to be attempting to escape demands and situations through inappropriate behavior.

The following accommodations were then put in place: Nelli had a ten-minute break when she first entered school. She was also given a fifteen-minute break halfway through the day and another fifteen-minute one at the very end of the day. An alternative lunch was arranged to help with her regulation and her social anxiety. A visual timer was used for nonpreferred tasks so that she could see when they would end, as well as a visual schedule so that Nelli knew what to expect of her day. The teacher also previewed any novel events for any given day.

Since Nelli also exhibited perfectionism around drawing and spelling, she was given a portable spell checker. Her teacher would also write the words Nelli needed on a sticky note on the child's desk. How-to-draw cards or stencils were helpful for her in drawing. Twice a week, a social worker also worked with Nelli on social skills and flexible thinking. Social skills were practiced daily with a classroom aide and with peers during lunch-buddies sessions.

Nelli also needed to practice self-calming strategies—typically, yoga positions—daily in the school counselor's office, which was where she would be escorted if she exploded. The teacher would ask Nelli to do body checks throughout the day, giving her constant feedback on her anxiety level. Nelli also used the emotional thermometer; this visual aid had strategies listed on the side and was taped to her desk.

Nelli created her own calming box after being given many items to choose from—including scented lotion, small figures of fairies, a portable music player, and a small flannel blanket. When she used the calming box—or another calming strategy—she earned time to play cards with a friend.

For interaction strategies, her teachers began responding to sudden changes in behavior with supportive responses. They also provided noncontingent reinforcement: teachers brought in pictures and magazines about fairies, ate lunch with her, and played basketball with her in the gym. She also became a "P.E. helper" for a kindergarten class once a week. Nelli continued to need sponges (i.e., as mentioned earlier, tasks to keep her busy) for downtime during transitions and to help with stopping a preferred activity.

Nelli did remarkably well with this FAIR Plan. She stopped all explosive behavior and was able to participate in all subjects, within a month of putting these strategies in place. By holding a small flannel blanket during challenging assignments, she was able to complete many tasks. She was using self-calming strategies and could recover from frustration within two minutes without inappropriate behavior, as noted in follow-up ABC documentation. What's best, she told her mother that she liked school, and teachers reported that they liked her, too. One said: "She's actually a pleasure to be with now!"

Chapter Summary

- Anxiety is hard to identify because there are few consistent outward signs.
- Students with anxiety can have inconsistent behavior patterns—antecedents can be inconsistent.
- Students with anxiety commonly have escape-motivated behavior.
- Students with anxiety can be inflexible, irrational, impulsive, emotionally intense, or prone to overreact.

- The first step in addressing a student with anxiety-based behavior is to create an observable definition of anxiety.
- Times of the day that might be hard for students with anxiety include unstructured times and transitions.
- Other circumstances that can make these students especially anxious are writing demands, social demands, novel events, and unexpected changes in routine. Accommodations should be considered in these areas as needed.
- Giving the student noncontingent, anxiety-reducing breaks throughout the day is crucial.
- Alternative lunch and recess should be considered.
- It is important for teachers to understand the four components of a transition and to make transition warnings match type of transition problem.

FAIR

Behavior Intervention Plan for the Student with Anxiety-Related Behaviors

Student's Name: _____   Date: _____

TARGETED BEHAVIORS (be as explicit as possible):

F   **Functional Hypothesis and Antecedent Analysis**

☐ Document all instances of targeted behaviors, using ABC data sheet (minimum of ten incidents)

☐ List antecedents from ABC data or observation to be addressed in this plan *(look closely at unstructured times, transitions, writing demands, social demands, novel events, or unexpected changes in routine):*

☐ Form a hypothesis about the function of behavior (circle one or more): attention, escape, tangible reward, sensory satisfaction. *Escape is a common function of behavior for students with anxiety.*

☐ List any pattern of consequences, using the ABC data:

☐ List any setting events of note:

A Accommodations

Environmental

- ☐ Provide safe space in classroom
- ☐ Schedule regular breaks
- ☐ Allow for breaks outside the classroom
- ☐ Arrange alternative lunch
- ☐ Arrange alternative recess

Executive functioning

- ☐ Teach "reading the room"
- ☐ Use Time Timer
- ☐ Narrate passage of time
- ☐ Use segmented clock
- ☐ Consider untimed test
- ☐ Use visual schedules
- ☐ Put organization time in schedule
- ☐ Present only a few problems or items at a time
- ☐ Preview nonpreferred tasks in the morning
- ☐ Consider accommodated or modified homework

Curriculum

- ☐ Use pictures to help students think of and maintain a topic when they write
- ☐ Have student use word processing
- ☐ Consider spelling accommodations
- ☐ Have student use self-monitoring writing strategies checklist
- ☐ List other technology resources:

Replacement behaviors (examples for escape-motivated behavior):

- ☐ Teach asking for a break appropriately
- ☐ Teach asking for help appropriately during demand

Teaching underdeveloped skills explicitly

- ☐ Positive thinking

- ☐ Executive functioning
- ☐ Self-regulation
- ☐ Thinking traps (cognitive behavioral therapy)
- ☐ Social skills
- ☐ Power cards

Regulation of self and self-monitoring

- ☐ Have student use regulation scale (i.e., emotional thermometer)
- ☐ Prompt for "body check" cues throughout the day
- ☐ Encourage daily self-calming practice in or out of the classroom
- ☐ Have student develop and use calming box
- ☐ Have student use self-regulation chart: "what to do when I feel"
- ☐ Schedule breaks—noncontingent escape to prevent avoidance behavior (specify before, after, and during activity and how many per day)
- ☐ Have student use mobile device for self-monitoring
- ☐ Use the self-monitoring sheet (appendix F)

I Interaction Strategies

- ☐ Respond to any sudden change in behavior with supportive response
- ☐ Use concise language
- ☐ Apply noncontingent reinforcement
- ☐ Use leadership-building and self-esteem-building activities
- ☐ Work on explicit relationship building
- ☐ Develop transition warnings and strategies

R Response Strategies

For escape-motivated behavior

- ☐ Avoid responses that would reinforce escape-motivated behavior, such as time-outs, removal from class
- ☐ Avoid requiring the student to earn escape/breaks. Provide breaks noncontingently.
- ☐ Prompt student to use a strategy when student shows signs of anxiety

- ☐ Assign rewards or points when the student demonstrates a self-regulation skill
- ☐ Avoid rewards or consequences based on consistent or set behavior criteria
- ☐ Label the student's anxiety level when the student shows signs
- ☐ Remind the student of previous success at calming
- ☐ Exposure: If a student exhibits low tolerance for work, start in small increments and reinforce with escape from work (break), and build up

CHAPTER 4

"You're Not the Boss of Me!"

The Student with Oppositional Behavior

As Ms. Graves handed out math worksheets to the class, she noticed that Emily looked particularly unkempt today. Her hair was uncombed, and she had breakfast (syrup, it appeared) smeared on her face. Ms. Graves breathed deeply and hesitated before handing Emily her worksheet, saying, "Go ahead and get started." Emily began to write her name on her paper. Ms. Graves gave a sigh of relief.

Within five seconds, Emily ripped the math paper and put a small piece of it in her mouth. A student sitting next to Emily shouted, "She just ate it!" Ms. Graves rushed over and asked Emily to please clean up the pieces she had ripped and to put them in the trash and get back to work. Emily screamed "No!" and climbed under the desk. She held the legs of the desk and banged them loudly against the floor. A child covered her ears, and two students asked to be excused to go to the bathroom. A teacher's assistant from the next room came in to help Ms. Graves coax Emily out from under the desk. Emily screamed "No!" again after each request. Because of all the commotion, the principal appeared. After two minutes of whispering with Ms. Graves, the principal led the class out of the room to the library. Ms. Graves, Emily, and the teaching assistant were alone in the room. Emily's behavior escalated. She yelled every time the teaching assistant made a suggestion like, "Why don't we go to Ms. Carson's office—she has a nice couch." Emily's responses included: "You're fat and ugly," "Don't tell me what to do," and "I'm going to punch you in the face!"

Eventually, the adults escorted Emily to the school psychologist's office so that the class could return. Emily returned to class two hours later. She never did the math worksheet.

Students who are oppositional are usually the most challenging to include in the classroom.[1] When a student is disruptive, the teacher can spend too much time focusing on how to deescalate the student's behavior, and productive learning takes a back seat as the teacher ends up repeating demands over and over again to a student who seems intent on undermining the teacher's authority.

According to a recent national survey, an estimated four million children engage in disruptive behavior at school, representing over 5 percent of all school-age children.[2] In special education classrooms, the numbers are much higher: two-thirds of students are diagnosed with an attention or disruptive behavior disorder.[3] Early intervention is critical because children who are noncompliant and oppositional when younger are at increased risk of developing aggressive and delinquent behaviors as teenagers.[4]

In this chapter, we outline how you can help a student with oppositional behavior comply and perform better academically and socially. Our definition of oppositional behavior includes students who are easily annoyed, seem to irritate others on purpose, exhibit explosive behavior, are consistently noncompliant, have difficulty taking responsibility for their actions, tend to break rules, and have difficulty with peers. Some students with anxiety may present with oppositional behavior, and additional strategies for addressing anxiety-related behaviors can be found in chapter 3. Other students who are depressed, withdrawn, and irritable can be quietly oppositional, and additional strategies in chapter 5 are helpful with these students.

A teacher can do much to improve oppositional behavior in students and prevent a standoff. As with all students with challenging behavior, the emphasis needs to be on preventing the behavior and responding early to change unproductive patterns.[5] Traditional behavior plans are not always helpful with students with oppositional behavior.[6] The FAIR Plan for students with oppositional behavior starts with creating a supportive classroom environment. The emphasis is on identifying antecedents and building strong relationships with these students. In this chapter, we recommend ways to communicate more effectively with these students and to teach them underdeveloped skills so that you, and they, can prevent further oppositional behavior.

CAUSES OF OPPOSITIONAL BEHAVIOR

There is no single cause of oppositional behavior. However, children with oppositional behavior disorder are more likely than those with no diagnosis to have parents report family violence or overly harsh and inconsistent discipline, or to have been in foster care or experienced frequent moves.[7] If teachers take the time to build a relationship with the family and provide empathic support, parents may be more willing to mobilize to get the additional guidance to change their own behavior (e.g., learning how to give praise, reinforce positive behaviors, and use effective communication).[8]

It is also important that these children be referred for a careful evaluation to determine if they have a treatable psychiatric disorder (depression, anxiety, or attention deficit disorder [ADD]). While as many as a third of children with oppositional behavior in some studies also have ADD, it is key to remember that not *all* children with oppositional behavior have ADD.[9] Table 4.1 shows some of the disorders that are associated with oppositional behavior. Sometimes, teachers conclude that a child needs ADD medication for his or her oppositional behavior. While

TABLE 4.1

Disorders associated with oppositional behavior

Disorder	Features
Oppositional defiant disorder	Consistent pattern of noncompliant and hostile behavior toward authority figures that seriously interferes with ability to function in school and at home. Symptoms can include frequent tantrums and angry outbursts, mean and hateful talking when upset, excessive arguing with adults, questioning rules, and often blaming others for one's mistakes.
Conduct disorder	Repetitive and persistent pattern of behavior in which the basic rights of others or major age-appropriate societal norms or rules are violated. Behaviors include aggressiveness toward people and animals, intentional destruction of property of others, deceitfulness or theft, serious violation of rules (e.g., setting fires, stealing, lying, and truancy).
Attention deficit disorder (ADD)/ attention deficit hyperactivity disorder (ADHD)	Difficulty with attention and organization. Impulsive behavior begins before the age of seven and is seen in at least two settings. Runs in families.

Source: adapted from American Psychiatric Association. *Diagnostic and Statistical Manual of Mental Disorders* 4th ed., text revision (*DSM-IV-TR*) (Washington, D.C.: American Psychiatric Association, 2000).

much evidence suggests that a medication can make a difference in a child's impulsive behavior if he has ADD, medications are not usually effective for treating oppositional behavior not caused by ADD. Regardless of whether a psychiatric disorder coexists with the child's oppositional behavior, teachers' and parents' responses can have a powerful influence on the trajectory of these children.

TYPICAL ATTRIBUTES OF THE STUDENT WITH OPPOSITIONAL BEHAVIOR

Noncompliance refers to times when an adult makes a request of a child and the child either actively or passively does not perform the requested behavior.[10] Occasional noncompliance is not unusual in typical children (reported by 25–65 percent of parents in various studies). Children are most likely to be noncompliant around two to three years old, when they are testing limits, and again in early adolescence, when they are separating from their parents. But in most children, the noncompliance is not frequent or severe (frequent or severe noncompliance is reported by only 1–9 percent of parents), and as children mature, they generally become more cooperative.[11] We are focusing on children who are consistently noncompliant, oppositional, and openly hostile to teachers. This persistent behavior impairs their ability to function academically, because of an inability to follow directions and classroom procedures. These children usually can't participate in unstructured activities, including games and field trips, because of their underdeveloped social skills, inflexible thinking, and need for control.[12]

When a student persistently argues, teachers may feel badgered and become frustrated that the student always has to have the last word. Teachers can feel disrespected and then may fail to realize that the student's inflexibility represents a skill deficit. In his influential book *The Explosive Child*, psychologist Ross Greene explains that it is important to make the key distinction between "she can't" versus "she won't."[13] He emphasizes that if a child *could* behave better, she *would*, and he stresses that the job of adults is to help identify the student's underdeveloped skills and provide choices when possible. If teachers build a strong relationship with these students, the children may become more aware of when they are arguing and may tolerate changing their agenda.

Many students with oppositional behavior are cognitively inflexible. They get stuck thinking there is only one way to solve a problem.[14] Consequences can appear ineffective, as these students frequently repeat their past mistakes. They can act impulsively, which makes it more likely that once they are caught in a struggle, their oppositional behavior will quickly escalate. In our earlier example, when Emily was asked to start her math, she responded by shoving her math paper into her mouth. When she was given an additional demand to clean up, she started to scream and hide under the desk. When she wasn't able to problem-solve effectively and thus got stuck on her aversion to doing the math, her behavior progressed quickly to inappropriate behavior.

Students with oppositional behavior can have all-or-nothing thinking, where they think in extremes, with no middle ground. A teacher is either for or against them, loves them or hates them.[15] Once they've made up their mind about a teacher's being mean or unfair, they don't easily change it. The teacher is left fighting an uphill battle all year. If students with oppositional behavior have a history of inconsistent or harsh discipline at home, they are more likely to have difficulty with authority figures in school and feel a desperate need to be in control. They can be relatively indifferent to consequences in the school setting if they were abused at home, as they were exposed to far harsher consequences at home.[16]

In addition to arguing with teachers, students with oppositional behavior are also often in conflict with their peers, socially rejected by them, and at risk for bullying towards other students.[17] Students with oppositional behavior frequently make mistakes in interpreting social information and then react aggressively, which further isolates them. They usually gravitate to peers who are also defiant as a way to get their social needs met. Social skills training can teach them how to join a group, ask questions, and deal with their anger more appropriately.[18] Yet their peers still can remain wary and have trouble forgiving these students' past negative behavior, and so these students can remain stigmatized with a bad reputation.[19]

FUNCTIONS OF OPPOSITIONAL BEHAVIOR

It is important to understand the function of the student's oppositional behavior so that the teacher doesn't respond in ways that reinforce the problematic behavior. The student can demonstrate more desirable behaviors if the environment is structured so that the desirable behaviors are more reinforcing or satisfying than the disruptive behavior. However, teachers can have difficulty choosing appropriate targeted interventions because there are multiple possible functions of oppositional behavior: attention, escape, or some tangible motivation.

Students are not always conscious of seeking certain responses from a teacher, even when their behavior looks premeditated. A teacher can resent these students for appearing to seek negative attention on purpose when they irritate others or break rules. If these students argue whenever the teacher gives a direction, they usually get negative attention. If they throw an object off their desk and a teacher rushes over to them, they get the attention they crave, even if it is negative.

Many students with oppositional behavior also attempt to escape teachers' demands. A student might, for example, rip up a worksheet to avoid completing it or bolt from the classroom so as not to clean up after an activity.

When a student tries to obtain a certain object through inappropriate behavior (e.g., grabbing a toy or stealing), this is an illustration of the tangible function. The tangible function is also demonstrated when a student is stuck on her own agenda (she wants what she wants when she wants it) and then can engage in inappropriate behavior to get what she wants. If a student lies to teachers about completing homework so she can go to recess, ignores the teacher's request to sit down because she wants to talk with her friend, or cheats in a game so she wins, the student is demonstrating tangibly motivated behavior.

WARNING SIGNS

Most students show signs that their inappropriate behavior is escalating before they explode. Each student will have a finite repertoire of warning signs that a teacher should observe and record after each behavior incident. Warning signs are small behavior changes and other signals that typically precede the student's explosion. After a few episodes, the teacher should create a list of warning signs that the student displays so that anyone working with the student will know he's getting close to the boiling point. Warning signs may include grunting, clenched fists, clenched jaw, using a loud voice when speaking, breathing heavily, rocking back and forth, and pacing. When a teacher notices any of the student's warning signs, it's time to act quickly. The teacher should remind the student of a regulating strategy, for example, asking the child, "Do you need a break?" or suggesting, "Take some deep breaths." The teacher can also remind the student that he has been able to calm himself before. Some students do best when the teacher avoids too much verbal interaction with them while they are escalated.

Many of the students described in the various sections of this book can be explosive and aggressive at times. Teachers can see a range of behaviors, from a quiet shutdown; to book- and desk-throwing; to hitting, biting, and kicking. Students with oppositional behavior are no exception. If a student has previously demonstrated an unsafe behavior, administrators and mental health experts need to work with the teacher to create an organized safety plan. The plan should include staff training, planned responses, and guidelines on when to involve parents, police, and transportation for an evaluation. The plan should be agreed to by parents and staff before a major crisis occurs. Staff working with a student who has the potential to be unsafe need to be trained in crisis prevention techniques.

THE FAIR PLAN FOR THE STUDENT WITH OPPOSITIONAL BEHAVIOR

Let's now tailor the FAIR Plan for the student with oppositional behavior. Many students in this book can exhibit oppositional behavior, so the following strategies may be used for a variety of students. Some of the strategies discussed in chapter 3 can apply to students with oppositional behavior as well, because students with anxiety-based behavior and students with oppositional behavior often have similar underdeveloped skills, including executive functioning, self-regulation, and cognitive flexibility.

Functional Hypothesis and Antecedent Analysis

Every time a student acts in a way that is inappropriate and that interferes with her learning (socially or academically), your teaching, or others' learning, it is important to write it down in ABC format (table 4.2 is an example of the ABC sheet that Emily's teacher filled out). A minimum of five incidents is necessary to observe a pattern. Remember to note any known setting events, as they can greatly affect student behavior. As with all students but especially those who are easily frustrated, make sure to rule out basic needs as antecedents. Hunger, thirst, fatigue, needing to go to the bathroom, and not feeling well can be antecedents for an outburst. Ask the student periodically if she is hungry or about other primary needs, especially if she is showing warning signs of oppositional behavior. Watch out for the following antecedents in students with oppositional behavior:

- Peer interactions without adult facilitation
- Unstructured activities (e.g., recess and lunch)
- Interactions with an adult who has an authoritative style or a history of conflict
- Situations when the student is asked to wait
- Teacher places a demand on the student
- Transitions
- Times when the student is told no
- Whenever the student is playing games with peers

When you are reviewing the consequence column of an ABC chart for patterns, look for responses that provide attention, escape, or tangible motivation (the students get their own way or get an object), as those are typical functions of students with oppositional behavior.

In the antecedent column of table 4.2, we see patterns of antecedents in Emily's behavior. Tally the incidents in antecedent patterns on your own ABC chart, so that you can refer to them later (see figure 4.1 for an example). Some incidents are counted in more than one category. Emily had difficulty during times of social demand, writing demand, transition to a social activity (lunch), and when given a directive in an authoritative, direct way.

Look for patterns in the consequence column as well. Tally the incidents. In the consequence column, we see that Emily is successfully gaining attention and is escaping a demand in all five of the noncompliant incidents. The antecedent information helps the teacher to choose interventions that support Emily. The consequence data helps teachers choose how to respond to Emily's behavior. According

FIGURE 4.1

Tallying the antecedents and consequences in Emily's ABC chart

Antecedents		Consequences	
Social demand (math):	/	Avoided demand (math, lunch, art, spelling):	////
Writing demand (spelling, writing) :	//	Avoided demand briefly (writing):	/
Transition (lunch):	/	Received one-on-one adult attention (all incidents):	##//
Given a directive (art, spelling):	//		

TABLE 4.2

ABC data sheet for Emily, a student with oppositional behavior

Date, time, duration	Setting event(s)	Activity	Antecedent (what happens immediately before behavior)	Behavior (description of behavior)	Consequence (what happens immediately after behavior)
9/12, 9 a.m., 7 min	First full week of school for the year	Math	Ms. Graves pairs kids to play a math game.	Emily takes two pencils and starts loudly tapping them like drumsticks on the desk. She does not go to the table with her partner.	Ms. Graves asks Emily to stop and go sit with her partner. The teacher tells her the peer will have to work alone, but Emily doesn't budge.
9/13, 10 a.m., 5 min		Writing	Ms. Graves passes out journals and tells students to write about their summer vacation. She hands Emily her journal.	Emily walks to the corner of the room and kicks the bookshelf and then sits on it.	Ms. Graves asks Emily three times to get started and then walks over to Emily and tells her she'll help. Ms. Graves sits with Emily for most of writing class.
9/14, 8:37 a.m., 11 min		Transition to lunch	Ms. Graves asks the class to line up for lunch.	Emily breaks a pencil in half and is quiet and unresponsive to questions while she breaks all the colored pencils from her desk.	Ms. Graves asks the classroom assistant to stay in the room with Emily as she takes the rest of the class out to cafeteria.
9/20, 2:15 p.m., 8 min	Class pictures at 12:15	Art	Art teacher sternly tells Emily to put away her coat.	Emily pulls her hood over her head and puts her head on the desk, screaming, "I'm not doing it, you cow!"	The art teacher calls the counselor, who comes and brings Emily to his room.
9/27, 1:45 p.m., 3 min		Spelling/ dictation	Ms. Graves is dictating the first spelling word and tells Emily, "You need to take out your pencil now. Hurry!"	Emily walks into the hallway and sits on a chair across the hallway.	Ms. Graves follows her and repeatedly asks her to go back into the classroom.

Note: adapted from Sidney W. Bijou, et al. *Journal of Applied Behavior Analysis* 1, no. 2 (1968); Beth Sulzer-Azaroff and G. Roy Mayer, *Applying Behavior-Analysis Procedures with Children and Youth.*

to the data, Ms. Graves should try to avoid giving Emily negative attention and allowing Emily to avoid demands.

Accommodations

With students who demonstrate oppositional behavior, it is important to create a classroom environment that is structured and predictable, but that also allows flexibility and choice on the part of the student. Once you have identified the antecedents that occur before the student's oppositional behavior, you can accommodate the student's specific challenge—for example, if there appears to be a pattern of inappropriate behavior during recess, then you need to implement specific recess accommodations. You may find you need to make accommodations to the classroom throughout the school day to help the student function optimally. Accommodations and modifications sometimes need to be made in the following areas for students with oppositional behavior: the school environment, executive functioning, curriculum, and training in underdeveloped skills.

Environment

If you can, develop a daily schedule that alternates nonpreferred and preferred activities for the student with oppositional behavior. This alternation can help the student to be more patient and to have more flexibility with the next nonpreferred activity. This schedule, however, may be unrealistic, since schedules are shaped by competing demands (e.g., specialists' availability). If it is not possible to set this sort of schedule, then embed a reinforcing activity within the nonpreferred subject area prior to the start of the next nonpreferred activity (e.g., allow the student to do a reading computer program at the end of reading period before math).

Students with oppositional behavior are constantly asked to shift from their agenda to engage in less preferred activities and to comply with authority, which may be exceptionally difficult for them. They benefit from breaks, which help them refuel and which can prevent outbursts. Try to schedule these breaks to be preventative, as opposed to reactive, whenever possible. The breaks need to highlight an escape from demands. To emphasize this with students with very low frustration tolerance and frequent outbursts, we have scheduled a midday break (or two) for students and named these breaks "Terrence-is-the-boss time" or "King Terrence time." The student gets to choose the activity, and the teacher tries to give attention but not give demands. Teachers will even ask, "What are we going to do now?" or "Where should I sit?" to make the point. Unfortunately, breaks are often underused for students with oppositional behavior.

Most students with oppositional behavior resist taking breaks, even if it might be beneficial. They might be suspicious of the word *break*, because of their history of being required to take a break from the classroom when they misbehaved. Alternative terms are *free time* or *choice time*. Incentives can also be helpful to encourage them to try breaks.

To ensure that the breaks are effective for attention-motivated students, provide one-on-one, exaggerated attention to the student. For all students, make sure the breaks are structured, with a clear beginning, ending, and agreed-upon activity and location. Short (five-minute) breaks within the classroom can include using the calm area of the room (for students who aren't attention-seeking) or an activity that can be done at the student's desk, like drawing, playing with a mobile device, listening to music, or using putty. Some activities suggested for the longer breaks (up to twenty minutes) are watching videos of the student's favorite sports team, drawing or arts and crafts (as long as the student doesn't get easily frustrated doing those activities), exercise (e.g., swings, trampoline, or running laps in the gym), or playing appropriate games on a computer or phone. Don't include activities that can dysregulate the student, such as aggressive video games or any activity that is competitive, as the student might become angry when he or she loses.

Alternative recess should be considered for students with oppositional behavior, as they have difficulty with unstructured times and playing with their peers. The majority of students with oppositional behavior are more likely to interact positively with peers in a small, quiet, highly structured activity, as opposed to a typical crowded, busy recess. The students should have adult supervision in an alternative location. If alternative recess is not available, adult supervision should be considered at regular recess.

Alternative lunch should also be considered, as students with oppositional behavior may need constant monitoring and need adults to coach them through social interactions like playing games, waiting for the water fountain, or lining up. A small lunch group in an alternative setting allows an adult to easily monitor and facilitate social interactions by giving explicit instructions. During this time, games and activities that support social skills instruction, such as perspective-taking skills, can also occur.

A personalized calming box in the classroom, as described in chapter 3, is also helpful for students with oppositional behavior. They use the items in the box to learn to self-calm when they are frustrated.

Students with oppositional behavior typically do not do well with transitions. Moving from a preferred activity to a disliked one is the most difficult transition for these students. Giving a student a task or a purpose during the transition is helpful. For example, if a student refuses to go to the library, asking him to take the book to the librarian will give him a task to complete and will get him making the transition to the library. (Chapter 3 gives an overview of the components of a transition, which may be helpful to refer to when you are thinking about strategies for transitions.)

When the transition is from a preferred activity to a nonpreferred activity, the first stage of a transition, *ending the first activity*, is not easy for these students, who can get stuck on one activity and not want to stop at what they perceive is in the middle. It's important to give a transition warning that allows for a natural closure to the task. Rather than "Turn off the computer; it's time to start spelling," try "Find a stopping place." Or to predict the end of a task, you might say something like "You have time for five more words!" Another component of a transition, *initiating a task*, is also a challenge for these students. "It's time for social studies!" may elicit a student's inappropriate response. Use transition warnings that address both components (the end of one activity and the beginning of another) of transitions when necessary: "When you finish drawing that robot, there will be two minutes until we start math."

Downtime is another part of a transition. This unstructured time can be difficult for students with oppositional behavior because of poor self-control and poor self-regulation. Downtime in a transition can also be thought of as waiting time. Waiting is difficult for students with oppositional behavior, because of their inflexibility and their inability to tolerate delayed gratification. They want what they want *now*. Teachers commonly overestimate these students' ability to wait, since most students develop this skill in preschool. A wait-time bag of tricks is essential for staff working with students who can't wait. We recommend that teachers have items in a small bag readily accessible during these times. Until these students learn better self-regulation, it is helpful to provide them with distractions (e.g., a computer tablet, a wipe-off board, Mad Libs, or a small bag of Legos) or to give them a task that helps them tolerate the wait for a desired activity.

Executive functioning

All of the executive functioning strategies discussed in chapter 3 apply to students with oppositional behavior as well. In addition to these strategies, some additional executive functioning skills should be explicitly taught.

Self-talk is an essential skill for students to learn to identify a troubling situation and to ultimately prompt themselves to use appropriate strategies and to learn to self-regulate. Many students can apply a strategy previously taught by having a teacher prompt them in the moment: "You look frustrated. What can you do?"

Whether it is a picture schedule for young students or an electronic minute-by-minute schedule on a mobile device, visual schedules can be very helpful for the student who becomes inflexible when uncertain of demands. If the student previews the schedule at the beginning of the day, it can prevent her from deciding on her own schedule and becoming inflexible.

Curriculum

Students can become very stressed by academic expectations. Writing, pencil-and-paper tasks, and any other academic area that is a relative weakness for the student can be especially difficult for the student with oppositional behavior.

It is helpful to be open-minded about how to deliver academics to your most inflexible students. Embedding choice in academic demands will help a student comply. Examples include allowing the student to pick the order of assignments, the materials to use, or a place to sit for working. Assignments that emphasize process and quality rather than quantity and the end product are a better match for these students. Open-ended demands that allow the student to exert some control are easier for the child to comply with than straightforward, less fun demands. We have had students do a PowerPoint presentation or a rap song rather than write a traditional essay for teachers. Hands-on projects such as science experiments, making a social studies poster, and creating a video can be great alternatives to more-traditional reports and projects. If you can do project-based instruction for the whole group at times during the year, it reduces your need to plan a separate project for the student. Instead of having your students write a creative narrative, have them create a cartoon or write a song. There are no right answers in such open-ended assignments, which helps the student to engage. Many teachers find that this open-ended style is favorable to most students. This kind of preparation takes a lot of extra work and creativity, but it is effective. Whenever you consider it appropriate, alternate easy and difficult academics. During an academic period, any time the student has independent work (as opposed to group work), have the student start with an easy academic activity. Get math sheets from a younger grade, and intersperse them with harder worksheets.

Technology can help these students to access curricula that would otherwise cause the students to shut down or become defiant. Sometimes it can be more palatable or motivating for the student to get directions from a computer than from the teacher. Students with low tolerance for frustration may show inappropriate behavior to escape doing worksheets, but there is often less escape-motivated behavior when a student learns with technology. Many long reading assignments in textbooks can be supplemented with videos or PowerPoint presentations, electronic books, or interactive Web sites so that the students can access the content in a form that is perceived as less demanding or maybe even enjoyable. See appendix D for a list of technology-supported instruction choices.[20]

The teacher and any other team members working with the student need to decide which curricula should be accommodated with technology and what types of creative projects need to be completed. The teacher's goal for the student should guide this process. If the goal is to meet all third-grade benchmarks, for example, then the way the student learns the material can be flexible as long as she is meeting the criteria. However, if the goal is to improve the student's stamina with traditional academics, the team may want to have a combination of traditional pencil-and-paper tasks, special projects, and computer-based instruction.

Teaching underdeveloped skill

All self-regulation strategies discussed in chapter 3 on anxiety apply to students with oppositional behavior as well, since students with oppositional behavior are attempting to regulate intense feelings.

Many students with oppositional behavior have trouble taking responsibility for their behavior and don't accurately assess their behavior or self-monitor.[21] They are likely to rate themselves as performing better than they are, so that they can receive a reward. Teachers can also rate the students' behavior and explain the rating so that the students can learn to monitor their behavior more accurately. Students can also learn to process a behavior incident. It is best for them to complete a processing sheet called "Taking Responsibilities for Choices" (see appendix G for an example) after they have calmed down, even if it is postponed until the following day.

Psychologist Alan Kazdin recommends "positive opposites" in behavior programs.[22] Instead of telling the student all the behaviors he should stop doing, encourage the behaviors that he needs to perform to be successful. Instead of saying, "Don't interrupt," tell the student to raise his hand when he has a question. Instead of saying, "No hitting," tell the student to use safe hands. It is important to use these positive opposites on a self-monitoring sheet—"safe body" rather than "no hitting," for example.

Many students with oppositional behavior tend to blame others rather than themselves for their actions. They can learn to evaluate how their behavior affects their successes and failures. Students with oppositional behavior often have difficulty playing games (they may cheat, have difficulty taking turns, or change the rules to give themselves an advantage) and need supervision while learning these skills. Other social skills that need to be addressed are how to work in groups, how to make friends, conflict resolution, understanding the feelings of others, and how to respond appropriately. Understanding their own strengths and emotions and dealing with anger and frustration are other skills that need to be explicitly taught.[23] Since students with oppositional behavior are demanding and focused on their own needs, they are difficult to like at times. Teaching them basic skills like complimenting others and saying please and thank you can help them make social connections.

Interaction Strategies

Schools are often reactive to students' oppositional behavior. We recommend the following antecedent management strategies be implemented as part of the students' day to prevent oppositional behavior. The strategies include relationship building, adding scheduled breaks, and providing appropriate support around transitions. Although some of these strategies are suggested for students with anxiety and depression, there are different reasons how and why they are implemented in those cases.

The relationship building between the teacher and the student with oppositional behavior is crucial to the student's overall social, academic, and behavioral success.[24] For example, kindergarten children who have highly negative relationships with their teachers demonstrate, two years later, more behavior problems and fewer behavioral competencies than do their peers who have highly positive relationships with kindergarten teachers.[25] Sondra Birch and Gary Ladd also found that conflict with the kindergarten teacher predicted declining prosocial behavior and slightly increased aggressive behavior with peers through first grade.[26] There is ample evidence to demonstrate that working with parents and providing guidance is better than only working with the child and makes a big difference in altering the child's behavior.[27] We are going to recommend these same strategies for teachers to build relationships.

First, it is important to examine your own perceptions of your students with oppositional behavior, as students can be astute at detecting teachers' negative feelings and will often respond with increased oppositional behavior. They are not the easiest students to work with and not the easiest to like because they are constantly testing limits. To make substantive change with these students, you need to provide positive attention and change how you respond to these students' annoying behaviors. You need to be aware of your nonverbal messages when interacting with students as well. Charlie Appelstein, author of *No Such Thing As a Bad Kid*, encourages teachers to be tolerant and patient. As the book title declares, he asserts that there are no bad kids, just bad luck and bad choices.[28] He shares the insight of a former oppositional student named Gus: "Kids aren't bad. They're just screwed up. The kid who's pushing you away the most is probably the one who needs you the most. Every time we get blasted for being 'manipulative' (or any other such term), our self-concept suffers. We take on that word—we internalize a sense of badness. Yet the kid you call 'manipulative' might have come to your facility with a history of manipulating his way out of getting beaten. So, maybe manipulating ain't so bad. Maybe it simply needs to be understood in the context of a child's situation. Maybe people don't need to use these words anymore."[29] As a way of perceiving the student in a more positive light, change the language used to describe the student. Table 4.3 lists some pejorative ways of describing people and then offers equally informative, but less offensive alternatives for these terms.

Creating time within the day for one-on-one relationship-building activities is essential for these students.[30] The students need to know that the teacher likes and respects them, because many of these students are not comfortable trusting people with authority and they need concrete proof that the teacher is on their side. We

TABLE 4.3

Strength-based beliefs and terminology

Pejorative label	Positive, hope-based reframe
Obnoxious	Good at pushing people away
Rude, arrogant	Good at affecting people
Resistant	Cautious
Lazy, uninvested	Good at preventing further hurts or failures
Manipulative	Good at getting their own needs met
Just looking for attention	Good at caring about and loving themselves
Close-mouthed	Loyal to family and friends
Stubborn, defiant	Good at standing up for themselves
Tantrum, fit, outburst	Sending someone a big message
Learning disability	Roadblocks

Source: adapted with permission from Charlie Appelstein, unpublished document (2011).

suggest creating opportunities for both small one-on-one moments of relationship-building and bigger, more significant activities throughout the year.

We recommend that teachers make the extra effort to connect with these students throughout the day. Before any intervention will work, students need to know the teacher likes them and wants what's best for them. One-on-one activities can be done during times of calm (not immediately after the student acts out, as it may reinforce the behavior) throughout the year to build a strong relationship. These joint activities can have the additional advantage of reinforcing a student's calm and cooperative behaviors.

For some students, it helps to do more significant, memorable relationship-building activities that go beyond the norm. Some of these activities may seem a bit extreme, but we suggest considering them especially in the beginning of the school year (or after vacations) to jump-start a positive relationship. The effort on your part is worth it when you see how the student becomes more engaged in the learning process and is more productive. You and the student could eat take-out food together or have a picnic on the school lawn. One teacher's spouse even dropped off the family dog at school so that the teacher and student could walk the dog during the school day!

Parent permission needs to be given in writing for activities off school property, and we recommend organizing transportation through the school department under "community trips" or going somewhere within walking distance. If the student has a history of explosive, bolting, or aggressive behavior, the teacher needs a safety plan for how to get help when an activity is off school property.

Strategies for giving demands

Giving demands to a student with oppositional behavior in a way that will promote compliance is an art. Teachers can unintentionally respond in ways that escalate a student's behavior, promote defiance, and counteract a positive teacher-student relationship. You can learn to give demands differently so as to avoid power struggles and to encourage these students to comply. Certain interactive approaches are more helpful for students with oppositional behavior. If you change the way you deliver a demand, the student's behavior can change to become more cooperative.

The *Cambridge Dictionary* defines *power struggle* as "an unpleasant or violent competition for power."[31] A power struggle can be created when a teacher gives an immediate demand that has an ultimatum quality to it, such as asking the student to do or stop doing something immediately: "Give me the pencil," or "Stop laughing right now." If the student says no to the demand, the teacher is in a tough position. If the teacher wants to gain control or power in this scenario, he or she might repeat the direction—"I said give me the pencil"—or ultimately punish the student and send the child to the office. There is no real gain with creating a power struggle, especially since, in most cases, the student is less flexible and more invested in gaining control than the teacher. As the old Spanish saying goes, "When one will not, two cannot quarrel."

Students with oppositional behavior have difficulty with authority, and they like to be in control. Using a severe, authoritative tone when speaking to a student with oppositional behavior will increase the likelihood that the student will refuse any request. Remember to use a neutral and calm tone, even when you are feeling frustrated. Saying "please" may sound deferential, but it makes the request less demanding. It is also extremely important to avoid yes-or-no questions as a method of making a demand, such as, "Do you want the class to be late for recess?" or "Are you ready for science?" This is a way of giving a direction, but students may think it's a choice or they may take the opportunity to be contrary. Similarly, some people have the habit of putting the question word *OK* at the end of a sentence: "Time for music, OK?" Try to avoid this with these students, unless it's acceptable for them to say no.

We encourage you to use choice as frequently as possible when interacting with a student with oppositional behavior. Research demonstrates that the use of choice promotes appropriate behaviors with peers and adults, reduces challenging behaviors, and improves the students' communication and social skills.[32] Give students a choice whenever possible throughout the day. By embedding choice in the direction, you allow the student to exert his agenda in a small way. Instead of telling the student to line up, ask him, "Do you want to stand in the front of the line or the back of the line?" And instead of "Start your math," ask, "Do you want to do your math with a pencil or a pen?" It takes some creativity, but it avoids a potential battle.[33] Table 4.4 gives further examples of choices you could give students.

Using declarative language instead of authoritative language can make a demand more tolerable to a student.[34] Declarative language is used when a person verbalizes his or her thoughts.[35] It allows teachers to point out the situation in a way that elicits the student to come up with her own plan to solve the problem. The teacher simply states the facts, which encourages the student to think of the next steps. Commenting on a shared experience can highlight information the student needs to act. Saying, "This table looks really messy. It's going to be hard to eat snack here!" is a good use of declarative language, which will be more likely to provoke a compliant response than "Clean up the table now." Since it is the student's "idea" to clean the table, she is much more likely to comply. Table 4.5 gives some more examples of declarative statements.

Giving demands in an indirect way can also avoid an oppositional moment with a student. One method is to write down the demand instead of delivering the message verbally. Putting a note that says "Please stop tapping your pencil" on the student's desk can prevent a student from arguing. In addition, it allows the student to save face when complying with a teacher's request, rather than being seen to back down by all his classmates. If a student is a nonreader, show him a picture of "quiet"

TABLE 4.4

Types, definitions, and examples of choice-making opportunities

Type	Definition	Example
Where	The location where the student will work or play	Choice of chairs, location on the rug, seat at table (e.g., "Would you like to sit on the blue chair or the red chair?")
When	The time the student will begin to work or play	The choice of when to start an activity (now, in five minutes, after snack)
Within	The specific materials the child needs to complete play or work	Colors of markers, pencil, or pen; write using computer or paper; types of materials (scissors, adhesives, etc.)
Whom	With whom the student is going to work or play	Choice of teachers or peers to work with
What	What the student is going to work on first	Choice between math sheet or math game
Terminate	The time the student is going to stop playing or working	Asking a student if he or she is finished with the activity; establishing a "stopping place" together
Future	What the student is going to play or work on in the future	"After your finish playing dominoes, what are you going to play with next?"
Tangible	Specific items the student needs either prior to, during, or after playing or working	Giving a student a choice of what he or she may want (e.g., to hold a fidget toy on his or her lap at desk or group time)
Refusal	Whether to begin/finish playing or working	Asking a student if he or she would like to continue or finish an activity (e.g., "Need one more minute?")
Alternative	The method the child will use to complete playing or working	Choice of ways the student will complete a project (e.g., draw the picture or use stamps)

Source: adapted with permission from Kristine Jolivette et al., "Naturally Occurring Opportunities for Preschool Children With or Without Disabilities to Make Choices," *Education & Treatment of Children* (ETC) 25, no. 4 (2002).

or tap an icon as a less invasive way of reminding him of the demand. We have seen students crumple or rip up the note, but they still refrain from arguing!

Another indirect method of giving demands is to remind other students nearby of the rules and expectations, without directing the statement to the particular

TABLE 4.5

Authoritative versus declarative statements

Authoritative statement	Declarative statement
"Line up."	"All the kids are lining up. Must be time to go to recess."
"Write your name on your paper."	"Oh, I hope I can remember who this paper belongs to."
"Pass in your math paper."	"Looks like I have almost all of the math papers here on my desk."
"Ask before you go to the bathroom."	"I'm confused. I don't know where you are going right now."
"Pick up the pencil."	"There's a pencil on the floor."

student: "Oops, some of you still need to put your names on your paper," or "Isaac, make sure you remember to use spell check."

With any demand, remember to deliver the direction and move away—don't hover near the student, and don't maintain eye contact. If you say, "Please raise your hand," while standing in front of the student and engage in eye contact, the student is more likely to argue or give a verbal response. If you say, "Please raise your hand," and walk away quickly (several feet away), especially if you immediately engage yourself in another conversation or activity, the student is less likely to respond. We recommend using the delivery strategies such as leaving a note on the student's desk, paired with moving away quickly, to optimize a cooperative response from the student.

Giving a student extended time to comply ("Put your folder on my desk before lunch") is more effective than an immediate demand ("Put your folder on my desk now"). This approach gives the student time to deescalate (students can't comply if they are escalated).

Reinforcing appropriate behavior

One of the motivating forces behind oppositional behavior for many students is getting attention. Teachers may need to step up their typical ways of giving positive attention for these students. Even if a student is initially motivated by escape or a tangible reward, she is at risk for getting negative attention for her behavior. Attention often becomes an additional motivator for students with oppositional behavior. After receiving negative attention for a long while, students learn that their oppositional behavior gets them not only the escape or tangible rewards they initially desired, but also attention from an adult.

We recommend using a combination of positive attention, intermittent reinforcement, and noncontingent reinforcement.[36] The most effective form of positive attention used in schools is praise. H. K. Reavis and colleagues suggest that praise should be immediate, frequent, enthusiastic, descriptive, and varied and should involve eye contact.[37] The ratio of positive statements (praise) to negative statements made to an oppositional student should be two to one.[38] We recommend giving students over-the-top positive attention as often as possible throughout the day after a student does an appropriate prosocial behavior: "I like how you waited your turn for the basketball," or "Nice job holding the door for Alice."[39] Try to deliver the praise immediately after the student's appropriate action and with enthusiasm as if the student did something very difficult—which he did! Think about responding as if a student with typically poor grades got 100 percent on a spelling test. Immediate positive reinforcement after every appropriate behavior has been demonstrated to be the best way to teach a new skill. This is referred to as *continuous reinforcement*. Role-playing is a great way to teach a student a new skill while providing immediate and continuous reinforcement. Have the student pretend that someone wasn't nice to him at recess, and show how he talked with the other student. When the student practices the new skill, the teacher's praise should be given exuberantly and immediately.

Intermittent reinforcement is a powerful way to increase appropriate behavior once a teacher knows how to use it.[40] Intermittent reinforcement is reinforcement delivered randomly—not after each incident. Catching the student being good is the key.[41] Since the students are working on appropriate behavior, a teacher could positively reinforce a student for doing *anything* other than inappropriate behavior. No behavior is too small to be praised: "I like the way you are sitting in your seat," "Patrick, nice job writing your name on your paper," "You hung up your coat perfectly." Teachers can give students praise, send a note home, or brag about them to a colleague in front of the student. We have also used "caught being good" certificates that teachers randomly give the student throughout the week. Once the student has demonstrated positive behavior momentum, teachers may decide to raise the bar and deliver reinforcement for more sophisticated behaviors.

Adding noncontingent reinforcement is also a must.[42] As described earlier, noncontingent reinforcement is random acts of kindness, doing or saying something nice not for what the student has done but rather for just being her. Giving the student positive attention throughout the day regardless of her behavior will reduce the student's need to act poorly to receive attention—she already has it. In the beginning of the year or if a student has recurring behavior problems to seek attention, we recommend attending to the student frequently. Negative attention is much more predictable and consistent, efficient (faster and may take less effort to obtain), intense and dramatic, obvious (voice volume, proximity, heightened emotion) than positive attention. To compete with the powerful reinforcing aspects of negative attention, teachers need to deliver attention with these components in mind.

We had a student start the year in fourth grade demonstrating constant inappropriate negative-attention-seeking behavior, such as arguing, swearing, insulting the teacher, and not complying with the teacher's directions. We strategized with the teacher's assistant and decided to "kill him with kindness" and give him intense and frequent attention throughout the day. The teacher's assistant set a timer to vibrate every two minutes as a reminder to attend to him. The teacher's assistant gave him a thumbs up, put her hand on his shoulder, asked him a question (even as simple as "Can you see if it's cloudy? I can't see out the window"), told him a joke, gave him a compliment, or made eye contact and smiled. This strong dose of attention along with relationship-building activities (she had a picnic with him: both of them took their lunches to eat on the bench in the front of the school) changed his behavior dramatically. His inappropriate comments were reduced to occurring monthly, and he stopped swearing and insulting her.

The use of humor is essential when you are working with students with oppositional behavior. Humor is a great way to help students listen to directions. When a student says, "I'm not going to art," saying something like, "Please don't make me carry you—I'm way too old," or "You're tired? What, were you up late dancing?" can provide comic relief. If done with consideration, any comment that provokes a laugh or a smile can help the student who is stuck. Make sure that the child understands the humor. For example, children with Asperger's syndrome and who are very oppositional may not understand subtle humor. Avoid the use of sarcasm, as it can be misunderstood easily. Making direction-following into a game is also a helpful strategy: "Let's pretend we're mice when we walk down the hall, and see if we can surprise the librarian with how quiet we are," or "Do you think you can do the first math problems before I do?"

Response Strategies

One day, we observed a class where a student was constantly arguing and negotiating with the teacher. The teacher was in the middle of a math lesson when the student called out, "Can we work with a partner?" The teacher ignored the student and continued to give the directions to the math activity. "Yesterday, you said we could work with a partner. So can we?" The teacher told the student to stop interrupting. The student answered, "I'm not interrupting, I'm asking a question." The teacher responded, "You are interrupting, and now you are making the students wait for the directions." The student retorted, "Why are you always picking on me? Why did you lie and say we would have partners today?" The teacher sent him to the office and told him to come back when he was ready to apologize for interrupting the learning in the classroom. "Apologize for what? I just asked a simple question."

It is helpful to be aware of this typical progression of teacher-student interactions with a student who argues constantly. There are two types of repetitive questions to recognize: information seeking and challenging.[43] Information-seeking questions are less confrontational: "Ms. Calvert, when is recess?" "How many more problems do I have to do?" "Why do I have to do this?" The best strategy for dealing with this type of question is to simply answer to the question. Ignoring the student and waiting for the child to stop asking is not likely to reduce this behavior, since the student is prone to get stuck on the thought. The child will probably repeat the question over and over or escalate. Answering the question can help the student to move on. If a student is asking information-seeking questions repeatedly, answer the question once. If the student persists, then you may want to end the interaction by saying, "We are all done talking about that."

The second form of questioning is more confrontational: challenging questions. These questions are often challenging the teacher's directions or authority: "Why do I have to?" Don't indulge the interaction. These questions don't need to be answered, as the student is not seeking information—he is purposefully challenging. Students will ask challenging questions for many reasons, such as anger, a feeling of injustice, and noncompliance. Regardless of the origin, redirecting and setting a limit is the best response for these types of questions: "It's time for math. Get started, or you can do it during snack time."[44] When setting limits, make sure they are reasonable, enforceable, and clear.[45] If a large fifth-grade student is told to go to the hallway and refuses, what options does a teacher have? Teachers need to make sure they can follow through on limits they set. Limits need to be reasonable (within the student's ability), clear, and concise. "First, then" is a good format for clear, concise limits: "*First* finish the last math problem, and *then* you can have a break."

Rewards and consequences

Students can still have behavior outbursts despite your preventative efforts. Traditional approaches with set criteria for rewards do not work well with students with oppositional behavior. Avoid plans that are all or nothing, as this type of plan often backfires. For example: "If you are quiet and don't interrupt this morning, you can go to lunch recess"—if the student interrupts at 9:15 a.m., she has already lost recess and has no motivation to follow the rules for the rest of the morning.

An incremental system is better and much more flexible. For example, the student earns two minutes of choice time every time he raises his hand, or loses a minute for every minute he's noncompliant. This type of response rarely puts the student in a position of having nothing to lose, so he stays motivated.

We recommend reinforcing new skills or self-regulation strategies with rewards when students demonstrate appropriate prosocial, compliant behavior. If the student is learning to self-regulate by taking a break instead of yelling, she needs to be rewarded for demonstrating the strategy. To teach a new skill most effectively, implement the rewards through tokens or points or the actual reward immediately following a demonstration of a prosocial or regulating strategy.

Response Strategies

In the following sections, we provide some steps for effective responses to students' oppositional behavior. Remember to have the response to the behavior match the function of the student's behavior, as seen in the ABC chart.

Negative-attention-seeking behavior

1. If the student is motivated by negative attention, make sure he doesn't receive negative attention for demonstrating inappropriate behavior, or this behavior will be reinforced. Here are the basic steps for responding to attention-seeking behavior: Remove attention from the student who is acting inappropriately, and acknowledge classmates who are demonstrating the expected behavior.

2. Remind the student of the expected behavior, and praise the change in the behavior when it occurs.

3. Remind the student that she will earn a reward for using a strategy like asking for a break.[46]

Noncompliance

Even after a teacher diligently implements the strategies for optimal ways of delivering demands, noncompliance may still occur. When a student is not complying with a direction (whether by ignoring the teacher, by quietly putting his head on the desk, or by outward defiance such as screaming or swearing), there are responses that will minimize the impasse and encourage the student to calm down and eventually comply. In this section, we encourage teachers to use less intense responses and to progress to more directive responses if the oppositional behavior persists. Start by seeking more information when the student is noncompliant; move on to reminding students of naturally occurring reinforcing activities. Finally, progress to a more involved response incorporating rewards and consequences.

Remember that a student's noncompliance is her way of communicating. The first step when a student refuses to follow a direction or demand is to gain more information from the student. If a student responds with opposition to a request to join a reading group, the teacher should inquire why the student doesn't want to go. Incorporating listening, validating the student's feelings, providing clarification, and giving reasonable choices (e.g., "Maybe you can pick your seat today," or "Do you want to set a timer to keep track of time?") can get the student past the moment.[47]

Providing choices and empathetically listening to and validating the student's feelings when the student digs in his heels are key, as well as having different teachers takes turns attempting to manage the situation. In many instances, when the student is noncompliant with one teacher, it works to switch to another teacher, who will try talking to the student. "Hey, buddy, what's going on? You don't want to go to reading?" Many times, the student will comply because this gives him an out from having to comply with the instructions of the first teacher.

Whenever possible, use natural consequences as a motivator (e.g., if the student chooses not to wear her coat to recess, she will be cold). It's best to use declarative statements ("Oh, I wonder if you will do well on the spelling quiz if you don't do your spelling today"), as opposed to an authoritative directive. For younger students, the teacher can talk to another adult to relay this information indirectly: "Miss Praught, do you think the principal will allow kids to be her special helper if they don't clean up their desk?" another helpful approach is to join with the student and say something like "I so hope you are able to get computer time; I was looking forward to playing with you."

When a student is noncompliant but tangibly motivated (wants what he wants when he wants it), a response with incremental consequences can often be effective. The following is an example of how it could work: Establish two demand-free breaks per day, one at midday and one at the end of the day, so there is always something to strive for. Remember to establish the breaks as no-demand, all-about-the-kid time. The breaks should include a very reinforcing activity and over-the-top enthusiastic attention from an adult. He is the center of the universe during this break! Before making the breaks contingent, give the student about three breaks noncontingently to establish buy-in. This is a great marketing strategy that companies use to get someone invested in their product (e.g., the cable company gives away a free movie channel for a month—then, once you love it, the company lets you know you have to pay to keep it). This plan won't work unless the plan is highly reinforcing and incorporates the student's desire for attention and control.

Once this is established, the breaks will become contingent on the student's complying with demands. The process for doing this is described in the following steps (the teacher needs a timer that counts up by seconds for this strategy): Students in kindergarten may not do well with this plan unless they have enough sense of time loss.

1. If the student is given a direction (e.g., "Write your name on the paper") and he doesn't comply, despite the strategies we've discussed, the teacher repeats the direction ("You need to write your name on the paper, or I'll start the timer").
2. If the student still does not comply, the teacher says, "OK, I'm going to start the timer."
3. The teacher will cheer the student on while the timer is counting. "You can do it. You were able to do it this morning!"
4. Remind the student of the reward time: "Oh, I really want to play with you at break time. I hope we have enough time!"
5. When the student finally complies, the teacher stops the timer. The student loses the amount of time lost off his reward time.

Although this is a consequence, it works well when other strategies have not. The incremental aspect of this plan is important so that the student is only losing seconds.

Attention-motivated and tangible-reward-motivated behavior

In many cases, students don't realize they are arguing, because they are so fixated on the point they are stuck on. The first step to teaching a student to stop arguing is to teach her what arguing is. The best way to do this is to point out when she is doing it in the moment. Label: "Zhanna, you're arguing right now," and remind her of the goal: "I need you to be flexible." If a student has trouble with flexibility, you can be transparent on what she needs to work on. Tell her that she needs to work on being flexible and that she will be rewarded every time she uses a strategy and shows flexibility. We define flexibility to students as "stop, stay calm, and make a new plan." Cue the student to take deep breaths or to use a strategy to stay calm while she tries to make a new plan. Remind her of the reward. Also, help her think of alternatives, such as letting it go, talking about it later, or getting what she wants at another time. Every time the student stops arguing and is flexible, let her earn a token or a marble in a jar, and deliver praise.

Escape-motivated behavior

Students with oppositional behavior can refuse to do academic tasks or act inappropriately to avoid them. To flip this dynamic, have the student earn a break (avoidance) after doing his work. For a student who has little tolerance for demands, start small. Have him do relatively easy and preferred academics for a short while, and then reinforce the on-task behavior by giving the student a break. For example, the student starts with twenty minutes of work, and then receives ten minutes of a break. After a period of success (no less than a week), the breaks can be minimized and the work can increase in difficulty.

How you respond to a student with oppositional behavior is critical to whether the child becomes entrenched in habitual responses or is encouraged to find a different way to communicate his needs and be successful. When you implement many of the strategies recommended, such as adapting the curriculum, consistent praise, and investing in building the relationship, the student can learn to respond to authority in a way that allows him to learn necessary skills, gain trust, and build competencies.

A FAIR PLAN FOR EMILY

Emily's ABC data revealed that she had a combination function of escape and attention. She had difficulty with social demands, writing, transitions to a social activity (lunch), and directives given in an authoritative, direct way. After all such incidents, she either was able to escape and/or receive negative attention.

Accommodations put in place included making a safe space in the room, and Emily got points for using it. The staff also arranged for her to have an alternative recess and lunch to help her experience positive interactions with peers and with an adult present to remind her not to bully peers or cheat at games. In this way, she could practice prosocial skills.

Emily was also given scheduled breaks at midday and the end of the day. Because she found listening to teachers stressful and frequently complained about it, the breaks helped her maintain stamina throughout the day. Because there was no aide in the classroom, the principal had an aide from another room supervise Emily during the two fifteen-minute breaks. It was just Emily and the adult. Had other children been present, the break would not have been free of demands (she would have had to compromise or take turns, two activities extremely hard for Emily). She looked the most calm, and reported to feel the most calm, during breaks when she got to be the boss and did not have to take turns or "worry about" losing a game.

She was taught how to the read the room when prompted, and the teachers used a segmented clock to monitor her longer tasks like writing. A visual schedule she used every day allowed her to preview unexpected changes and nuances in the schedule, like indoor recess or no computer lab on certain days.

For the curriculum, the teachers created a 20-5 schedule (twenty minutes of work and five-minute break) and split the math class so she did math with the kids for half the time and then the same lesson on the computer in game form for the duration of math. She did her writing on a computer and began to make PowerPoint slides instead of writing paragraphs. The teacher used the writing strategies checklist and open-ended writing assignments whenever possible. Her homework was done on the computer only; Emily's mother would watch her and report to the teacher she did her homework.

Teachers also began explicitly teaching Emily self-monitoring and social skills and had her use power cards (see chapter 3) prompting her to take deep breaths when frustrated and to ask for help. They also used the emotional thermometer and prompted her to check her frustration level by how tense her body felt (body checks) throughout the day. An aide from another room helped her practice self-calming once or twice a day in the counselor's office.

When interacting with Emily, Emily's teacher avoided yes-or-no questions, embedded choice in her instruction, and used declarative language and humor whenever possible. She also tried to give her extended time for compliance with requests, as well as positive and noncontingent reinforcement. In addition, her teacher's assistant brought her a take-out lunch twice in the fall. The teacher also sat with her during alternative lunch about once a month.

In response to inappropriate behavior, teachers answered Emily's simple answers and redirected other questions. They gave Emily rewards for using strategies and demonstrating prosocial behavior instead of oppositional behavior. They avoided giving her negative attentions. Her 20-5 schedule also helped Emily build her tolerance of frustration.

Within five weeks, Emily had stopped bullying peers during games and stopped making unkind comments to peers. Although she still had outbursts about once every two months, she recovered more quickly—within five minutes—and her outbursts did not include aggressive behavior. She began working productively on the 20-5 schedule and continued to complete writing assignments on the computer all year.

Chapter Summary

- Oppositional behavior could have one or all of the following functions: escape, attention (negative), tangible rewards.

- Common antecedents to oppositional behavior are the following:
  - Peer interactions, especially without adult facilitation
  - Unstructured activities (e.g., recess and lunch) and transitions
  - Interactions with an adult who has an authoritative style or a history of conflict
  - Situations in which a student is asked to wait, is given a demand, or is told no

- The emphasis for teachers is on preventing oppositional behavior and building relationships with the student.

- Students with oppositional behavior can have several difficulties, including cognitive inflexibility, all-or-nothing thinking, difficulty with authority, and social problems with peers.

- Most students with oppositional behavior show warning signs that they are escalating. Keep a list of warning signs, and when a student demonstrates them, act fast!

- If a student has demonstrated unsafe behavior previously, the team should create a safety plan, including staff training, planned responses, and when to involve parents, police, and transportation for an evaluation.

- Demands are very hard for students, so consider breaks throughout the day.

FAIR

Behavior Intervention Plan for the Student with Oppositional Behavior

Student's Name: _____   Date: _____

TARGETED BEHAVIORS (be as explicit as possible):

F **Functional Hypothesis and Antecedent Analysis**

☐ Document all instances of targeted behaviors, using ABC data sheet (minimum of five incidents)

☐ List antecedents from ABC data or observation to be addressed in this plan *(look especially at interactions with peers and certain adults, unstructured and waiting times, transitions, and demands):*

☐ Form a hypothesis about the function of behavior (circle one or more): attention, escape, tangible reward, sensory satisfaction. *Attention, escape, and tangible functions often motivate oppositional behavior.*

☐ List any pattern of consequences, using the ABC data:

☐ List any setting events of note:

A   Accommodations

We have included strategies and interventions from other chapters that you may consider.

Environmental

- ☐ Provide safe space in classroom
- ☐ Modify schedule
- ☐ Schedule breaks
- ☐ Allow for breaks outside the classroom
- ☐ Arrange alternative recess
- ☐ Arrange alternative lunch

Executive functioning

- ☐ Teach self-talk
- ☐ Teach "reading the room"
- ☐ Use Time Timer
- ☐ Narrate passage of time
- ☐ Use segmented clock
- ☐ Consider untimed test
- ☐ Use visual schedules
- ☐ Put organization time in schedule
- ☐ Present only a few problems or items at a time

Curriculum

- ☐ Embed choice
- ☐ Alternate easy and difficult assignments
- ☐ Have student use word processing
- ☐ Consider spelling accommodations
- ☐ Have student use self-monitoring writing strategies checklist
- ☐ Assess quality, not quantity, of work
- ☐ Offer hands-on, experiential lessons
- ☐ Give open-ended, flexible assignments
- ☐ Use student's own interests in curriculum

☐ Other technology resources:

Teaching underdeveloped skills explicitly

☐ Positive thinking
☐ Self-monitoring
☐ Positive opposites, cognitive flexibility
☐ Executive functioning
☐ Self-regulation
☐ Social skills
☐ Power cards

Replacement behaviors (examples for escape-motivated behavior):

☐ Teach asking for a break appropriately
☐ Teach asking for help appropriately during demand
☐ Other:

Regulation of self and self-monitoring

☐ Have student use emotional thermometer
☐ Prompt for "body checks" throughout the day
☐ Encourage daily self-calming practice
☐ Have student develop and use calming box
☐ Have student use self-regulation chart
☐ Schedule breaks—noncontingent escape from demands to minimize frustration (specify before, after, and during activity and how many per day)
☐ Use the self-monitoring sheet (appendix F)

▌ Interaction Strategies

☐ Use strength-based terminology
☐ Work on explicit relationship building
☐ Develop transition warnings and strategies
☐ Offer positive reinforcement
☐ Offer intermittent reinforcement

- ☐ Offer noncontingent reinforcement
- ☐ Use leadership-building and self-esteem-building activities

Strategies for giving demands

- ☐ Avoid power struggles
- ☐ Avoid yes-or-no questions or saying, "OK?" when making a demand
- ☐ Embed choice in the demand
- ☐ Use declarative language
- ☐ Give indirect demands
- ☐ Give demand, and move away
- ☐ Give extended time for compliance
- ☐ Use humor when appropriate
- ☐ Make it a game

R Response Strategies

- ☐ Assign rewards or points when the student demonstrates a self-regulation or prosocial skill when student is anxious or frustrated
- ☐ Answer simple questions
- ☐ Redirect challenging questions, and provide a limit
- ☐ Set limits that are enforceable, reasonable, and clear and simple
- ☐ Use incremental rewards and consequences
- ☐ Frustration tolerance: If a student exhibits low tolerance for work, start in small increments, and reinforce with escape from work (break), and build up

For escape-motivated behavior

- ☐ Avoid responses that would reinforce escape-motivated behavior, such as time-outs, removal from class

For attention-motivated behavior

- ☐ Avoid responses such as one-on-one talks or repeatedly telling student to stop

For tangibly motivated behavior

- ☐ Avoid responses such as giving an object or allowing student to do something after the student screams and demands it

CHAPTER 5

"I Don't Care"

The Student with Withdrawn Behavior

Mr. Lawson was heading to pick up his second-graders from art class when the substitute teacher approached him, concerned that no one knew what to do with Jack, who was sound asleep on the art room rug. The art teacher didn't want to wake him up. Mr. Lawson sighed. Not a day went by this school year where Mr. Lawson didn't worry about this boy. Jack was the only student who wasn't represented on the All About Me bulletin board. Despite Mr. Lawson's multiple attempts to encourage Jack, the teacher couldn't get Jack to tell him his favorite color, animal, or food or draw a picture of his family. "Nothing" was all he could squeeze out of the little guy. In the teacher's twenty years of teaching, Jack was also Mr. Lawson's only second-grader who never giggled or laughed, even when Chester the magician came to the class and pulled colorful handkerchiefs and coins from behind his ears. The only time Jack would occasionally smile was when he played tag during recess.

Mr. Lawson needed to decide whether to wake Jack and risk his being cranky for the rest of the day or to allow him to sleep for a while and miss academic time. He couldn't ask the school counselor for advice, since she didn't work on Fridays. He turned to the substitute teacher and said, "I'll come up and wake him. Wish me luck."

When a student is shut down and withdrawn, teachers can feel sympathetic to the student's apparent distress. But after spending extra time trying to cheer up a withdrawn student who continues to have low energy, to be irritable, and never to express joy, they can become discouraged that their attempts at comforting and engaging the student seem to make minimal difference.

We've found few resources on practical ways to address withdrawn behavior in the classroom. Much of the literature about students who may be withdrawn because of depression or anxiety is geared toward therapists and parents.[1] Teacher training related to students' withdrawn behavior emphasizes identifying and referring children who may be depressed or suicidal. Although these are important skills to develop, teachers also need concrete strategies to help such withdrawn students in the classroom. Effective treatment is often difficult to access, and even then, it may take considerable time for the student's classroom functioning to improve.

Students with withdrawn behavior are not typically disruptive or explosive in class, and this may explain the dearth of advice. For the teacher, withdrawn behavior is a relatively "good behavior problem," as these students are manageable and don't distract other students. But despite their quiet demeanor, students with withdrawn behavior are a concern to teachers and staff, who are eager for interventions that will help. Some students with depression can be irritable and oppositional as well as withdrawn, and additional strategies for working with these students can be found in chapter 4.

When children exhibit withdrawn behavior, it is often a sign they are depressed. Withdrawn behavior may also be a student's temporary response to a major life change (e.g., divorce or a transition to a new school), a characteristic of shy temperament, a symptom of anxiety, or a reaction to trauma. In this chapter, we will focus on children with depression, but the strategies are also applicable to children who are withdrawn for other reasons. We begin this chapter with information about symptoms of depression and then provide a FAIR Plan with practical strategies to develop a nurturing classroom environment and help these students to perform better academically and socially. Given the right tools, teachers have the power to make these students feel better and be more engaged in school.

RECOGNIZING DEPRESSION

Although depression is relatively common (found in 3 to 5 percent of children and adolescents), teachers and parents can have a hard time recognizing it.[2] Like anxiety, depression can be a hidden disability. Teachers may assume a child is lazy if the student is not trying in school, rather than realizing that the child's lack of energy, interest, or motivation to do the work may be a symptom of depression.

Unlike adults, children may not be able to identify that they are depressed. They are more likely to show, rather than tell, how bad they feel. Withdrawn behavior is one of the key ways their distress is manifested. Young children with depression often experience nonspecific physical ailments such as stomachaches or headaches; they may also refuse to go to school, act clingy with a teacher, be irritable, or be preoccupied with the thought that something bad will happen. Older children may sulk, act bored much of the time, lose interest in friends and activities, get into trouble at school, or be negative and irritable.[3] Generally, these behaviors represent a marked change from how the child had been in the past.

Irritability is an extremely common symptom of depression in children and adolescents. Adults usually do not recognize a child's irritability and associated behaviors (such as increased shouting, refusal to follow teachers' directions, arguing, and disrespect of authority) as a possible symptom of depression. Table 5.1 lists both obvious and underrecognized signs of depression in children. To break the code and understand the student's behavior, teachers must consider that some of these behaviors may be caused by depression and learn to respond effectively.

All children can be sad, irritable, or moody at times, but clinical depression is distinct because the irritability or depressed mood is pervasive, lasts for a long time, and affects the student's ability to function. If a child is irritable most of the day for two weeks or more and she is having trouble functioning in school, this should prompt a consultation with the school counselor and discussion with parents about an evaluation. Table 5.2 shows the various psychiatric disorders that may cause depressive or withdrawn behavior.

Depression is often unrecognized and untreated, so if a teacher can alert mental health staff and the family, and if the child and family can get access to treatment, this can make a significant difference in the student's trajectory.[4] If a child has untreated symptoms of major depression, the average length of an episode is seven to nine months, although it can be up to two years. This can have a profound impact on a child, as he can fall behind during an entire academic year or two if he doesn't receive the help he needs. Depression is a treatable illness, and treatment can improve cognitive function, social development, and academic performance, as well as decrease suicidal thoughts.[5] Sadly, children who develop depression will

TABLE 5.1

Signs of depression in students

Obvious signs	*Under-recognized signs*
• Unreasonable fears	• Excessive complaining
• Poor self-esteem	• Decline in grades (not due to a learning disorder or medical illness)
• Expressing feelings of sadness, guilt, help-lessness, worthlessness	• Giving up easily
• Loss of interest in previously enjoyed activities	• Irritability, restlessness
• Lack of energy (feeling fatigued)	• Difficulty concentrating, remembering details, making decisions
• Loss of appetite, and weight loss or weight gain	• Persistent boredom
• Frequent crying and looking sad	• Social isolation—disengaging from peers
• Talk of suicide or self-harm	• Complaints of physical illness or aches and pains
	• Not caring about appearance or hygiene
	• Perfectionism
	• Lethargy (e.g., falling asleep in class or low energy)

Source: adapted from American Psychiatric Association, *Diagnostic and Statistical Manual of Mental Disorders* 4th ed., text revision (*DSM-IV-TR*) (Washington, D.C.: American Psychiatric Association, 2000).

often have recurring episodes of major depression if they do not receive adequate treatment, and this can be incapacitating. If teachers know that a child has had depression in the past, it is key for them to closely attend to the child's emotional state, noting whether the student becomes withdrawn and less motivated to do work, which could potentially signal a relapse. Getting treatment quickly can help to prevent bigger problems.

What Causes Depression in Children?

Children's vulnerability to depression can come from both environmental stress-ors and biological causes. Compared with children of parents without depression, children of depressed parents are three to four times more likely to develop a mood disorder.[6] However, stressors in the environment can also precipitate depression

TABLE 5.2

Some subtypes of depression in children

Disorder	Features
Major depressive disorder	Depressed or irritable mood with impaired function plus four of the following symptoms for two weeks: • Sleeping too little or too much • Loss of interest • Guilty feelings or feelings of worthlessness • Energy decline • Difficulty concentrating • Change in appetite • Slowing down of thought and physical activity (psychomotor retardation) • Restlessness (agitation) • Suicidal ideation
Dysthymic disorder	Less severe than major depression, but a more chronic disorder, with depressed or irritable mood present for at least one year, with two or more symptoms of major depressive disorder
Bipolar depression	Major depression with a history of at least one manic episode
Adjustment disorder with depressed mood	Stress-related, usually resolves within six months; emotional or behavioral response of sadness, anguish, and distress to an identifiable stressor—response appears within three months after the stress (e.g., death of a parent, birth of a sibling, changing schools)

Source: adapted from American Psychiatric Association, *Diagnostic and Statistical Manual of Mental Disorders* 4th ed., text revision (*DSM-IV-TR*) (Washington, D.C.: American Psychiatric Association, 2000).

in vulnerable children. Students can react strongly to their environment and can become depressed after their parents' divorce, being bullied, the death of a family member, or any other major life event (this is referred to as situational depression). When students experience trauma such as physical or sexual abuse, neglect, or domestic violence, this can undermine their sense of safety, and they can become depressed, withdrawn, and anxious in the classroom. Additional strategies for working with children who have anxiety can be found in chapter 3.

Help Outside the Classroom

Teachers should never worry alone about their students with withdrawn behavior. When you suspect you have a student with depression, make sure that you tell the principal and the mental health specialist (e.g., school psychologist, social worker, or adjustment counselor) immediately. School mental health clinicians are a crucial resource and can help obtain outside treatment and evaluations for students. These professionals can also provide guidance about how to work with depressed and withdrawn students in the classroom.

Good communication is key to ensure that family, school counselors, and outside providers have any relevant information. You might find it useful to schedule a weekly or monthly meeting time with the school mental health specialist to check in and share concerns about the student. Don't assume the counselors know as much as you do. In fact, a student is more likely to give teachers information, as the child is with them more of the day. Unfortunately, this key step of collaboration between the teacher and counselor is often overlooked, leaving the teacher unable to complement what the student is learning in the counseling sessions. For students with frequent physical complaints and frequent visits to the nursing office, the school nurse may be a valuable source of information and insight regarding the student as well. We include more information in the box "Suicidal Warning Signs in Youth." Chapter 7 also discusses suicide warning signs and how to support reintegration of a student after hospitalization.

A child with depression warrants a comprehensive evaluation by a child psychiatrist, social worker, psychologist, or pediatrician to see how serious the depression is; what suicide risk there is; and whether there are other contributing factors, such as a learning disorder, an anxiety disorder, a medical condition, or family difficulties, that need to be addressed. In rare cases, a child may be prescribed an antidepressant to improve her function, particularly if she has been suicidal or made a suicide attempt, had a steep decline in functioning, or has a family history of depression.[7] Medications should never be the only treatment for a depressed child.[8] The child and family should also participate in therapy to address possible family responses that may be contributing to a child's depression. Usually, a child will also benefit from play therapy (if she is under ten) or cognitive behavioral therapy (if over ten). Group therapy can enhance students' social skills, which may allow the children to build a more supportive network of peers.

Suicidal Warning Signs in Youth

Always take suicidal warning signs seriously. Report your concerns to an administrator or a counselor quickly, and follow school protocol. Never leave the student alone.[9]

- Talking or writing about thoughts of suicide, drawing suicide-related pictures, or acting out suicide (e.g., pretending they are going to jump out the window or putting something around their neck and making a choking expression)
- Signs of depression or a sense of hopelessness
- Giving away possessions
- Death themes in classroom drawings, journals, or homework
- Focusing on, or discussing, suicidal plans and methods
- Increasing focus on, or access to, guns or other weapons

Cognitive Behavioral Strategies

Individuals with depression can get caught in a cycle of negative thoughts and experiences, which perpetuates their low mood. Many studies show the efficacy of cognitive behavioral therapy (CBT), a cornerstone of treating depression in adolescents and adults.[10] The treatment has been adapted to be developmentally appropriate for children, though they usually need to be at least ten years old to grasp some of the concepts and do the reasoning required. When children are depressed, it is helpful for them to learn these skills with a counselor, either at school or at a clinic, and then have these skills reinforced in the classroom by the teacher (more information can be found in the "Accommodations" section of this chapter).

In CBT, children first learn to monitor how they are feeling and to make the key connection that their thoughts can have an impact on their feelings. Building on this skill, they learn to recognize *thinking traps*, or automatic thoughts that can be debilitating.[11] Common thinking traps for people with depression are these: magnifying the negative aspects of a situation while overlooking the positive aspects (sometimes also referred to as thinking on the downside); catastrophizing (when a small setback is viewed as the end of the world); or seeing things as all-or-nothing.[12] People with depression can have negative thoughts such as "It's all my fault," "I can't do anything right," and "I *never* have friends." Students may also have a repetitive pattern of blaming others (parents, teachers, or peers) for problems they are experiencing. These types of thoughts usually make children feel worse and tend to lead them to withdraw from others.

With help from the school counselor or an outside mental health clinician, children can learn how to recognize these thinking traps, challenge the accuracy of their initial thought, and construct a more adaptive alternative. If their initial thought is supported by the evidence, then they come up with an action plan. These children may also need support with their social skills, as they may be too timid to initiate contact with other students, be extremely sensitive to peer rejection (e.g., taking mild joking as a severe criticism), and focus on the negative. Role-playing can help them practice communication skills such as how to initiate conversations, make new friends, build on what others say, and problem-solve.

Thought stopping and positive self-talk, two other techniques learned in CBT, allow students to combat negative thoughts and stay engaged. In thought stopping, a student learns that she has control over her thoughts and that when she is having an upsetting thought, she can replace it with positive imagery or calming self-statements. Children can distract themselves from repetitive thoughts by replacing distressing thoughts by singing or rapping a positive statement.[13] Power cards can be used to help students practice positive self-talk and can include a positive or calming image.[14] Self-talk refers to the ongoing internal conversation a person has that affects his or her mood. Positive self-talk will usually lead to positive mood and self-esteem in the student.[15] Thought stopping needs to be practiced repeatedly. Table 5.3 gives some examples of positive self-talk, which teachers may find as a useful strategy to encourage students who are withdrawn and who get easily discouraged.

A FAIR PLAN FOR THE STUDENT WITH WITHDRAWN BEHAVIOR

Students with withdrawn behavior require a combination of a supportive, nurturing classroom environment and teachers who understand them and respond to their behavior in a productive way. They also need opportunities to build their underdeveloped skills with school-based clinicians or outside therapists and have these reinforced in the classroom.

TABLE 5.3

Examples of positive self-talk

Self-talk strategy	Example
Talking yourself through a difficult task	"If I just take my time, I'll be able to do it."
The use of humor	"If I were paid a dime for every mistake, I'd be rich!"
The expression of hope in the face of disappointment	"That's OK; I'll do better on math next turn. It's important to keep trying."
The preservation of self-esteem in a difficult situation	"I may be bad at this game, but I'm really good at basketball."
The need to take a time out from a difficult situation	"I'm too upset to play anymore. Let me think of something else to do."

Functional Hypothesis and Antecedent Analysis

Every time a student makes a negative statement, cries, doesn't produce work, exhibits inappropriate behavior (e.g., yelling, aggression, property destruction, bolting), asks to go to the nurse or complains of ailments, or exhibits other behavior that is concerning, it is important to keep a record of the behavior in the ABC format discussed earlier. It's especially important to start taking data if any behavior interferes with the student's learning, other students' learning, or the teacher's instruction. As we noted before, a minimum of five observations is necessary to observe a pattern, but more are even better. Table 5.4 provides an example of an ABC data sheet for Jack, whose story began this chapter.

Don't forget to record setting events, which are incredibly important to record and recognize for all students. A student's withdrawn behavior can be directly related to occurrences that happened well before the behavior is exhibited as well as directly before an event. Look for patterns in both the antecedent and the consequence columns, tallying them so it is easier to review the information (figure 5.1).

Looking at the ABC data and tallies, we can see that Jack made many negative statements during times of the day when he wasn't receiving attention from an adult or a peer. During a small-group activity, he fell asleep on the table. Three out of five incidents occurred when he was doing an independent activity. In light of

TABLE 5.4

ABC data sheet for Jack, a student with withdrawn behavior

Date, time, duration	Activity	Setting event(s)	Antecedent (what happens immediately before behavior)	Behavior (description of behavior)	Consequence (what happens immediately after behavior)
3/7, 9:15 a.m., 10 sec	Math		Jack is working independently.	Jack exclaims, "I'm stupid," and breaks his pencil.	Mr. Lawson pats him on the back and tells him he's good at math. Then he does the next three problems with him.
3/10, 8:10 a.m., 3 min	Morning meeting	His sister is home sick.	Jack sits in morning meeting looking at his teacher.	Jack starts to hold his stomach and moan.	Mr. Lawson asks him what's wrong repeatedly and then sends him to the nurse.
3/15, 1 p.m., 5 min	Art class	He is late to school as he had a doctor's appointment.	Jack is independently drawing at a table with five other students.	Jack blurts, "I hate art," and tears up his paper into tiny pieces.	Art teacher sits next to Jack to help him with his next drawing and pats him on the back. Art teacher reports incident to teacher.
3/15, 2:10 p.m., 7 sec	Quiet reading		Jack is reading a book he chose at his desk.	Jack cries and says, "I can't take it anymore."	Mr. Lawson pulls Jack aside and talks with him.
3/19, 12:45 p.m., 10 min	Reading group		Jack is asleep with his head on the snack table.	Jack won't wake up or acknowledge the teacher.	Mr. Lawson lets him sleep for ten minutes.

Note: adapted from Sidney W. Bijou, et al. *Journal of Applied Behavior Analysis* 1, no. 2 (1968); Beth Sulzer-Azaroff and G. Roy Mayer, *Applying Behavior-Analysis Procedures with Children and Youth*.

FIGURE 5.1

Tallying the antecedents and consequences in Jack's ABC chart

Antecedents		Consequences	
Independent work (math, drawing, reading):	///	One-on-one adult attention (math, meeting, art, reading):	////
Whole-group activity (meeting):	/		
Small-group social activity (slept through snack and reading group):	/	Received help from a teacher (math, art):	//
When not getting attention (all):	////	Successfully avoided small group of peers (snack/reading):	/

these observations, Mr. Lawson learned that Jack was seeking attention with his withdrawn behavior and that Jack might also be engaging in negative thinking when alone (i.e., when Jack was not distracted or engaged in an activity with help from another person). Jack avoided small-group social time (the snack and read-aloud aspects of reading group) by sleeping.

Mr. Lawson found that reading the notes in this ABC format helped to uncover the patterns of how he responded to Jack. He realized that he was giving a lot of one-on-one attention when Jack was passive. With support from our team consultation, the teacher started to narrate (described aloud what he saw Jack was doing: "It looks as if you two are coming up with a nice poster, Jack and Bob") when Jack was doing partner work. Later in this chapter, we offer more suggestions for narrating. Mr. Lawson also worked with the counselor to help Jack come up with some positive self-statements. When the boy got discouraged, Mr. Lawson helped him with how to feel more comfortable when joining groups.

Accommodations

Students with withdrawn behavior need special accommodations through a supportive classroom environment; creative, low-stress curricula; and extra help in improving poor social and other skills. Let's look at some of these approaches in detail.

Environment

It is important to provide a safe, calm space in the classroom for a student with withdrawn behavior. This is a place for her to go to self-regulate when she is feeling sad or frustrated. The space can consist of a beanbag chair, comfortable pillows, and activities to distract a student from her negative thoughts.

Some depressed students may desperately want to be noticed and have someone to talk to, while others just want to be left alone. You may need to intervene actively to help the student engage with other classmates. An alternative lunch plan may help with those students who are always sitting alone during lunch or a student who repeatedly says, "Nobody likes me." Starting with only one other student at first is important, especially if the student tends to withdraw in a small or large group. This is an opportunity for students to learn how to join a conversation and build on what another student says. Games should be available, as this may encourage a withdrawn student to interact. Emphasize what the two students have in common whenever possible (e.g., "You both like movies," or "You both seem to like to draw!"). This can help the student with withdrawn behavior feel more connected to the other student.

Providing staff support at recess or creating a buddy system with a peer can give the student with withdrawn behavior additional support to engage in activities. Students with withdrawn behavior, especially those with social skills challenges, may need a schedule and a concrete recess plan that a teacher helps them to fill out before going out to recess (such as in figure 5.2). The plan includes who they are going to play with, how they are going to ask the student to play, and what activities they would like to do. Sometimes, as we have mentioned, it may be useful to support the student in choosing a compatible partner, possibly by approaching the other student first. For older students, in fourth through sixth grade, remove the pictures from the recess plan, and include more age-appropriate recess activities such as wall-ball or jump rope.

Executive functioning

Students with withdrawn behavior have difficulty with several executive functioning skills, including task initiation, working memory, organization, and attention. When a person is depressed, qualities like initiative, attention span, and organization—critical to executive functioning—often fall by the wayside. Many aspects of CBT can help students who might be hindered by self-doubt or other negative thoughts. A school counselor or an outside counselor can help a child monitor his or her feelings, fight thinking traps, engage in positive self-talk, and engage with others. With an improved emotional state, the child can often better develop her

FIGURE 5.2

Sample Recess Plan

1. What activity should I pick?

   Jumprope

   Ring Toss

   Play ball

   Chalk

2. Who would be a good choice to play _____ with?

   _____

   _____

   _____

3. Ask your friend _____ . . .

   Do you want to play _____ with me _____ ?

4. Tell a teacher _____ if you need help.

Source: Pics for PECS™ images are used and adapted with permission from Pyramid Educational Consultants, Inc. (www.pecs.com). Pyramid Educational Consultants, Inc. reserves all rights to the Pics for PECS™ images.

executive functioning skills, which serves as a positive feedback loop when these skills improve the child's overall performance and thereby increase her self-esteem.

Curriculum

Because students with depression often have decreased interests and motivation, it is more important to identify what they are interested in and start there so that they can build momentum. Whenever possible, the curriculum should be creative and project-based. Multisensory lessons (i.e., those that incorporate all learning styles: visual, tactile, auditory, and kinesthetic) are more likely to keep the student aroused, attentive, and, most importantly, learning, because these lessons are more stimulating. Teachers are fighting an uphill battle to motivate a withdrawn student, so if he shows some interest in a particular topic, focusing on that subject will make teaching him easier. If, for example, the teacher assigns a written report on Martin Luther King, providing the student with choices on how to complete the project can optimize his interest. If he is artistic, having him create a diorama on Rosa Parks can demonstrate his knowledge of the content.

Using technology to supplement instruction is a great way to motivate and engage a student with withdrawn behavior. Online lessons, games, and activities correlate with academics for almost all grade levels. Technology can be incorporated in a whole-class lesson or individually. Some districts have an inclusion specialist who can help to modify the curriculum for the student with withdrawn behavior.

Allowing extra time for assignments is an important accommodation since students with depression struggle to stay motivated enough to complete work. Some students with depression can have slowed thinking and need more time. However, others may find it more difficult when they have extra time, because they just think obsessively and second-guess themselves. In the latter situation, a teacher could interview the student to discover the student's distress level and to determine if extra time is unhelpful.

For students whose thinking may be slowed because of depression, teachers and parents should decide if the children need accommodation in the form of a temporary homework reduction, as it can take time to respond to treatment. This is especially important in the older grades, where homework may comprise a large part of the student's overall grade. The student may stop making any effort, because she feels she has fallen so far behind that it is hopeless to try to catch up.

Teaching underdeveloped skills

Students with depression can have many underdeveloped skills, such as positive thinking and cognitive flexibility. If a student is on an IEP, the special education team identifies the clinician who teaches the student the underdeveloped skills. Skills that may need to be strengthened are positive thinking, self-advocacy, cognitive flexibility, social skills, and executive functioning. If these skills are not explicitly taught, it is difficult for students to improve their behavior. Appendix B lists a number of curriculum resources that can be used to help the student improve her underdeveloped skills.

Teachers' observations are vital in shaping how the counselor supports these students. Regular communication between the teacher and the counselor is essential. If a child often isolates himself and misinterprets overtures of friendship or doesn't initiate contact with other students, then the counselor may role-play with him or offer a friendship group to help facilitate social skills. When a student prematurely quits a game with self-defeating comments, the counselor can coach him on positive self-talk that encourages him to persist.

It is also helpful if the teacher adopts the same language as the counselor to reinforce the student's effort. Whenever possible, if a teaching assistant is available and parents give permission, have the assistant join the student in her school counseling session. This is most appropriate when the counselor is teaching the student a new skill, such as positive self-talk or how to relate better to others. The assistant can then help the student use the same language and practice her skill throughout the day.

For example, if Maria usually withdraws after a comment such as "I *never* do anything right," a teacher's assistant who has learned the techniques and language Maria is using with the counselor can say, "Are you sure you never do anything right? This sounds like a thinking trap. How about if we think together whether this is a hundred percent true, or if there are times you get things right?" This continuity of language helps Maria learn to take the strategies she learned in therapy and put them into place when she is overwhelmed in the classroom.

Self-regulation and self-monitoring

These are underdeveloped skills for students with withdrawn behavior. Use the self-monitoring sheet in appendix F, and in the top box, write down the strategies that you want to teach. When a student uses a replacement strategy like asking for help from a teacher to get attention *instead* of a self-degrading statement, then he earns a bonus point.

Whenever possible, the counselor or teacher can introduce technology for self-monitoring (being aware of your own behavior and accurately perceiving when certain behavior is inappropriate) and self-regulating (managing to keep yourself at a functional level of arousal—not letting yourself get too upset). Rather than a paper self-monitoring sheet, the student can use a mobile device (e.g., an iPod Touch or a smartphone) to self-monitor and self-regulate.[16] For example, if Pete is in music class and starts to feel frustrated, he can use his mobile device. The first screen asks, "How do you feel?" and gives visual choices. Pete touches the icon for frustrated, and the program cues him to pick a strategy. He picks "Ask to get a drink of water in the hallway." Once he returns, the program prompts him to rate if this strategy helped him. If he is still frustrated, he can pick another strategy. Some programs even allow Pete to give himself points for using a strategy. The emotional thermometer (seen in chapter 3) can be put on a mobile device as well to promote self-regulation. Not surprisingly, a mobile device or another electronic tool for self-regulation and self-monitoring is much more motivating to students than paper, but both are effective.

Another way to promote self-monitoring and more accurate reporting is for the student to fill out a reflection sheet at the end of each school day (figure 5.3). The sheet requires the student to write something that occurred that day and was challenging and to write down something she liked. You may initially need to provide some scaffolding for the student to come up with something positive on the sheet. This form can also be created electronically and put onto a mobile device for the student.

Proprioceptive exercises and alerting strategies

Students with withdrawn behavior typically have low energy. Physical exercise is effective at reducing a student's risk of becoming depressed and may help improve symptoms of depression in some students.[17] Incorporating movement breaks throughout the day can help the student stay attentive. Big, proprioceptive exercises (i.e., heavy work or exercise done against resistance that engage muscles and joints) last the longest. Smaller alerting strategies (activities that will help a student feel more alert) may be used during class if the student is showing low energy—these don't require the student to get up from his desk or to stop working. Table 5.5 lists some of these strategies and exercises. Before the teacher allows a student to rest, or if the student is acting sluggish, it's helpful to encourage alerting strategies as a way to prevent sleeping during school.

FIGURE 5.3

Sample reflection sheet

Date: _____

Student's Name: _____

1. What activity today was your least favorite?

2. What activity today did you like? [Or, What was your favorite activity today?]

3. What was something you were good at today?

4. What was something that was difficult for you today?

TABLE 5.5

Alerting strategies and proprioceptive exercises

Alerting strategies	Proprioceptive exercises
• Loud music with a fast beat	• Wall or chair push-ups
• Have students rub their arms or legs vigorously	• Wipe the board or table
• Chew crunchy food, drink cold water	• Heavy work: push in chairs, put chairs on desks
• Move-and-sit cushion (inflated seat cushion that allows students to move around while sitting)	• Carry heavy books to a neighboring teacher
• Citrus or peppermint scents	• Move desks
• Brightly colored paper or highlighting text	• Wheelbarrow walk
	• Running
	• Jumping jacks
	• Pull-up bars

Sources: D. Saunders, "The Importance of Sensory Processing," Web page, 2005; revised April 30, 2006, http://dsaundersot.webs.com/resources.html; Sasha Fureman and Tiffany Sahd, "Strategies for Sensory Success," *Washington Parent*, April 2005.

Interaction Strategies

Children who are withdrawn need particular investment from the teacher to build a relationship and help to bolster their self-esteem.

Relationship building

The most important preventative strategy for students with depression is relationship building. This process takes time—maybe months, but it is integral to students' being engaged enough to learn. Many students with depression isolate themselves or, through negative behavior, prevent people from getting close to them. Some students may play alone at recess, eat by themselves at lunch, and stop playing with friends after school. If students are irritable, they may be quick to insult other students, misinterpret or blame other students and staff when bad things happen, or whine a lot. When you take extra time with these students, you can often break the cycle of self-fulfilling rejection.

Direct conversation may be too intimate for some students, so a more indirect way of building a relationship is to spend time together playing a game or doing a task in the classroom (e.g., helping the teacher to decorate the blackboard or write a newsletter). This may be a more comfortable way for them to know that a teacher cares. Opportunities for outreach might be playing a board game during recess time or asking the student to help decorate a bulletin board. These small overtures can have huge payback. Robert Pianta, a prominent developmental psychologist, refers to this as *banking time*: storing up positive experiences to help the teacher–student relationship withstand problems or conflict in the future.[18]

Make sure to narrate a bit during relationship building times (e.g., "You and I are having special time together"). Otherwise, a student with withdrawn behavior might not register these experiences or may misinterpret them, because of her predisposition to remember the negative experiences over the positive.

Noncontingent reinforcement, a technique mentioned in other chapters, is very effective in increasing feelings of self-worth.[19] This means random acts of kindness by the teacher. When the teacher does something nice for the student without its being contingent on good behavior, this helps the student feel as if someone knows him. If the teacher offers, say, a sticker or trading card of a student's preferred television character, it is reassuring that someone has bothered to notice his interests. Over time, the student will associate the reinforcement with "just being myself" as opposed to registering, "The teacher only likes me when I'm good."

Specific positive reinforcement

In addition to giving positive reinforcement in a way that is comfortable for the student, give specific positive reinforcement and praise for the behavior you want to see more of. "You're a great kid" or "You're smart" is the type of blanket statement that can easily be rejected by some students with withdrawn behavior. Precise praising statements are likely to be more credible and more memorable to a student: "I like the way you helped your friend" or "You finished your work so quietly, thank you."[20] When speaking to a younger student with withdrawn behavior, you may want to be enthusiastic with a somewhat exaggerated tone when praising her. Praising a student for working hard rather than for a trait (e.g., being smart) helps the depressed student focus on what she has control over and can do again.

Be cautious when using humor with students who are depressed and withdrawn. These students do not often feel joy or laugh, and they can be quite sensitive. Humor can be misunderstood as sarcasm, and the student may feel picked on or that you are laughing at him, rather than with him.

Giving positive feedback

Even though students with depression may need praise from teachers as a way to help improve their harsh self-critical tendencies, these children can be extremely sensitive to how teachers give praise. It is important to notice how these students respond to praise and to ask them what is the most comfortable way for them to get positive feedback. For example, Colleen was a withdrawn, quiet fifth-grade student. Her teacher, Ms. Khalef, knew that she had a history of depression and had been in treatment with an outside counselor for three years. Colleen was a fabulous writer and handed in some of Ms. Khalef's favorite pieces. Ms. Khalef noticed that Colleen's writing became alarmingly poorer in quality and was concerned that this decline could be a sign of Colleen's depression worsening. She contacted the social worker, who confirmed that this was an accurate observation. In consultation with us, Ms. Khalef learned how students with depression may respond to praise. The teacher realized that she had often praised Colleen publicly. Ms. Khalef met with Colleen to figure out how she preferred to be praised. "When I'm impressed with something you have written," Ms. Khalef asked, "how should I let you know?" Ms. Khalef gave Colleen some options such as writing her a note, giving a silent thumbs-up, patting her on the back, or waiting until they were alone. They agreed that Ms. Khalef would write her a note in her homework folder instead of praising her publicly.

Leadership opportunities

One technique teachers can utilize is to give the student leadership tasks at strategic times throughout the day. A withdrawn student may become more motivated, given the opportunity to help the secretary put out mail after recess or read to a younger child at the beginning of school. Providing these opportunities at strategic times during the day can turn the tide from an initial negative feeling to a more positive feeling. Allowing the student an opportunity to have control and leadership helps to improve self-esteem (the child feels he or she has become good at something) and will counter learned helplessness over time.[21]

Narrating a student's experience

Students who are depressed often overlook positive experiences and exaggerate the negative, which further reinforces their sense of isolation and prevents them from participating in activities that could make them feel better. We have found that some teachers on occasion challenge or debate a student who is overly hard on herself. They believe that they can persuade the student to see it differently. A more effective approach is to narrate what the child is doing as a way to help her to improve her own observation skills. In our experience, this can have surprisingly dramatic results.

A way to help a student remember experiences more accurately is to narrate the experience in the moment for the student.[22] This strategy is more feasible if there is another staff member available to dedicate some time to watch the student and periodically quietly narrate. If there is not enough staff to give one-on-one attention during an entire activity, even narrating a small portion of the activity is helpful. Even when a teacher dedicates five or ten minutes of recess or math class, it can make a difference. To do this effectively, just like a narrator in a movie, the teacher states out loud what is actually occurring while the student is engaged in an activity: "You've done five math problems already, and three kids haven't even started yet," "You are smiling and Will is laughing," or "Will laughed at your funny story." If the student appears annoyed at being singled out or talked to randomly, the teacher can narrate for the whole group or for more than one student. "You two are smiling and talking while you eat your lunch," or "You are all almost halfway done with spelling, and you are ahead of schedule." For older students, such as fifth- and sixth-graders, the narration technique needs to be done more subtly to avoid sounding condescending: "You two have been smiling for five minutes. What's so funny?" The student is more likely to remember factual events with the narration than without it. Narration can also be done indirectly by making the statement to a colleague: "Mr. Carson, look at Jack and Jen. They have been giggling for five minutes!"

After we consulted with Mr. Lawson (Jack's teacher in the first example in this chapter), his teaching assistant, Ms. McDonald, specifically narrated events quietly when Jack was interacting with other peers or participating in class activities. After she did this for three weeks, Jack wrote a personal narrative for the first time. He wrote that he played a math game with two peers, that he was the only one who knew how to spell *psychedelic*, and that his friend shared a snack with him. Although Mr. Lawson and Ms. McDonald thought the narrating approach seemed awkward and initially took a lot of extra time and effort, they were excited that it encouraged Jack to participate more and that he continued to improve.

Reframing

It's critical to reduce the student's negative behavior and statements. Additional negative statements and behaviors can generate more-negative feelings about themselves. When a teacher reframes, he or she substitutes the student's generalized negative statement "I suck at math" with a distilled factual response such as "Multiplication is not your favorite." This substitutes for a coddling response from the teacher, like, "What? You're great in math!" which could accidentally reinforce negative-attention-seeking in some students. It also helps the student not to minimize good events and helps her to build memories that are more positive. By creating a more accurate and positive memory of that activity for the student, reframing improves her observation skills and challenges her tendency toward all-or-nothing thinking. The teacher's factual statement can help the student realize over time that she just didn't like the spelling list that day, for example, not that she is horrible at writing. Table 5.6 shows some examples of reframing.

Helping the student with evidence to dispute negative perceptions

Another strategy for responding to negative statements is to offer the student evidence that his negative perception of events is inaccurate. If a student complains that you *never* call on him, your teaching assistant can make a tally of every time the student is called, or you can put a paper clip from your right pocket to your left pocket every time you call on the student throughout the day and present this paper

TABLE 5.6

Reframing a student's negative statement into a positive one

Negative statements by students	*Teacher's reframing statements (neutral and calm tone)*
"I can't write."	"Spelling was challenging today."
"I'm stupid!"	"Sounds like you're frustrated opening your snack container."
"Art is stupid. I am the worst artist in this class!"	"Working with clay is not your favorite activity."
"I stink at reading."	"That was a very long reading passage today."

clip chain to the student at the end of the day. This technique can also be used to provide the student with factual information about how many kids talked to him, how many compliments the student received for his project, or any other issue. To respond to the common statement "I'm stupid," you can (with a student peer's permission) show the student with withdrawn behavior a sample of a respected peer's work and point out that she makes mistakes, too: "Bindi got number four wrong, too. Do you think she's stupid?" The concrete proof can help the student be less self-critical.[23]

Another powerful way to provide a student with proof that she has friends and has positive social interactions is to take photos of the student interacting with friends (with photograph permission from her classmates) throughout the week. Sharing these with the student and her family can help to minimize the student's negative self-concept.

Prompting the student effectively

When a person is in a situation where he has little control over the outcome, he may learn that his responses are ineffective. Students can feel powerless and develop a "what's the use" syndrome.[24] When a student displays this type of learned helplessness, teachers often offer a good deal of attention and help—sometimes too much. *Prompt dependence* is a phrase that refers to students' overreliance on teachers' help.[25]

Instead of overprompting, prompt the student in a way that encourages independent problem-solving skills. Help the student to take control, to plan, and to execute a task. Avoid directives such as "Get out your math folder," instead prompting the student to be aware of his surroundings: "What are the other students doing?" or "What do you need for math class?" This encourages the student do the work of figuring out what he needs.

Many times, a teacher in a rush will do some of the steps for a student or ask another peer to help, but when possible, it is better to resist the reflex to help the student too much. For example, if Anita stands frozen in front of her locker as class is about to start, most teachers would prompt her to put away her belongings so the class can get started. It is surprising the number of directives that can be given in this situation: "Hang up your coat." "No, on that hook." "Now open up your backpack." "Unzip it." "Go sit in your seat." During this time, Anita doesn't need to think or plan and is engaged minimally in the task.

Response Strategies

We encourage teachers to respond to a student's inappropriate behavior in an empathetic way that encourages students to change their behavior.

Negative attention

Be careful not to provide negative attention to the student with withdrawn behavior if the ABC notes show a pattern of this type of consequence. There are two essential steps in responding to negative behavior in students with depression. First, *stop* responding in a less productive way, that is, with immediate one-on-one attention. Second, either ignore the student when she is showing negative behavior (this is only possible in a one-on-one situation or if she is only motivated by adult attention), or respond in a neutral, factual way, reframing the statement briefly and concisely with a neutral tone and minimal eye contact.

Social misperception

When a student with withdrawn behavior misperceives a social interaction with a peer, commonly as a result of the student's negative thinking, you can explain the facts of the social interaction through comic strip conversations. Draw the social interaction frame by frame in cartoon form, putting thought bubbles for each character. This is a great way to illustrate for the student what the characters were thinking throughout the interaction (e.g., "She was not thinking you were stupid—she was not even looking when you dropped the ball!" with a picture of the peer looking away, thinking about something else). See appendix D for several Web sites that assist with cartoon making.

A FAIR PLAN FOR JACK

Looking at Jack's ABC data, his teacher realized that Jack made many negative statements during times of the day when he wasn't receiving attention from an adult or a peer. Once during the year, during a small-group activity, Jack even fell asleep on the table. Three out of the five incidents of unacceptable behavior occurred when he was doing an independent activity. Jack also avoided social times of the day. Looking at the data, the teacher also realized he, the adult, was giving a lot of one-on-one attention when Jack was passive.

For accommodations, the teacher provided a recess buddy, created a recess plan, and rewarded Jack for following it with special privileges like playing with special Legos. The teacher also put in place a visual schedule with time guidelines and specific instructions to help Jack organize belongings. The teacher used a timer and narrated the passage of time during nonpreferred tasks.

For accessing the curriculum, Mr. Lawson found pictures to help Jack think of a writing topic. The teacher made a particular effort to use pictures of animals that Jack had shown an interest in. He gave the boy extra time for these assignments and taught with a multi-sensory approach, knowing that hands-on activities would especially engage this student.

Mr. Lawson also began teaching Jack positive thinking and self-advocacy, such as using his words with peers when he didn't like something because he was at risk for being bullied. He prompted Jack with the alerting strategy of getting a drink of cold water when Jack asked to rest or looked as if he was about to fall asleep. The teacher also asked him to use an emotional thermometer and regulation chart throughout the day and an iPod for self-monitoring. Finally, Mr. Lawson had Jack fill out the reflection sheet daily.

Mr. Lawson began eating lunch with Jack once a month and found ways to give him leadership opportunities, including delivering packages and restocking the paper in the office copy machine. Jack agreed to a thumbs-up for a positive reinforcement signal throughout the day. In order to give Jack more accurate and positive information about himself, Mr. Lawson took pictures of Jack playing tag with friends at recess and narrated the boy's positive interactions during snack time.

When Jack did make a negative statement, Mr. Lawson tried to avoid giving him special attention and reframed the boy's statements neutrally. The teacher also gave him extra time with the nurse when Jack used a regulation strategy such a pulling out a power card.

As a result, Jack gradually reduced the number of negative statements. In addition, Mr. Lawson reported seeing him respond positively to peers during structured games like math bingo, participate in all subjects, complete his work, and sit with other students at snack time.

Chapter Summary

- Students with withdrawn behavior can be negative-attention-seeking.
- They may also avoid positive attention.
- Some students with withdrawn behavior are diagnosed with depression.
- Students with depression may engage in negative thinking and perceive situations negatively.
- If you notice any suicidal warning signs, always take these signs seriously. Report your concerns to an administrator or a counselor quickly, and follow school protocol. Never leave the student alone.

FAIR

Behavior Intervention Plan for the Student with Withdrawn Behavior

Student's Name: _____ Date: _____

TARGETED BEHAVIORS (be as explicit as possible):

F Functional Hypothesis and Antecedent Analysis

☐ Document all instances of targeted behaviors, using ABC data sheet (minimum of five incidents)

☐ List antecedents from ABC data or observation to be addressed in this plan:

☐ Form a hypothesis about the function of behavior (circle one or more): attention, escape, tangible reward, sensory satisfaction. *Attention function often motivates withdrawn behavior.*

☐ List any pattern of consequences, using the ABC data.

☐ List any setting events of note:

A   Accommodations

We have included strategies and interventions from other chapters that you may consider.

Environmental

- ☐ Provide safe space in classroom
- ☐ Schedule breaks
- ☐ Allow for breaks outside the classroom
- ☐ Consider alternative lunch
- ☐ Provide recess accommodations: facilitation by adult, buddy system
- ☐ Have student complete a concrete recess plan

Executive functioning

- ☐ Teach "reading the room"
- ☐ Use Time Timer
- ☐ Narrate passage of time
- ☐ Use segmented clock
- ☐ Consider untimed test
- ☐ Use visual schedules
- ☐ Put organization time in schedule
- ☐ Present only a few problems or items at a time

Curriculum

- ☐ Use pictures to help student think of and maintain a topic
- ☐ Have student use word processing
- ☐ Consider spelling accommodations
- ☐ Give extra time for assignments
- ☐ Other technology resources:
- ☐ Assess quality, not quantity, of work
- ☐ Teach multisensory, experiential lessons
- ☐ Give open-ended, flexible assignments when possible
- ☐ Use student's own interests in curriculum

Teaching underdeveloped skills explicitly

- ☐ Positive thinking
- ☐ Self-advocacy
- ☐ Motivation (CBT)
- ☐ Cognitive flexibility
- ☐ Executive functioning
- ☐ Self-talk-power cards/scripts
- ☐ Thinking traps
- ☐ Social skills
- ☐ Thought-stopping

Replacement behaviors (example for attention motivated behavior):

- ☐ Ask for a break appropriately
- ☐ Ask for help appropriately

Regulation of self and self-monitoring

- ☐ Have student use regulation scale (i.e., emotional thermometer)
- ☐ Have student use self-regulation chart
- ☐ Have student use exercises and alerting strategies
- ☐ Have student use mobile device for self-monitoring
- ☐ Use the self-monitoring sheet (appendix F)
- ☐ Have student fill out reflection sheet

I Interaction Strategies

- ☐ Work on relationship-building
- ☐ Use noncontingent reinforcement
- ☐ Offer specific positive reinforcement
- ☐ Be cautious in using humor
- ☐ Give positive feedback in a comfortable way
- ☐ Use leadership-building and self-esteem-building activities
- ☐ Narrate events in the moment
- ☐ Reframe student's negative perceptions

☐ Offer evidence to dispute negative perceptions
☐ Photograph positive social interactions
☐ Prompt the student effectively: in a way that will reduce dependence on prompting

R Response Strategies

☐ Avoid responses such as one-on-one talks immediately following behavior
☐ Avoid overhelping or overprompting the student
☐ Assign rewards or points when the student demonstrates a self-regulation skill
☐ When a student misperceives a social situation, try comic-strip strategy

CHAPTER 6

"I Didn't Mean To . . ."

The Student with Sexualized Behavior

Ms. Kent, the substitute teacher, was relieved when she finally reached sixth period, close to the end of a long day. She was, however, nervous about covering this group of sixth-grade students, particularly because of Max. Ms. Kent had never worked with Max, but she knew he had already been suspended twice this year. After giving instructions about the science lab the students needed to complete, Ms. Kent asked if they had any questions. Max raised his hand. Ms. Kent called on him. "Do you know that your nipples are poking through your shirt"? The class gasped and one student exclaimed, "Oh, no, he didn't!" in disbelief. Ms. Kent could feel her face flushing, and she quickly crossed her arms in front of her. "Max, you need to go see Mr. Kaufman. Now!" Max gathered his belongings and sauntered out of the class. "Don't worry, Ms. K, we all like it!" were his parting words.

WHAT IS SEXUALIZED BEHAVIOR?

In this chapter, we are specifically addressing students who display sexually inappropriate behavior. This includes saying sexual words or phrases to peers or teachers, making sexual gestures, making noises, or engaging in pretend play that simulates sex, making sexual invitations to others, inappropriately touching another person, or masturbating in the classroom. There is no clear research on how many students display this kind of sexualized behavior in schools. However, in our own experience and from what we have learned through talking with teachers, these behaviors seem to be relatively rare, but can be very upsetting. Teachers often don't know what to do.[1] We have found that displaying sexualized behavior can put the student on a fast track to a self-contained classroom or out-of-district placement because of understandable concerns about protecting other children. Decisions about these interventions, including decisions about removal, placement, or restrictions on contact with other students, need to be made on a case-by-case basis.

Students display persistent sexualized behavior for a host of reasons, and there is not a single common profile. Nor is there much published work on how to successfully work with these students in school.[2] In this chapter, we draw on our clinical experience to describe different types of students who display these behaviors, particularly impulsive students, students with social deficits, and students with trauma histories.

Teachers' instinctive response to a student's sexualized behavior is often to make it clear that the behavior is inappropriate and needs to stop. For many students, this will be all that is needed. Others, however, will demonstrate persistent sexualized behavior that requires more specific interventions. This chapter provides a framework for teachers to understand these students and shares information on how to constructively intervene with support from school mental health staff. An appropriate teacher response and therapy can help children with these behaviors learn to respect personal boundaries, form healthy relationships, and function better in school.

Despite the concern that children with sexualized behavior may go on to become criminal sexual offenders as adults, there is minimal long-term risk for this dire consequence, particularly if they receive appropriate short-term outpatient treatment with their family.[3] Children with sexualized behavior do respond to treatment, and the involvement of parents or other caregivers is crucial.[4] Active support by schools is critical to address the needs of children with sexualized behavior, as schools can moderate some of the stressors in these children's lives while also keeping other students safe.

NORMATIVE SEXUAL BEHAVIORS IN CHILDHOOD

Although our understanding of normative sexual development in children is still limited, teachers need to consider age-appropriate, "normal" sexual behavior in children to recognize problematic sexual behavior.[5] Preschoolers are interested in how their body parts function. It is not abnormal for them to touch their own genitals to relieve anxiety or for pleasure (even in public), stand too close to other people, try to view peers or adults nude or in the bathroom, or expose their genitals to peers.[6] Whereas half of preschoolers are noted by parental observation to touch their genitals, this number drops to about a third of children between six to nine years old.[7] Children normally touch themselves less in school than at home and less in elementary school than in preschool.[8] By grade school, some children continue to touch or masturbate, but they have usually learned that this is done privately and that it is socially taboo to do this in public settings such as school. As they get older, children may also show interest in the opposite sex, ask questions about sexuality, look at nude pictures, draw sexual body parts, and use sexual words.[9] Children may explore using sexualized comments to others, but this normally stops when adults set limits on what is appropriate.

Elementary-school-age students joke about body parts and elimination processes (often with the expected sound effects), and this is a common way of expressing curiosity while testing boundaries, bonding with peers, and addressing anxiety about matters related to sexuality. These jokes may be disruptive and are inappropriate in a classroom setting, but they are normal.

Young children play "doctor" or "mommy and daddy" games that involve observing and sometimes touching each other's body parts. This kind of behavior is relatively common and is rarely motivated by the child's desire for sexual stimulation.[10] According to the Task Force on Children with Sexual Behavior Problems, "normal childhood sexual play and exploration is mutual and noncoercive when it involves other children and it does not cause emotional distress."[11] After kindergarten, most children know that the classroom is not the place for sexual play and that, if teachers saw "doctor games" taking place, this behavior would not be permitted.[12]

CAUSES OF SEXUALIZED BEHAVIOR IN SCHOOLS

Anxiety, self-soothing, the need for attention, and imitation are some of the motivations for sexualized behavior.[13] Multiple variables, including physical or sexual abuse, exposure to parental violence, and family adversity (e.g., family income and total life stress), can contribute to sexualized behavior. If a child is exposed to adult sexual behavior or overstimulation (e.g., X-rated movies) in a home that lacks boundaries, he may also demonstrate sexualized behavior. Children who display sexualized behavior may also have other disruptive behavior problems (including disregard for others and difficulty respecting adult authority and following rules).[14] These sexualized behaviors occur across all socioeconomic levels, cultures, and family structures and are not related to the student's sexual orientation.[15] Boys are more likely to be referred for sexual behavior problems than girls, though research has not shown consistent gender differences in community samples.[16]

In our clinical experience consulting to schools about students who exhibit sexualized behaviors, there are three main factors that are often linked to sexualized behavior in schools:

- Interpersonal social skill deficits
- Impulsiveness
- Exposure to trauma

In this chapter, we will categorize students' sexualized behavior according to these three main factors and will discuss the students in that context. Students whose sexualized behavior is the result of copying sexual behaviors seen at home (e.g., a student has seen family members having sexual intercourse and does not understand that he should not be repeating those acts) will not be discussed. In this situation, the family and child need guidance about appropriate boundaries. However, some of the responses that we advocate also apply for these children. We also recognize that some children can use sexualized comments or acts as a form of intimidation and harassment and that school protocols need to be followed.

Adults often assume that if a child is exhibiting sexualized behavior, he has been sexually abused. We want to highlight that most children who have been sexually abused do *not* develop sexualized behaviors and many children with sexualized behavior do not have a known sexual abuse history.[17] We caution teachers to stay curious about why students exhibit sexualized behaviors and not to automatically assume that the student was sexually abused. However, it is crucial to remember that teachers are mandated reporters—if they suspect or have reason to believe that a child has been abused or if a child has revealed that she has been violated, they must file a report with child protective services and follow school protocol.

Sexual behaviors in the school setting elicit strong emotional reactions, which can lead to actions that leave both parents and teachers feeling isolated, angry, and ashamed. Nevertheless, it is important not to jump to a conclusion of sexual abuse, especially with impulsive students. A psychiatric evaluation and diagnosis is not the school's responsibility, but automatically assuming abuse as the underlying issue can harm the relationship with parents as well as delaying the appropriate interventions.

School staff are usually adept at identifying a student who has trouble with sexualized behavior, but they often fail to consider that the child may have bipolar disorder (even if there is extreme irritability, grandiosity, and hypersexual behavior). Researchers have found that for children under twelve years old diagnosed with bipolar disorder, over 43 percent present with hypersexuality, and only 1 percent have a history of sexual abuse.[18] According to these findings, hypersexuality is most likely a manifestation of mania.

A FAIR PLAN FOR JANELLE

Kindergarten teacher Ms. Adair reported that her student Janelle could destroy the classroom in a matter of minutes when upset by hitting one particular girl most days and swearing at anyone who tried to stop her. During group reading time, Janelle smacked her own bottom and grabbed two figurines and had them kiss. She would often complain of being hot and pull her clothes over her head.

The school was concerned that Janelle's sexualized behavior was caused by sexual abuse at home and filed a report with social services. Janelle's mother was very upset and avoided coming to school. We were asked to evaluate the child, and determined that Janelle had early-onset bipolar disorder. We referred the family to appropriate treatment, which included a medication trial and a new behavioral plan in school.

When the reasons for a child's sexualized behaviors can be identified, professionals can devise a specific intervention targeting the behaviors and their causes. The reasons for a child's sexualized behaviors cannot always be determined. In those cases, the general responses outlined in this chapter can still be helpful. It is key to recognize that many of these children, given the appropriate FAIR Plan strategies (e.g., enhancing communication skills, learning personal boundaries, and learning to delay impulses), can move beyond these behaviors and learn to make better decisions.[19]

Students with Social Deficits

Students who have social deficits have trouble understanding the unwritten, non-verbal rules that govern social interaction. They have difficulty processing nonverbal aspects of communication, such as body language, facial expressions, or tone of voice. This can lead to an inability to distinguish serious threats from playful teasing, or missing cues that can help them know how to behave in a situation.[20]

Who are the students with social deficits? Students with nonverbal language disabilities (also called nonverbal learning disorder, or NVLD) have skill deficits affecting their ability to learn academic skills and to acquire social skills (because of difficulty processing nonverbal information).[21] Students with Asperger's syndrome and autism spectrum disorder also have social deficits.

Sexualized behaviors may be seen in these students when they are unable to determine which behaviors are appropriate in a given situation. They may be unable to maintain a socially appropriate physical distance from others; may make repetitive, sexually inappropriate, or intrusive comments; or may inappropriately touch other peers or teachers. For example, a child may hug every child he sees, kiss adults on the lips, or touch strangers' hair or clothing. These behaviors range from strange or annoying to frankly sexual, frightening, and unacceptable.

Not all students with social deficits exhibit sexualized behavior. There are three main dynamics that can lead students with social skills deficits to engage in what would be considered sexualized behavior. Sexualized behavior can:

- Result from a lack of understanding of what is OK to say and do, and what isn't
- Serve as an efficient, predictable, intense, and obvious way to assure a response from a peer or an adult
- Be a way to express frustration and anger in students who have learned that sexualized comments are taboo

Sexual behavior from a lack of understanding

These students may not have any idea of the negative emotional impact sexualized behavior can have on the other person or may be unable to distinguish between a mild social transgression (telling someone publicly they have bad breath) and a major one (telling someone to take their pants off). Students with social deficits often underattend or miss relevant subtle social cues, which impedes their integration into their peer group and thus curtails their social growth and development.[22]

Students with social deficits are not good judges of what behavior is appropriate in a particular situation. Without the ability to discern what is acceptable, they often say the wrong thing to the wrong person at the wrong time. Teachers recognize that students with social deficits can make comments that are inappropriate, such as "You're the fattest person I ever saw" or "Why do you have black circles under your eyes?" These students can learn through explicit instruction that these are inappropriate or unexpected statements or that "it's OK to think that, but you can't say it."[23] With these students, sexual comments fall under the same category of social mistakes. Unfortunately, sexual comments are often more offensive and have more significant consequences. If a student says, "Your breasts are really juicy" to a classmate or goes to touch her, the other student feels violated, and the consequences of this behavior can be significant. As the student moves up through the grades, parents and school staff have to take these offenses more seriously, because they become upsetting to other students and some of the student's inappropriate comments may be misinterpreted as stalking.

Isaac, a sixth-grade student, had a "mad crush" on a girl in his class, Nicole. Because of his lack of understanding of appropriate boundaries, he would stand too close to her in the cafeteria and follow her around the school (even following her to the bathroom once). Not surprisingly, Nicole told her friends that she thought he was "creepy." Because she was not responding, he escalated his behaviors and followed her home from school, sitting in her front yard and looking into her bedroom window. While moving from class to class, he hid his phone from the teacher and texted Nicole. The girl's parents were frightened for their daughter and filed a restraining order against Isaac. When the principal confronted Isaac about his behavior, the boy had no idea his behavior was scary. He began to work with the school social worker on specific social skill instruction and role-playing.

Students like Isaac require explicit rules about appropriate behavior. The interventions for these students include making fundamental social rules (e.g., no touching peers) more understood and explicitly teaching them how to interact appropriately. Although teachers and students alike can misconstrue behavior like Isaac's as malicious, it is not deliberate disobedience and there is no desire to hurt.

The student has an underlying skill deficit that is relatively invisible and needs support to gain the necessary skills to behave in an appropriate way.

Sexualized behavior as an efficient and obvious way to get a response

Many students with social skills challenges are hungry for social interaction, but have few ways to obtain it. Their typical peers are getting social interactions all day long, while they feel more and more left out.[24] They often have a history of many failed social experiences associated with attempts to gain positive attention. They also may fail to notice positive attention from others as it is more subtle than negative (i.e., positive attention may be a smile or wave, as opposed to negative attention, which may be a peer shouting, "Stop, go away!"). Over time, some students resort to maladaptive means as the most successful way of getting attention. They learn that one effective way to engage in concrete and obvious social interaction is to provoke a negative response, even though they are not always conscious of doing this. Negative attention can be better than no attention. It is also more efficient (predictable and easier), intense, and obvious. For example, if Tim says, "I have hairs on my penis," to a peer, his peer will give a much more obvious response, such as exclaiming "Gross," "What the heck," or "Cut it out," than if Tim just said "Hi." Tim, who has trouble with subtle cues, has no problem registering this more intense, albeit negative, reaction as a response from a peer.

Sexualized behavior as a way of expressing frustration

Some students with social deficits *do* know that sexual comments are taboo and unwelcome, and they use sexual language when they need to express anger and frustration—just as other students use slang or swear. They may not correctly understand the emotional impact on others when they make these sexualized comments or act in sexualized ways. Jim, a sixth-grader, was frustrated that he was eating alone so often in the cafeteria. He raised a commotion when he stood on a table and started to gyrate as if he were having sexual intercourse. He liked the attention, and it was his effort to let his classmates know that he was sick of eating by himself. However, he did not understand how this type of behavior further isolated him from his peers. Jim needs social skills training focusing on learning about the impact of his behavior on others, as well as how best to make friends.

Impulsive Students

Students who are severely impulsive (acting before they think) can demonstrate sexualized behavior. Impulsive students often say things that they know are inappropriate, but they just can't stop to think before blurting them out. Their peers may have the same thoughts, but are able to keep these thoughts to themselves. While impulsive students don't control themselves in the moment, they can usually process the incident later and do feel remorse.

For example, many boys (typically over the age of eight) may have sexual thoughts when they see girls, but most boys show restraint and act appropriately, either saying nothing or giving an appropriate compliment. An impulsive student, however, may express the thought the minute it passes through his mind, saying something like, "I like your butt." Many boys may need to touch their genital areas during the school day, because they are nervous or feel stimulated, but they are likely to do it discreetly (e.g., putting their hands in their pockets or hidden under big shirts). Impulsive students may lack this planning capacity and thus be seen touching themselves or masturbating openly. Students with severe ADD may fall into this category.

A FAIR PLAN FOR CARTER

In another case example, Carter lived with his grandmother and three siblings. He often tried to run away from his third-grade classroom. He needed to be prompted several times a day to stay on task and was verbally aggressive with sexual words if he was redirected.

Carter's teacher implemented a point system to encourage appropriate behavior. Soon after, however, the boy was suspended after he grabbed a girl during recess and told her he wanted to have sex with her. After the incident, he was extremely remorseful. His family had difficulty getting him to outside therapy, but the school encouraged his grandmother to have an evaluation with his pediatrician for his impulsivity and he was started on medication for ADD. With help from his school counselor and teacher, he learned how to communicate better with his friends and to monitor his impulses. Carter's story highlights that children's sexualized behavior usually does not occur in isolation and may reflect a combination of family stressors, difficulty regulating impulses, and oppositional behavior, all requiring intervention on multiple levels.

When students who have bipolar disorder are manic, they may make sexualized comments. Providing good supervision and redirection, as well as a FAIR Plan, is key while the student stabilizes. Jeremy, a fifth-grader with bipolar disorder, had this problem. He said things like, "You're hot and I don't mean the temperature," or "You could be in one of *those* movies" (said while smiling, referring to a pornographic movie). Jeremy had a particular interest in three female classmates, and when they were around, he would get giddy and full of energy and wouldn't sit in his chair. He would try to look down their shirts and would tell them they were pretty. Useful interventions included a referral for a psychiatric evaluation of his manic episodes as well as special class management. It was key to avoid seating him near these girls or placing the girls and Jeremy together in a small group, as it increased his impulsivity and prevented him from paying attention.

In many situations like these, the other students need coaching about how to tone down their responses when the student acts inappropriately toward them. For example, squealing "Eww!" gave Jeremy too much attention. It's also important to tell students that another student's behavior is not acceptable and that they need to advocate for themselves by calmly telling the student with sexualized behavior, "I don't like that," and "Please stop" (without giving the child too much attention) and telling a teacher if any incident occurs.

Interventions for these impulsive students differ from interventions for students with social skill deficits, because most students with impulsive behavior know what's right and wrong; they just can't control themselves. They don't necessarily need basic social skills instruction. Instead, for example, teach them to stop and think before speaking and to use self-regulation techniques when they feel excited.

Impulsive students with sexualized behavior may need close supervision during unstructured times, as this is often when they get into trouble. For example, Andrew was a fourth-grade student with bipolar disorder. During recess, he would gravitate toward a group of kindergarten girls "playing house" behind the custodial shed, just out of the teachers' sight. Older students do sometimes play with younger children during recess because they are developmentally immature, without any problems. In this case, staff were uneasy; because of Andrew's hypersexual behavior, he was at risk for upsetting these younger girls or even touching them. The staff made a rule that Andrew couldn't play with these younger girls and encouraged him to play with his peers. Teacher foresight and monitoring prevented what could have led to a traumatic situation.

Students with Past Trauma

When students have experienced sexual trauma and violation of their sense of personal safety, the impact can be long-lasting and devastating. All children who have experienced sexual abuse should undergo a psychological evaluation and may need ongoing counseling.

As discussed earlier, it is important to remember that not all sexualized talk or behavior is related to abuse experiences, and the majority of sexually abused children do not show any behaviors that bring to light their past or present experiences.[25] As we have emphasized, there are many reasons for sexualized behavior, and they need to be understood in the context of the child's age and developmental level, as well as psychological or psychiatric issues.[26]

Most parents of sexually abused children are reluctant to disclose the child's history to the school, fearing that it will lead to negative judgment. It is thus likely that there are many classrooms with "silent" sexually abused children. These children may show anxiety, avoidance, or other signs of distress that only they, with the help of a therapist, can trace back to their abuse. However, some children with a sexual abuse history do show behaviors that identify them as having been abused. Some compulsively repeat the acts they saw or were subjected to (sometimes concretely), use sexual language, compulsively masturbate, or seek relationships that are inappropriate. Specific symptoms of sexual abuse can be repetitive sexual talk and play and age-inappropriate sexual behavior (sharing sexual knowledge that is beyond their years or showing adultlike sexual behaviors), as well as fears of specific situations that remind them of the abuse.[27]

Many students who have experienced sexual trauma are familiar with sexual attention from others. Getting attention in a sexual way can become a learned behavior. Sometimes, the adult who was abusive was the only person who gave the child special attention, even though it was confusing and harmful.

Students who have experienced trauma and have sexualized behavior can have poor interpersonal boundaries and may not know how to protect themselves.[28] They may not have the safety reflexes other children have, which puts them at risk of encountering sexual predators. Students with sexual trauma may try to have an inappropriate close relationship with teachers or classmates. For example, when an older boy touches a younger girl's hair and says something sexualized, most girls would get anxious and move away. A girl with a history of trauma wouldn't necessarily recognize this as a red flag and may not respond by moving away to protect herself. Many of these children have learned that it is useless or even dangerous to resist, and they would just go along with a boy who initiated contact like this. Judith Cohen, a prominent researcher and clinician in treating these children, explains that traumatized children may also repeatedly try to reverse their experience by seeking out inappropriately close relationships with peers or adults who may not be safe in this regard.[29] Their hope is that this time, they will get the attention and love they need without abuse.

Other sexually abused children have powerful reactions if someone invades their space, even inadvertently. They may lash out at a peer who whispers a compliment in their ear or touches them unexpectedly. These students may get into trouble for hitting and fighting. The child may be aware of a connection to the abuse, but often is not able to say why she overreacted.

Understanding and minimizing triggers for students with a history of trauma

Students who have experienced trauma respond to internal triggers (flashbacks) and external ones. The triggers can be aspects of the school environment (e.g., people, sounds, words, or smells) that bring up memories of their past trauma. Regular aspects of the school day may be overstimulating and lead the child to act out without his being able to explain why. Because the connection between trigger and reaction is mostly unconscious and the child cannot explain his behavior, the teacher is the one who needs to look for changes in behavior as a possible clue to triggers. Some of these triggers can be removed from the child's day to help the traumatized child experience school as a safe place. Triggers can become overgeneralized so that, for example, a child abused by his father will react to any image of a father as dangerous.

If the child's abuse history is known, and there is a therapist to consult with, the teacher can target and remove specific environmental triggers. It is impossible to create a trigger-free environment. A consultation between therapist and teacher may also identify appropriate code words that will prompt a removal to a less threatening environment while the child learns to manage his anxiety.

A seven-year old student, Craig, was the victim of both sexual and physical abuse. He showed increased sexualized behavior after certain occurrences in the classroom. When the teacher, Ms. Markson, read a book to the class and turned the page to a picture of a father and son playing together, Craig had immediately written "suck my dick" on the floor with a marker he had taken off an easel. After the lesson, Ms. Markson asked Craig to help her wash the floor as they talked about what to do the next time he felt uncomfortable. The school social worker asked Ms. Markson to keep a running list of environmental triggers that led Craig to make sexual comments or act inappropriately. She noted that in addition to pictures in books, Craig was also affected by the use of words such as *father, girlfriend, boyfriend, husband, romance, underwear, bikini, hug, kiss,* and *love*.

Together, Ms. Markson and the social worker developed a plan to keep the classroom free of as many trauma cues as they could. She made Craig his own personal book bin of books that did not have provoking pictures depicting fathers as characters. This was the kind of support Craig needed while he was learning how to cope with his anxiety.

As it is impossible to create a trigger-free environment and stop all classmates from using words that are part of daily conversation, Craig needs to learn to self-regulate. His teacher and the school social worker created a list of activities for the moments when he felt overstimulated by these triggers. The calming activities included writing in a notebook, taking a break, visualizing a safe place, and listening to his favorite music.

Being aware of the students' triggers and making all staff aware can reduce the student's exposure to them. Staff awareness is important initially for students like Craig to feel safe. Over time, with the help of therapy and a coordinated effort at school, they will learn that there are no longer any real threats to their safety. Their overgeneralized anxiety (which in Craig's case, made him see innocuous pictures or words as distressing) will be reduced. Gradual exposure to traumatic cues is important, so that students can learn to tolerate being in a safe, but nevertheless feared situation (e.g., reading a book about a man and child) without undue anxiety and without acting out. This will allow students to function better in school and to learn.

Emotional response to students with histories of trauma

The information teachers have available about the trauma history of their students varies. As stated earlier, teachers may have a sexually abused child in their classrooms without knowing it, or they may have some knowledge of the situation. Knowing about a child's sexual abuse usually leads to strong reactions in all professionals. When teachers do know, their reaction may be overwhelming and may lead to obsessing about the child, which can distract them from problem-solving constructively. It is painful to think of a child being violated. For teachers who care about their students, it can be devastating to hear the details of the abuse.

Another student, Michael, was the victim of sexual abuse by his cousin during a summer. He was also severely abused by his father and witnessed his mother's abuse. He was allowed to eat only after everyone else did, only if there was enough, and was forced to sleep on the floor. When he moved into a new school system after a successful foster placement, the majority of the staff was aware of, and deeply affected by, his story. Michael was a charismatic and bright student with some sexualized behavior. In some explosive incidents, he would say to the staff extremely violent things that he had learned in his biological home, such as "Don't make me take a knife and carve your f—ing breasts right off your chest." He also made sexualized comments (talking about what he wanted to do with other female students), which would get him suspended. School staff had many emotions: empathy as well as horror in reaction to his life experiences, and fear and anger at his behavior and statements in school.

Reacting to tragic stories about students you work with and care for is understandable, but it is important not to let this emotional reaction cloud your response to the student's behavior. Be cautious of the tendency to be more permissive and coddling to a student with this kind of behavior. Remember that the child needs firm but appropriate limits to learn to behave appropriately. When we consulted with Michael's teachers, we helped them refocus on holding Michael accountable for his outbursts and providing him with skills to behave appropriately rather than excusing his behavior because of his past trauma. We also encouraged teachers in this position to take care of themselves, because students with this type of problem can be very emotionally challenging, and teachers can suffer from compassion fatigue.

Creating trauma-sensitive school environments

Students with sexualized behaviors put schools in a difficult position. Most schools have a zero-tolerance policy for sexualized behavior. However, some consequences of these policies can accidentally reinforce the unwanted behavior from the student (e.g., strong reactions such as "Oh my gosh, it is *never* OK to say that!" or laughing and gasping from peers). Negative attention can be a reinforcing response for students with social deficits and impulsivity. Students with trauma histories may be revictimized by harsh punishments for behaviors they do not understand, or the negative reactions may be just what the students are used to and reinforce an adversarial child-authority dynamic.

Obviously, ignoring these behaviors is not an option. The goal is to find a balance between protecting all students and staff, holding kids accountable for their actions, and helping a child who exhibits behaviors over which she has little control. It is critical that schools provide a sanctuary for all children—those who may act out, those who may suffer in silence, and the rest of the children. Schools can strive to be a place for children to communicate their distress without either being victimized further or victimizing others. Addressing the role that trauma is playing at school requires a broad-based approach woven into every aspect of the curriculum. The Massachusetts Advocates for Children's (MAC) report "Helping Traumatized Children Learn" provides a good starting place, outlining how schools can create safe environments and establish the infrastructure needed to support all children, regardless of whether they have been traumatized.[30]

THE FAIR PLAN FOR THE STUDENT WITH SEXUALIZED BEHAVIOR

Various FAIR Plan interventions are helpful for students with sexualized behavior. Let's now look at some of these approaches that teachers can use to help students learn to respect personal boundaries, form healthy relationships, and do better in school.

Functional Hypothesis and Antecedent Analysis

Every time a student makes a sexualized statement, exhibits sexualized behavior (i.e., grinding against a chair, thrusting the pelvis toward a peer), or displays other behavior that is of concern, it is important to write it down in ABC format. Only five incidents may be necessary to observe a pattern, but more are better. Table 6.1 shows an ABC data sheet for Travis, the fifth-grade student with bipolar disorder who exhibits sexualized behavior. Remember that setting events are important to notice and to record. Students are very affected by life changes and other events; a child's behavior may be directly related to these factors.

In the antecedent column, some patterns to look for include these: unexpected changes (e.g., a substitute teacher), times when the students are in close proximity to one another (e.g., sitting on the rug or standing in line), and unstructured times (e.g., the cafeteria, transitions, or downtime). As you look at these antecedents, keep a tally to help you review the information later. Some behavior incidents might fit into more than one category and thus be counted more than once. These antecedents will help you determine the best way to intervene. From Travis's tally sheet, it looks as though he needs support during unstructured times, especially when there is not enough support, and when he is near a female student (Figure 6.1).

Also look for patterns in the consequence column. Since gaining negative attention is often one of the functions of sexualized behavior, look for patterns in the teachers' or peers' reactions. Travis successfully gained negative attention from teachers and peers for his sexualized behavior, as shown in the consequence patterns. It is important to minimize attention when delivering a consequence for Travis, as the attention is reinforcing the sexualized behavior.

Table 6.2 shows another ABC chart for the first-grade student, Craig, with known trauma. Craig's teacher tried to discern patterns of antecedents that might be external triggers for him, to minimize them when possible. The ABC chart shows some patterns that seem to be external triggers: the words *husband* and *boyfriend*, pictures of a father and child hugging, and seeing students hug.

FIGURE 6.1

Tallying the antecedents and consequences in Travis's ABC chart

Antecedents		Consequences	
Physical proximity to female students (special activity, P.E.):	//	Peer attention (special activity, chorus, snack):	///
Unstructured times (chorus, snack):	//	Teacher attention (math, P.E., snack):	///
Low adult-to-student ratio (chorus, math, P.E.):	////		

TABLE 6.1

ABC data for Travis, a student with sexualized behavior

Date, time, duration	Activity	Setting event(s)	Antecedent (what happens immediately before behavior)	Behavior (description of behavior)	Consequence (what happens immediately after behavior)
3/6, 1:15 p.m., 4 sec	Special activity		Students are sitting on the rug waiting for the movie to start, and light is turned off.	Travis makes kissing noises at female peer sitting right next to him.	Two students yell, "Hey, stop! You're gross!"
3/10, 11 a.m., 2 min	Chorus	Travis comes in to school late.	Female student has a solo.	Travis puts his fists under his shirt, simulating breasts.	Students giggle.
3/12, 10:15 a.m., 5 min	Math	Teacher in the doorway is talking to another teacher.	Students near Travis are talking to each other with their backs to him.	Travis draws a penis on his math sheet.	Teacher talks to him in the hallway.
3/15, 9 a.m., 2 sec	P.E.		Children are playing freeze tag.	Travis tags a female student on the buttocks.	Another student tells the teacher. P.E. teacher speaks sternly to Travis and sends him to the office.
3/17, 12:12 p.m., 5 sec	Snack	Aunt and uncle are staying with the family for a week. Teacher's assistant is at lunch during snack.	Girl next to him is squeezing yogurt out of a tube into her mouth.	Travis says, "You're good at that, huh?"	Students giggle. Another student tells the teacher, who speaks to Travis and sends him to the principal's office.

Note: adapted from Sidney W. Bijou, et al. *Journal of Applied Behavior Analysis* 1, no. 2 (1968); Beth Sulzer-Azaroff and G. Roy Mayer, *Applying Behavior-Analysis Procedures with Children and Youth.*

TABLE 6.2

ABC Data for Craig, a first-grade student with sexualized behavior and trauma

Date, time, duration	Activity	Setting event(s)	Antecedent (what happens immediately before behavior)	Behavior (description of behavior)	Consequence (what happens immediately after behavior)
4/10, 10:45 a.m., 4 min	Recess		Teacher says, "My husband let us borrow his parachute to play with," and takes out the parachute.	Craig holds a stick in front of his pants, pretending it is his penis.	Teacher tells Craig to put the stick down. Students laugh.
4/12, 11 a.m., 15 sec	Read aloud		Illustration in the book has a father and child playing and hugging.	Craig writes, "suck my dick" on the floor with a marker.	Teacher talks to him and has him clean the floor.
4/19, 12:15 p.m., 10 sec	Lunch	Craig's aunt is angry with school for calling so many meetings, and comes in yelling at principal.	Cafeteria assistant asks teacher how her husband is feeling.	Craig holds up a straw and says, "Look, it's my dick," to the boy sitting next to him.	Boy laughs. Teacher takes Craig back to the classroom so he can eat lunch with her.
4/22, 9:15 a.m., 3 min	Phonics		Student is talking about her mom's boyfriend's birthday.	Craig spells "blow job" with magnet letters on his desk and tells peer to look.	Two boys laugh and point. Teacher takes the magnet letters away from him and tells him that the words aren't acceptable.
4/29, 1:45 p.m., 1 min	Indoor recess	Craig reports his aunt is going to "sue the school."	Two girls hug each other.	Craig has two Lego characters imitate sexual intercourse.	Student says, "Craig!"

Note: adapted from Sidney W. Bijou, et al. *Journal of Applied Behavior Analysis* 1, no. 2 (1968); Beth Sulzer-Azaroff and G. Roy Mayer, *Applying Behavior-Analysis Procedures with Children and Youth.*

FIGURE 6.2

Tallying the antecedents and consequences in Craig's ABC chart

Antecedents		Consequences	
Hearing the word husband (recess, lunch):	//	Teacher attention (recess, read aloud, lunch, phonics):	////
Hearing the word boyfriend (phonics):	/		
Seeing picture or action of hug (read aloud, indoor recess):	///	Peer attention (recess, lunch, phonics, indoor recess):	////
		Materials removed (phonics):	/
		Student removed from peers (lunch):	/
		Student asked to clean floor (read aloud):	/

The consequence column shows that Craig received attention for his sexualized behavior in all of the behavior incidents (four out of five incidents generated attention from teachers, and another four out of five generated attention from peers; see figure 6.2). Teachers tried different consequences, including removing the student from peers, taking away materials used inappropriately, and requiring Craig to clean up after inappropriate writing. Minimizing attention to the student while having a consistent consequence will be the right combination for this student.

Accommodations and Modifications

Accommodations and modifications need to be considered for students with sexualized behavior to reduce antecedents that may be exacerbating or causing the behavior.

Environment

As we discussed before, students who have experienced trauma can be hypervigilant. When possible, engage the student in a conversation about where he or she likes to sit in the classroom. Remember that sexualized students can be drawn to each other. If there is more than one student with sexualized behavior in the classroom, they need to be separated whenever possible. Have them sit on opposite sides of the classroom but not facing each other. Because students might communicate nonverbally, it is important to avoid visual access, as well as physical access.

Increased supervision may be important for students with sexualized behavior throughout the school day. If the student has ever impulsively touched a peer or talked about touching a peer, then the staff needs to monitor the student more carefully. Involve the principal and other staff in the discussion about how to accomplish this. If the student has an individual education plan, specify the need for additional staff to monitor the student. At recess, be aware of *blind spots*: recess monitors usually stand in the same spots, and there are often some places on the recess yard they can't see, such as wooded areas, behind bushes, and around the corner of a building or playground structure. Reviewing bathroom supervision (i.e., having an adult make sure a communal bathroom is empty and then wait for the student to come out, while asking other students to wait) or an accommodated bathroom plan (i.e., using the nurse's or staff bathroom) is important as well.

Personal space in the classroom is one cue that can be easily controlled. When arranging the classroom, it's helpful to allow a student with a trauma history to choose where to sit. Some may prefer to be closer to the "safe" person (teacher). Others may feel more comfortable sitting in the back of the room with their back to the wall. This position may prevent the student who is hyperalert from constantly turning around if there is any small noise or movement. For younger children (grades K–3), allow the student to decide where to sit when the class is sitting on the floor, and ensure that all students maintain a wide girth of personal space. One way to do this is to control the spacing of students by designating spots on the rug with carpet squares, masking tape, or other materials. Providing ample personal space is in line with universal design since it not only helps students with trauma histories, but is also good for all students.

Waiting in line is another time when personal space is important. Here again, concrete markers on the floor can help the students remember to space themselves from each other. Teaching them to stay one arm's length from each other at all times in line is another option. Additionally, allowing students with histories of trauma to walk in the back of the line means they do not feel they have to be constantly looking behind them or be aware of people in front of and behind them. It also allows them some control over how close they get to their peers, which is impossible when someone is behind them.

Students who have experienced sexual trauma may require more supervision in certain situations. Recess and lunch are often unstructured with not enough staff supervision. The team may want to consider increasing supervision during these times. Bathrooms are anxiety-provoking even for children without any of these problems, as this is where a lot of "normal" sexualized joking, comparison of body parts, teasing, and bullying happens. Communal bathrooms can be triggering for some students, especially for boys, since the urinals allow exposure to some nudity. If students are showing abnormal sexualized behavior, they should not use a communal bathroom unsupervised as they could act inappropriately. An accommodation for this can be to require the student to use the nurse's bathroom (if it's a single bathroom) or to use a single staff bathroom. This often can be an issue with the staff, so the accommodation needs to be arranged through the principal and then be announced at a staff meeting. Otherwise, the student might be reprimanded by an unknowing staff member.

The issue of how other students will react can be very complicated. If the student's impulsivity scares others, they will be relieved not to have to encounter the child in the bathroom. If the student is one who is likely to get teased, as many children with social deficits are, the student will need help to develop an explanation for why he or she does not use the regular bathroom (i.e., a medical reason). Make these accommodations on a case-by-case basis, weighing safety issues and peer dynamics.

Creating a safe place in and out of the classroom, and deciding on a consistent way for the student to request using the safe place, is also a way to promote self-regulation during the day. The safe space should be comforting, possibly with a beanbag or another comfortable chair. Students with trauma histories should be able to take breaks in the safe space when they feel triggered or anxious.

Teaching underdeveloped skills

For students with sexualized behavior, awareness and ability to keep appropriate body space between themselves and others are often underdeveloped. Specific social skills lessons about acceptable personal space, sometimes in the forms of social stories, are helpful.[31] Special education teachers or counselors can be the ones responsible for creating the stories, teaching the social skills lessons, and tailoring them to the student's age and need.

A helpful way to teach both about boundaries and about personal space is to use the Circles of Intimacy Curriculum.[32] This curriculum is geared to students who have experienced trauma, but can also be a nice visual teaching tool for students with social deficits. The circle diagram consists of a bull's-eye, where the center circle is labeled as *self,* and the progressively larger circles are labeled *family, friends, acquaintances, professionals,* and *strangers.* The student talks with the school counselor or psychologist to identify who is in what circle and to make a chart of acceptable language and physical proximity for each group. The names of the student's friends and family will be written in the corresponding circle so that there is no confusion. For younger students, put photographs or recognizable pictures of the people included in the circles, as the child may not be able to read all the names.

Next, make a chart of acceptable behavior, like the one filled in for Craig, the first-grade student mentioned previously, in table 6.3. The teacher can then use the visual privately (i.e., keep it in a desk drawer and take it out to show student privately) as a reminder of proximity and language expectations throughout the day: "Remember to stay one-arm distance from your friends during recess, and that saying 'I love you' is just for mom and your brother, OK?"

To make this kind of chart useful, it is critical to know as much as possible about the habits and expectations in the child's family. It is therefore important to meet with the child's caretaker and review what the cultural and family expectations for physical contact and expression of affection are.

Self-regulation and self-monitoring

Self-regulation and self-monitoring are underdeveloped skills for students with sexualized behavior. To help teach self-monitoring, you can use the type of self-monitoring sheet explained in chapter 3 to help the student monitor his own behavior and to reinforce the use of strategies throughout the day, specifically targeting the area(s) the student is struggling in. The targeted behaviors for a student with sexualized behavior may include using appropriate words, appropriate play, and appropriate personal space.

Use cognitive behavior therapy strategies, such as prompting the student to cue the teacher when he is feeling excited. Encouraging the child to take a break and self-calm is another great approach. Use a consistent scale to label the student's regulation state. Staff can use an emotional thermometer like the one in chapter 3, but we would suggest adding "excited" as an emotion, or use the Alert Program

TABLE 6.3

Intimacy chart for Craig, a first-grade student with sexualized behavior and trauma

Circle of intimacy	Language expectations	Proximity expectations
Self		It's OK to: • Touch your own genitals in private • Be naked in private
Family	It's OK to: • Say, "I love you"	It's OK to: • Hug • Kiss (not on mouth) • Be in underwear • Sit on aunt's lap • Hold hands • Be naked in the bath while aunt is in the bathroom
Friends	It's OK to: • Say, "I like you," or compliment them	It's OK to: • Stay one arm's distance away from friend • High five • Shake hands
Acquaintances	It's OK to: • Say, "Hi, nice to see you," or talk about certain subjects: school, movies, toys, food	It's OK to: • Stay one and a half arm's distance away from acquaintance • High five • Shake hands
Professionals	It's expected to: • Say, "Hi" • Make "small talk" on certain subjects: weather, school events	It's expected to: • Stay two arms' distance away from the professional • Wave
Stranger	It's expected to: • Don't say "Hi" or talk to them	It's expected to: • Stay more than two arms' distance away from stranger

language ("How is your engine running?").[33] If the teacher helps the student label his regulation state, the child will eventually be able to identify his state by himself and then learn to self-regulate independently. All staff working with the student should know the signs that the student is becoming dysregulated, as this is when the student may be more likely to act in a sexualized way. For example, when Mohammed starts giggling or showing extra motor movement (e.g., wiggling in his seat or moving around in line) or his voice gets louder, that is the time to cue him to use a self-calming strategy: "Mohammed, your engine is running fast—please use a strategy." Or prompt him to self-monitor: "Mohammed, how is your engine right now? What should you do?"

Some younger students with trauma history will ask for hugs and try to sit on the teacher's lap. Sometimes, a personalized handshake (done to give a student special attention without the physical intimacy of a hug) may not be sufficient for the student who is craving more contact. We recommend teaching the student to use sensory materials that could simulate a hug and, hopefully, could give him the input he is craving. One student, Erik, learned to roll himself up in a weighted blanket in the reading nook area of the classroom and hug his stuffed animal when he was craving intimate contact. We have had other students keep small flannel blankets or pillows in their calming boxes (see appendix E) so they could take them out and wrap up or squeeze them when needed.

The student showing sexualized behavior may have one or more of the following underdeveloped skills: awareness of personal space, controlling impulsive comments, appropriate language and interactions with different people in their life, handling hypersensitivity (students with PTSD), self-regulation, and self-monitoring. In appendix B, we have also provided a list of curricula for helping teachers, school mental health clinicians, and outside therapists teach these skills.

Interaction Strategies

Schools usually have rules about physical contact between teachers and students. In addition, it is helpful to be aware of how and when you make contact with a student, because you can never know if it could be a triggering event for the student. In the younger grades, hugging is controversial. If any student asks for hugs, you could instead create a personalized handshake to give the student some positive attention. We have also seen a "hand hug" used: you can shake hands but squeeze (which may not be good for all students). If for some reason you decide that hugging is OK once in a while (we don't advise this), make sure that you give a hug sideways while you are sitting. This way, shorter or younger students' heads are not near your chest.

Warn students when you are approaching them from behind: "I'm going to check your paper next, Charlie," or "I'm right behind you." Avoid surprising a student. In general, allow extra personal space for students who have experienced trauma. Get in the habit of talking to them from an extra six inches away. Note that eye contact can be uncomfortable for these students as well. Sometimes, teachers will assume that if a student is looking away, it is because the child is not listening. The student, however, might also be feeling overwhelmed and may need time to regain control.[34]

Remember, students often have shame associated with their experiences of trauma, so avoid negative statements such as "That was a terrible thing to do." Even if the students haven't experienced trauma, making them feel embarrassed is unproductive. Students who feel that they are bad are more likely to engage in negative-attention-seeking or rule-breaking behavior.

To break the cycle of negative behavior getting negative attention, try to make attention predictable. Putting one-on-one time on the student's personal visual schedule is a good way for the student to know when to expect her special time (if you only have a second, all you may be able to do is read the student's favorite page in a book). Whatever the length of time available, making it predictable is more important than length. Using a timer is another concrete way of making your attention predictable. When you are going to go help another student, set the timer and say, "I'll be back to check on you in ten minutes." The student is less likely to engage in negative-attention-seeking behavior in the meantime, because he knows when the teacher is coming back. Another idea for younger students is to try a token board. If the student does an activity quietly and appropriately every five or ten minutes he earns a token. Every time you give the student a token, praise him in a way that he is comfortable with and talk with him briefly. This way, the student knows that every few minutes, you will be over to attend to him. He will consequently be less likely to need negative attention. Remember that negative attention is not only more predictable than positive attention, but also more efficient (faster, easier), more intense, and more obvious (louder, more exaggerated affect). To make positive attention equally satisfying to the student, the positive attention needs to be greatly exaggerated.

Response Strategies

Responses to students' sexualized behavior should minimize negative attention from teachers and other students to prevent the risk of reinforcing it. The best responses vary, depending on the specific situation.

Students who make sexualized statements

When a student makes a sexualized statement, it's important to give little attention to the statement or to ignore it, but do not ignore the fact that a rule has been broken.

Let's take the example of Max from the first scenario in this chapter. When Max said, "Do you know that your nipples are poking through your shirt?" Ms. Kent reacted by sternly telling him to go to the office as the class gasped. Minimizing the response and taking away a privilege quickly will address the behavior but not give attention to the student. For example, Ms. Kent could respond by saying neutrally, "That is inappropriate [or you just broke a rule]. You lost X." She could also do this more privately by saying, "That is inappropriate," and putting a tally on the board (previously established with the student as an indication of a loss of a certain privilege).

Because of the distressing nature of students' sexualized comments or behavior, you may need to remove the student from the classroom to give yourself a moment to collect your thoughts and to calm the class before the student returns (more common for older students in grades 4–6). While walking the student out of the room, do not engage in talking with him. Try to minimize the attention he gets from this behavior. If the student can write, list the privileges he has lost, and ask him to fill out a processing sheet, with questions like "How did my behavior make others feel?" "What did I want out of the behavior?" "Did I get what I wanted?" "What was a better way to get attention?" and so forth. These prompted questions are appropriate for any student who makes sexualized comments.

When the student behaves appropriately and does not say something sexualized, the teacher should intermittently and preventatively give attention in an obvious way and bonus points for appropriate behavior.

Students with impulsivity or social deficits and who touch an adult inappropriately

If a student with sexualized behavior who has problems with impulsivity or social deficits touches an adult, it is important to follow the same protocol as described above and emphasize that the student has broken a rule, but teachers need to minimize the attention given to the student. The consequences will be more significant for older students than younger students, such as office referral, suspension, and legal prosecution for harassment. If a student touches a teacher's thigh, the consequences would be more severe than for a sexualized comment.

As with a student who makes sexualized statements, when he is behaving appropriately, the teacher should preventatively give positive attention to the student to reinforce appropriate behavior.

STUDENTS WITH KNOWN TRAUMA HISTORY AND WHO TOUCH AN ADULT INAPPROPRIATELY

If a student with a known trauma history touches a teacher, it is important to not shame the student and take away a privilege. The reasons for the child's behavior are not necessarily intentional, but usually attention-seeking. If the teacher says, "That makes me uncomfortable," and walks away from the student (at least six feet), the student will learn that touching is not a good way to get attention or to get close to a teacher. When the student is behaving appropriately and maintaining proper personal space near the teacher, particularly when they are working one-on-one and are seated close together, the teacher should intermittently and preventatively give attention and bonus points to the student.

Students who consistently invade peers' personal space

If the student has sexualized behavior and is consistently invading another student's personal space, use environmental support (i.e., chairs at circle, tape on the floor to space students lining up) and constant prompts for personal space. When the student maintains proper personal space *without* this environmental support, the teacher's response should be based on how much a student requires a reminder. If he needs constant reminders and prompts, he will do better if he receives a token every two minutes that he maintain personal space, along with praise. If he receives five tokens, he gets a reward. Students who need reminders only occasionally, when they are dysregulated, can receive bonus points on their self-monitoring sheet when they properly maintain their personal space.

Despite these preventative strategies, however, the student still may invade another student's personal space. For example, Mia leans into a student while watching the art teacher make origami. The teacher needs to cue her to use "personal space" and should give Mia praise and attention for complying. This will bring minimal attention to the mistake, cue the correct response, and reinforce her efforts to keep personal space. To reduce singling out the student with sexualized behavior, have personal-space rules consistent for the whole class. Younger children often lean into each other, touch each other, and so on, which can be considered normal. However, students with sexual behavior problems need more restrictions, as these children can act inappropriately and intrusively, but this is a tricky issue to figure out. Consultation with school mental health specialists is key.

Students who masturbate

If a student masturbates in a public space in school, teachers can encourage a replacement behavior, teach an incompatible behavior (behavior that occupies a student in a way that doesn't allow the student to engage in the inappropriate behavior), cue the student to be aware of when he or she is doing it, explicitly teach the student when and where it's appropriate, or apply several of these strategies.

If a student uses his hand to masturbate, the teacher should give him fidget toys and other objects to keep his hands busy. The provision of these objects promotes *incompatible behaviors*: the student can't use his hands to masturbate if they are busy doing something else.[35] The teacher can also reinforce "hands on your desk" with positive reinforcement (e.g., a token every two minutes that the student has his hands on the desk).

If a student masturbates by rubbing her body on furniture, the teacher can try to change the seating situation by adding an inflatable seat cushion on the chair to reduce feedback, or changing chairs.

Teachers need be neutral and matter-of-fact when discussing masturbation with students and not refer to the behavior with judgment (e.g., referring to it as bad behavior or saying, "Good kids don't do that"). Teachers should ask the counselor and the student's parent(s) how to refer to the behavior with the student, as some parents may not be comfortable with the word *masturbation*.

Impulsive students can be inattentive to their own behavior, which results in behaviors like picking noses or passing gas in the classroom. If a student masturbates and is not conscious of it, the teacher should establish a secret signal about all unwanted behaviors with the student. The teacher will say a word or will use a gesture to let the student know that he is engaging in the behavior and to stop. Having the student self-monitor for this behavior can also be very helpful. The teacher can do this on the self-monitoring sheet in a confidential way or can give the student a self-monitoring device. A vibrating timer (e.g., a mobile device app) or, for students who can't access a mobile device, a wristwatch that is set to go off every few minutes can silently cue the student to check to make sure he is not masturbating or to stop if he is. Make sure the timer isn't vibrating near the genital area, or it could be stimulating. Mobile devices can also have apps that will beep at intervals, signaling the student to self-monitor.

Teaching the student when and where masturbating is acceptable can happen in a one-on-one lesson or by using a social story.[36] Some teachers and counselors may decide to suggest that the student only masturbate at home.

Regularly reinforcing the student throughout the day for not masturbating is helpful. A clear way to reinforce the student for appropriate behavior is to use a token chart where the student earns a token every few minutes that she is not masturbating. The tokens can be cashed in for a reward at intervals during the day.

Chapter Summary

- *Sexualized behavior*, or sexually inappropriate behavior, includes saying sexual words to peers or teachers, making sexual gestures, making noises or engaging in pretend play that simulates sex, making sexual invitations to others, inappropriately touching another person, or masturbating in the classroom.
- *Normal sexual behavior* in childhood includes (in preschool) touching genitals, trying to view others nude, and exposing genitals to peers and (in elementary school) making jokes about body parts and elimination, and playing doctor.
- *Potential causes of sexualized behavior in school* include anxiety, self-soothing, the need for attention, and/or imitation.
- Sexualized behavior in a student does not necessarily mean he or she was abused.
- The three main factors associated with children who exhibit sexualized behavior are (1) interpersonal skill deficits; (2) impulsiveness; and (3) trauma (e.g., sexual or physical abuse, family violence, overstimulation).

- Teachers can understand and minimize triggers, removing known ones and teaching children to self-regulate when they are exposed to a trigger.
- Teachers can avoid being overwhelmed by their emotional response to a student's trauma story. The focus should be on proactive efforts.
- Three fundamentals for creating a trauma-sensitive school environment are (1) minimizing the amount of negative attention given the student, (2) keeping a neutral attitude, and (3) refraining from shaming the student.

FAIR

Behavior Intervention Plan for the Student with Sexualized Behavior

Student's Name: _____   Date: _____

TARGETED BEHAVIORS (be as explicit as possible):

| **F** | **Functional Hypothesis and Antecedent Analysis** |

☐ Document all instances of targeted behaviors, using ABC data sheet (minimum of five incidents)

☐ List antecedents from ABC data or observation to be addressed in this plan:

☐ Form a hypothesis about the function of behavior (circle one or more): attention, escape, tangible reward, sensory satisfaction. *Students with sexualized behavior usually have attention-motivated behavior.*

☐ List any pattern of consequences, using the ABC data.

☐ List any setting events of note:

Accommodations

We have included strategies and interventions from other chapters that you may consider.

Environmental

- ☐ Provide safe space in classroom
- ☐ Schedule breaks
- ☐ Allow student to have preferential seating
- ☐ Ensure a supervised and structured recess
- ☐ Provide a supervised and structured lunch
- ☐ Develop a bathroom plan
- ☐ Designate seating on rug or whole-group floor
- ☐ Designate personal-space markers to line up
- ☐ Allow student to walk in the back of the line

Replacement behaviors

- ☐ Teach asking for help appropriately
- ☐ Other:

Regulation of self and self-monitoring

- ☐ Have student use emotional thermometer
- ☐ Have student use self-regulation chart
- ☐ Have student use mobile device for self-monitoring
- ☐ Use the self-monitoring sheet (appendix F)

Teaching underdeveloped skills

- ☐ Personal space
- ☐ Self-advocacy
- ☐ Social skills
- ☐ Stop and think

I Interaction Strategies

- ☐ Work on relationship building
- ☐ Use noncontingent reinforcement
- ☐ Offer specific positive reinforcement
- ☐ Avoid hugs
- ☐ Use personalized handshake
- ☐ Use leadership-building and self-esteem-building activities
- ☐ Use sensory strategies to simulate hug
- ☐ Announce when you are behind student
- ☐ Avoid shaming or judgmental statements about student's behavior
- ☐ Give predictable positive attention

R Response Strategies

- ☐ Establish clear rules around touching and sexualized talk
- ☐ Avoid responses that would reinforce attention-motivated behavior, such as one-on-one talks, dramatic responses, or strong reactions
- ☐ When a student makes a sexualized comment, minimize attention and deliver consequence
- ☐ When a student touches you inappropriately, relay that you don't like it and walk away (remove attention)
- ☐ Assign rewards or points when the student demonstrates appropriate personal space, displays prosocial behavior, or uses a self-regulation strategy like putting hands in pockets or taking deep breaths when his or her energy is too high or the student feels excited
- ☐ If a student masturbates, try cueing a replacement strategy, giving the student a self-monitoring device, providing a social story about when and where, or cueing with a secret signal
- ☐ When a student misperceives a social situation, try a comic-strip activity

CHAPTER 7

Commonly Asked Questions

Some Answers, and a Challenge

Throughout this book, we have described a framework for understanding and working with students who demonstrate persistent, challenging behaviors. We have tried to explain to the best of our ability how to structure such work and have presented a number of strategies that we have found most useful in our work with students and classroom teachers. Along the way, we have been fortunate that many of the teachers we have worked with have also pushed us to explain how to best implement the FAIR Plan, given the day-to-day pressures and logistics that are part of a school day. The questions they have raised have helped to clarify our thinking and have helped to make our approach even better.

In this chapter, we answer twelve of the most frequently asked questions that we encounter. These questions include how to work with the families of challenging students, how to handle questions from other parents and students in the classroom, and how to prepare for special situations that sometimes arise, such as when an especially vulnerable student returns from hospitalization.

1. How can a teacher maintain stamina when he or she has a challenging student?

Working with a student with challenging behavior takes an incredible amount of a teacher's energy and can take an emotional toll that leaves the adult with little reserve to do all the other aspects of the job. Teachers need to take care of themselves during the school year, because their stamina is directly linked not only to their own health and well-being, but also to the success of their students. We do not want to lose good teachers to burnout or to develop a sense of reduced personal accomplishment.

An essential first step is to put the situation in perspective; rather than experiencing the student's behavior in a personal way (as a personal attack or proof of your own incompetence, for example), see it objectively, as if observing it from a distance. This is, of course, easier said than done. Students with challenging behaviors can easily threaten a teacher's feeling of competence. For this reason, it's important to remember two points. First, these students are very complicated, or we wouldn't have written a book about them. Second, even seasoned experts feel incompetent at times with challenging students! Start by understanding that the student's behavior is not a reflection of failure on your part, but a way for the student to communicate something to you in the only way the child knows how. In this way, the behavior becomes an opportunity for you to uncover forces driving the behavior and to help the student succeed.

Everyone experiencing stress can fall into all-or-nothing thinking. The tendency is to see oneself as a failure, if one is not having complete success. Teachers working with difficult students can easily fall into this pessimistic attitude. Part of practicing perspective is developing a capacity to see the gray areas. A great deal of the time work with young people with challenging behavior feels like two steps forward, one step backward. While some students show a dramatic and quick turnaround, most take weeks or months to demonstrate significant behavioral progress. During this behavioral marathon, focus on the small, incremental successes. Writing down the small successes you see with the student, or asking a colleague to remind you of them, can help prevent the isolated negative incidents from eclipsing the very real successes.

Like all caretakers, you need to take time to rejuvenate both physically and emotionally on a daily basis. Finding ways to let go of stress and nurture yourself is critical if you are to help your students adequately. You need to take care of yourself while caring for others.

Here are some self-care tips:[1]

- *Set healthy boundaries.* Do not overcommit yourself. Teachers are considered dedicated when they put in long hours and volunteer for *everything*. But overcommitment can lead to fatigue and illness. When you are working with a student with challenging behavior, setting boundaries is doubly important. Say yes when you mean yes, and permit yourself to say no.

- *Schedule breaks often.* Even just five-minute breaks throughout the day are helpful to keep tension at bay. Try to fit a break into your busy preparation blocks or lunch break if the rest of the day is too busy. Play music, get a snack, read a magazine.
- *Exercise.* Research shows that exercise can reduce stress and depression. Despite the exhaustion you feel after work, try to fit it in.
- *Know your own threshold for stress.* Understand your own stress signs (e.g., increased heart rate, irritability, headaches, fatigue, or change in appetite). These signs are your body telling you that you're stressed. Listen to these signals. Make sure you get enough sleep and eat well.
- *Find at least three activities that relieve stress.* Art, yoga, watching mindless TV—whatever works for you! Make sure you make the time in your day to do them consistently. You are worth it.
- *Don't struggle alone.* If you're feeling discouraged or overwhelmed, talk to a coworker or supportive supervisor. Let colleagues and administrators know when you need help.
- *Start your day on a positive note.* Take a walk, watch something funny on You-Tube, blast your favorite song—do anything that makes you feel positive. Try to avoid starting the day with that dreaded stressed feeling.

2. What's the best way for administrators to support a teacher who has a student with challenging behavior?

Having a student with challenging behavior in a classroom creates a high level of stress in teachers. In addition to supporting the student, the teacher needs support from administrators to avoid the path of frustration, burnout, and discouragement and, instead to mobilize the proactive methods suggested in this book.

A lot of extra responsibilities come with having a challenging student. When administrators delegate some of these responsibilities to other people in the building, the teacher's load is lightened. Regularly meeting with consultants (e.g., special educators, mental health professionals, and behavior analysts) can be essential for the student's progress, but also takes up the teacher's prep time. If possible, the administrator can arrange coverage so that the teacher can meet with consultants at times other than lunch and prep.

The building substitute or other flexible support staff if not otherwise assigned, are usually used to help the secretary or other classroom teachers with administrative tasks. This staff time can be channeled to supporting the teacher who has a very challenging student. Support staff can instruct small groups of children while the teacher works with the student with behavior challenges. Alternatively, these adults can take the student with behavior challenges to his or her calming break. Most classroom teachers can always use a hand addressing the needs of the class and the student with challenging behavior.

Because there are usually so many people involved with a struggling student, implementing a clear coordination plan can help keep the teacher's responsibilities at a manageable level. It may be helpful, as a team, to make a list of responsibilities and indicate who is responsible for them (see appendix H for a sample implementation plan).

3. The FAIR Plan seems like too much work and seems time-consuming. How can a teacher fit this into a busy day?

The pressures faced by classroom teachers today are staggering. These professionals face rigorous curriculum demands, time-consuming literacy and math blocks, standardized testing practice and instruction, full inclusion of students with special needs, meetings consuming preparation time, and parent meetings and other interactions, just to name a few pressures. Add one disruptive, possibly explosive student to the mix, and the teacher is now also responsible for squeezing in all the components of a behavioral plan for one student. The most frequent response we get when sharing strategies with teachers is, "When am I going to find the time to do that?"

This is a valid question. But in reality, this student is already taking a large amount of the teacher's time. To prove this point, we have sat in teachers' classrooms with a stopwatch and calculated the time the teacher dedicates to the student in question. Every time the teacher says the child's name; redirects her to stay in her seat; repeats directions to her as well as nearby students, who missed the directions because of the disruptive behavior; argues with the student about how much she has to do; negotiates with her on when she can go to get a drink . . . you get the picture. Teachers are always shocked at the total time that they are dedicating to the student in a reactive, unproductive way—even without a meltdown or violent episode, which can take hours away from the previously scheduled plan.

Implementing these strategies is *not* more time taken away from you. It will probably take the equivalent of, if not less, than the time it currently takes you to manage the student. By putting your time into proactive, productive strategies, you will reduce the problem behaviors over time. Learning new strategies for these students, building better relationships with them, and employing new responses to unacceptable behaviors until these responses become automatic is time-consuming in the beginning. These strategies are still likely to take less time than is already spent redirecting or attending to the student. Think of it as an investment in the eventual improvement of your student and the classroom learning climate.

4. How does a teacher talk to the other students after a student's explosive incident?

If other classmates witnessed a student's extreme behavior (such as throwing objects, trying to leave the classroom, swearing, making noises, self-stimulating, or being extremely oppositional when redirected), you may decide it is important to talk with the other students. They may be frightened, confused, and unable to focus on learning. It is better not to discuss the student's behavior with the class alone after an incident unless you feel comfortable doing so. You may want to invite the counselor, special education teacher, or principal to join the class. We advise teachers to tell the parent of the student who is being discussed that a whole-group conversation is warranted and is preventative so that the other students don't think the acting-out student is dangerous, strange, or bad. The main point of the talk is to educate the group and also reassure them that they are safe and that the student is safe. You can tell the class that the student is "working on staying calm."

Frequently, discussions with the group of classroom peers are best held both in the beginning of the school year and after a difficult incident. "We are all born differently. You may have noticed that Audrey sometimes screams in class. She doesn't do this to be bad or because she is hurt. She is working on a better way to tell us she is frustrated." Without such messages from respected teachers, students may come up with their own, more negative or dramatic interpretation (e.g., "He screams because he misses his mommy," or "He screams because he hurt himself"). Giving the students the facts in a neutral way will prevent them from coming to their own, inaccurate conclusions about the student's behavior and your responses to it. It's best to be accurate and allow students to ask questions.

How much should you say when providing an explanation to a classroom peer group? In finding a balance between saying enough and not saying too much, saying less is better. Do not reveal the student's disability unless you have parental permission and there is a specific reason for doing so (like disclosing and educating the class about Asperger's syndrome). If the parent does want to disclose the student's disability and discuss it, the student could be present and be part of the discussion. Otherwise, arrange to have the student go somewhere else when this conversation is taking place, or have it when the student is out of the room with a specialist.

You can also tell the other students how to be helpful when another incident occurs. "If you see Johnnie screaming, you don't have to get scared; we're going to make sure you are safe. He's not hurt. He's screaming because he's frustrated or angry. It would be really helpful to Johnnie if you can keep doing your work without staring or getting up and moving away. You only need to worry about yourself. Remember, if you have questions, you can ask us later."

5. Since family involvement is key in dealing with students with challenging behavior, what's the best way to communicate with the family of a student with challenging behavior?

Given that you will be communicating frequently throughout the year, a good start to the first conversation with a parent is, "When I need to get in touch with you, how do you prefer I do so?" Be open to e-mails or phone calls.

At the beginning of the year, maximize the efficiency of whatever form of communication the family prefers. Ask parents to let you know the kind of information about which they want to know. Otherwise, you may not be aware that the parents want to know if the student ate all his lunch or if he went to the bathroom. If the parents are focused on their student's social life or literacy, it is helpful to include such information. Focusing your communication on what the parents want to hear about will save you time.

A common form of communication with parents is a communication notebook, but sometimes, parents don't find these helpful. These tools are time-consuming and frequently filled out by the teaching assistant. However, we recommend the notebooks after you and the parents have discussed what information is important to communicate for a particular student.

Another communication option is to take digital pictures of the child interacting or having a successful moment and e-mail them home once in a while (make sure to receive photo permission from the parents of the class). When the child comes home, the parent can hold the picture and ask, "How was your day? Tell me about this picture!" It is helpful for the parents to see with their own eyes that their child has had many successful moments throughout the day. For students with withdrawn behavior, this technique can also help the children remember and retell something positive about their day. This type of relationship-building with the family, as well as with the student, is essential. Sometimes you may have to go the extra mile and talk with families in the evening or on the weekend if that is the only time they are available.

Another way to connect with the family is to refrain from calling with only bad news. If the child is in third grade, a parent may have received phone calls with bad reports for a couple of years, which may have made the parent mistrustful of the schools.[2] Parents may dread your calls, anticipating that they will hear that their child did something bad and that they may even need to leave work. A random positive call (e.g., "Elizabeth had a good week," or "She read aloud today") is great for relationship building. You're going to be working with these parents all year, and it is always worth the investment in a connection.

6. When a student with challenging behavior hurts a peer, how does the teacher talk to the peer's parent?

We recommend calling the peer's parent before the end of the school day. Talking to the parent before the student comes home and reports the incident is a proactive measure that will often elicit the calmest possible interaction. Report the facts of the incident concisely, and listen and validate when the parent states his concerns. It may sound like this: "We want to let you know Ellen is in the nurse's office. She's OK. Another student bit her on the leg. We are taking this very seriously. I am sure you have some questions, but let me tell you what happened. I want to make sure before you get off the phone that you feel comfortable that Ellen will be perfectly safe here."

Make sure to listen and validate all the parent's concerns. Do not reveal the other student's disability, as this is confidential. The parent may question the school about the perpetrating student and what consequences this student received. Parents may not understand why there are different disciplinary procedures for a student who has an IEP and why the child was not suspended but rather had accommodations. Responses such as "We're helping her work on her impulse control," with some detail to reassure the parent that their child will not be bitten again (e.g., increased supervision), or "As a school, we are supporting her to learn how to express her anger better" will preserve the confidentiality of the student. At the beginning of the year, the team should designate who will be making these phone calls.

7. What's the best way to deal with the issue of fairness? The FAIR Plan suggests giving students breaks, rewards, and so forth. How should this be addressed with other students?

The FAIR Plan involves many interventions that *are* unequal and could seem unfair to others. Students may think it's unfair that another student is getting special treatment, particularly around rewards, breaks, getting to eat somewhere other than in the cafeteria, or receiving extra adult attention. You may be concerned that it may appear unfair for a student to break a rule and not get the same consequences given to other children.

Having a whole-group discussion about the student's differences can prevent some confusion and resentment on the part of the student's classmates. In addition, a neutral, automatic one-line reply for in-the-moment questions is all that's needed in most cases to normalize the situation. For example, when Isaiah asks why Sally is listening to an iPod, a good reply might be, "I am learning to cook, and you are learning to read. She's learning how to stay calm, and listening to music helps. We are all learning, and we need different things to learn."

For older students, a more matter-of-fact answer will do. "She needs this iPod, as it is helping her to stay calm right now." In most cases, it is obvious that the student is different, making elaboration unnecessary. Usually this type of brief explanation will do the trick, but if a student perseverates and asks or challenges repeatedly, you might end the conversation by saying, "You need to worry about yourself right now."

Even if students understand the situation, they may be jealous. We often let other students have turns with special items such as iPods, by saying, "How about next time we have indoor recess, I let you play with it?" It can also be an opportunity to have the student practice sharing and may even paint the student in a good light with her peers.

8. What is the best way to use the safe or quiet space in the classroom? What if more than one student wants it at the same time?

Most of the students discussed in this book require self-regulation strategies, including the use of a safe space within the classroom. Once the student is initially taught to take a break in this convenient and soothing place, there should be a system for the student to access the space, such as using a pass or a nonverbal signal like raising her hand.

We recommend teaching the student more than one self-regulation strategy, such as taking a break and using the calming box, so that he is not overly reliant on the availability of the safe space. If two students want to use the safe space at the same time and there is enough space, it could be shared. Some students are not compatible (e.g., one wants to sit calmly and another wants to do yoga, or the two children have a history of clashing). In this instance, there should be a "closed/open" system in place (e.g., a red sign and a green one). The student can only use the space if it's open. If it's not, he can use another calming strategy or an alternative safe space outside the classroom. The teacher may want to set a timer so that the student currently using the space knows when her turn is up.

9. Aren't some disruptive students just spoiled or selfish or excessively needy?

No. While not all students who demonstrate challenging behavior meet the criteria for emotional and behavioral diagnoses, their behavior suggests they are stuck in some way and need helping getting out of a behavioral rut. For example, some students demonstrate demanding and entitled behavior because, with their caregivers, they are in a cycle in which they have learned that demanding behavior will get them what they want.[3]

10. What should a teacher do if he or she is worried that a student may be suicidal?

If students talk, write, or draw about thoughts of suicide or act out suicide (e.g., pretending they're going to jump out the window or putting something around their neck and making a choking expression), always take them seriously. The most important message is that no matter how young they are, you must never discount students' comments about wanting to die or hurt themselves. Children sometimes communicate in their writing how bad they feel. In their journals, their own stories, or their drawings, students may reveal thoughts of self-harm with comments such as "I would be better off dead," or by drawing a person jumping off a building. Refer to the suicidal warning signs in chapter 5. If a student is in immediate danger or is hurt, have your principal call 911.

Peers may share with you that they are worried about another student because she has confided that she doesn't want to live and may have a plan to harm herself. This is always a red flag and warrants prompt action. At one school we worked with, an eight-year-old confided to a teacher that when he got home, he was going to put his head in the oven so he could die. The teacher dismissed this as his wanting to get attention. Although it is extremely rare for young children to kill themselves, a child's repetitive talking about death or how she might try to end her life is a major sign of distress.[4] This is never normative, and a careful evaluation and intervention is necessary.

As a teacher, you are not expected to evaluate a suicidal student and it is standard for schools to have protocols for how to respond. We would recommend that you document what the student has said and not leave the student unattended at any time until mental health personnel or the principal can assess the student. If the suicide statement or act occurs at the end of the school day, a school adult should stay with the student until staff can connect with the parent and make a plan for where the student will go after school to be safe. It is important to validate the child's sense of distress; we caution against engaging in a conversation or eliciting more details. A helpful response could be, "You shared something important with me, and I want to make sure that you are safe because I care about you a lot. Ms. Smith is very good at making sure kids feel safe; let's go talk to her."

If a student is impulsive and you are also worried that, if his behavior escalates, he may use something in the classroom to harm himself, sharp objects such as scissors must be made inaccessible, and the student should be moved away from the window, or lock the windows. The student may need to be monitored at all times, including trips to the bathroom (personnel can stand in the hallway and do verbal checks).

11. If a student has been hospitalized, how can a teacher help the child with the return to school?

A student may return unannounced from a psychiatric hospitalization or an evaluation that assessed her safe to return to school. She may be self-conscious about how to respond when other classmates ask where she has been. She may also have started a new medication when in the hospital and could experience new side effects (sleeping in class, increased agitation, etc.).

Ideally, you should be informed prior to the arrival of the student so there can be a discreet discussion about how the student is going to catch up on her work. The student also needs help with what to say to other students or teachers about her absence. It is helpful if the student can practice an automatic response before her return to the classroom. Pull her into the hallway if you have no more time than that, and help her develop a respectful but private response such as, "I was sick, but I am feeling better now," or "It was something personal, but I'm OK now." Remember that the student may need guidance to stay private and not be too dramatic. You don't want a sixth-grader returning to school and announcing to everyone that she tried to kill herself. If a student is over-sharing, you may want to pull her aside and say, "That's private, and you may only want to tell your best friend and family about that. Let's think about a better response to kids' questions about where you were." It is critical to work closely with the student and the parents to figure out what work is essential to make up and what can be postponed or dropped. Sometimes, students who are depressed can become extremely disconcerted that they have missed lessons and have trouble prioritizing what they need to finish. Or they may feel overwhelmed and stressed and then experience a backslide in their mood.

It can be particularly difficult for you if a student was hospitalized after he had talked about being suicidal to classmates and his parents don't give permission to answer students' questions while he's in the hospital. Without the parents' permission, you can only tell students that he is safe and will hopefully be back soon.

12. Is there hope for these students?

Yes! The students with challenging behavior we've discussed in this book improve, sometimes remarkably. One teary-eyed mother summed up a transforming and successful year for her fourth-grade son: "I used to feel as if I was raising an animal I didn't understand and sometimes feared. Now, I have my son. Thank you for giving me back my son." Students with challenging behavior learn to breathe in a moment of panic; learn to say, "I'm frustrated," instead of screaming; learn to restrict the impulse to comment on a girl's breasts; begin to think positively about themselves; and laugh openly.

We want you to take these tools we have discussed and apply them to your students with challenging behavior. Doing so will give you the satisfaction of seeing these students gain a level of stability, harness their energy, and uncover their potential. The distilled advice on these pages will give you a roadmap and the confidence to persist if you have temporary setbacks with these students. By learning to understand what they are trying to communicate, you are encouraging them to find alternative behaviors so they can thrive. We are grateful for your commitment to these students with challenging behavior, knowing that the victory for these students comes from your disciplined, steady, creative effort. Breaking the behavior code and shaping the environment will allow these students to develop the necessary tools to thrive.

Sample Antecedent, Behavior, and Consequences (ABC) Data Sheet

Student: _____

Date, time, duration	Setting event(s)	Activity	Antecedent (what happens immediately before behavior)	Behavior (description of behavior)	Consequence (what happens immediately after behavior)

Source: adapted from Sidney W. Bijou, Robert F. Peterson, and Marion H. Ault, "A Method to Integrate Descriptive and Experimental Field Studies at the Level of Data and Empirical Concepts," *Journal of Applied Behavior Analysis* 1, no. 2 (1968); Beth Sulzer-Azaroff and G. Roy Mayer, *Applying Behavior-Analysis Procedures with Children and Youth* (New York: Holt, Rinehart and Winston, 1977).

Curriculum Resources

Even though these curricula are listed by behavioral profile, they can also apply to students with other behavioral challenges depicted in the book.

THE STUDENT WITH ANXIETY-RELATED BEHAVIOR

Flexible Thinking

Michelle Garcia Winner, *Think Social! A Social Thinking Curriculum for School-Age Students: For Teaching Social Thinking and Related Social Skills to Students with High Funtioning Autism, Asperger Syndrome, PDD-NOS, ADHD, Nonverbal Learning Disability and for All Others in the Murky Gray Area of Social Thinking* (San Jose, Calif.: Michelle Garcia Winner, 2005).

Decreasing Negative Thinking, Self-Monitoring, and Self-Regulation

Philip C. Kendall, *Coping Cat Workbook* (Ardmore, Pa.: Workbook Pub., 2006).

Matthew McKay, Jeffrey C. Wood, and Jeffrey Brantley, *The Dialectical Behavior Therapy Skills Workbook: Practical DBT Exercises for Learning Mindfulness, Interpersonal Effectiveness, Emotion Regulation & Distress Tolerance* (Oakland, Calif.: New Harbinger Publications, 2007).

Patricia K. Tollison, Katherine O. Synatschk, and Gaea Logan, *Self-Regulation for Kids K–12: Strategies for Calming Minds and Behavior* (Austin, Tex.: Pro-Ed).

William J. Knaus, *The Cognitive Behavioral Workbook for Anxiety: A Step-by-Step Program* (Oakland, Calif.: New Harbinger Publications, 2008).

Kari Dunn Buron, "The Incredible 5 Point Scale," www.5pointscale.com/.

Mary Sue Williams and Sherry Shellenberger, *How Does Your Engine Run? A Leader's Guide to the Alert Program for Self-Regulation* (Albuquerque: TherapyWorks, 1996).

Leah Kuypers, *The Zones of Regulation* (San Jose, CA: Think Social Publishing, Inc., 2011)

Executive Functioning

Center for Executive Function Skill Development, "Cognitive Connections," www
.executivefunctiontherapy.com.

Dawson, P., Guare, R. *Executive Skills in Children and Adolescents: A Practical Guide
to Assessment and Intervention*, Guilford Practical Intervention in Schools Series
(New York: Guildford Press, 2004)

Social Skills

Janet Z. Giler, *Socially ADDept: Teaching Social Skills to Children with ADHD, LD,
and Asperger's* (San Francisco: Jossey-Bass, 2011).

Nancy Leber, *Easy Activities for Building Social Skills* (New York: Scholastic Professional Books, 2002).

Brenda Smith Myles, Melissa Trautman, and Ronda L. Schelvan, *The Hidden Curriculum: Practical Solutions for Understanding Unstated Rules in Social Situations* (Shawnee Mission, Kans.: Autism Asperger Pub. Co., 2004).

Michelle Garcia Winner, *Think Social!* (San Jose, Calif.: Michelle Garcia Winner,
2005).

Michelle Garcia Winner, *Thinking About You, Thinking About Me* (San Jose, Calif.:
Think Social, 2007).

THE STUDENT WITH OPPOSITIONAL BEHAVIOR

Social Skills

David W. Johnson and Roger T. Johnson, *Teaching Students to be Peacemakers*
(Edina, Minn.: Interaction Book Co., 2005).

Tonia Caselman, *Teaching Children Empathy: The Social Emotion: Lessons, Activities and Reproducible Worksheets (K-6) That Teach How to "Step into Others'
Shoes"* (Chapin, S.C.: YouthLight, Inc., 2007).

Michelle Garcia Winner, *Social Behavior Mapping* (Kentwood, Mich.: The Gray
Center, 2007).

Carol Gray, *The New Social Story Book* (Arlington, Tex.: Future Horizons, 2010).

Jeanette L. McAfee, Amelia Davies, and Future Horizons Inc., *Navigating the Social
World*, (Arlington, Tex.: Future Horizons, 2003).

Carol Gray, *Comic Strip Conversations: Colorful, Illustrated Interactions with Students with Autism and Related Disorders* (Jenison, Mich.: Jenison Public Schools, 1994).

Jed Baker, *Social Skills Picture Book: Teaching Communication, Play and Emotion* (Arlington, Tex.: Future Horizons, 2001).

Ellsworth A. Fersch, Mary Smith, and Hamilton-Wenham Regional High School, *Project Adventure* (Hamilton, Mass.: Project Adventure, 1972).

Dealing with Anger

Elizabeth Verdick and Marjorie Lisovskis, *How to Take the Grrrr out of Anger* (Minneapolis: Free Spirit Pub., 2002).

Warwick Pudney and Eliane Whitehouse, *A Volcano in My Tummy: Helping Children to Handle Anger; A Resource Book for Parents, Caregivers and Teachers* (Gabriola Island, B.C., Canada: New Society Publishers, 1996).

Carolyn C. Wilson, *Room 14: A Social Language Program* (East Moline, Ill.: Linguisystems, 1993).

Judith Coucouvanis, *Super Skills: A Social Skills Group Program for Children with Asperger Syndrome, High-Functioning Autism and Related Challenges* (Shawnee Mission, Kans.: Autism Asperger Pub. Co., 2005).

Amy V. Jaffe and Luci Gardner, *My Book Full of Feelings: How to Control and React to the Size of Your Emotions* (Shawnee Mission, Kan.: Autism Asperger Pub. Co., 2005).

Teresa A. Cardon, *Let's Talk Emotions: Helping Children with Social Cognitive Deficits, Including AS, HFA, and NVLD, Learn to Understand and Express Empathy and Emotions* (Shawnee Mission, Kan.: Autism Asperger Pub. Co., 2004).

THE STUDENT WITH WITHDRAWN BEHAVIOR

Positive Self-Talk, Thinking Traps, and Thought-Stopping

Elisa Gagnon, *Power Cards: Using Special Interests to Motivate Children and Youth with Asperger Syndrome and Autism* (Shawnee Mission, Kan.: Autism Asperger Pub. Co., 2002).

Kenneth W. Merrell, *Helping Students Overcome Depression and Anxiety: A Practical Guide* (New York: Guilford Press, 2008).

Mary Ellen Copeland and Matthew McKay, *The Depression Workbook* (Oakland, Calif.: New Harbinger Publications, 2002).

Alanna Jones, *104 Activities That Build: Self-Esteem, Teamwork, Communication, Anger Management, Self-Discovery, and Coping Skills* (Richland, Wash.: Rec Room Pub.,1998).

Kathy L. Korb-Khalsa, *Taking Depression to School* (Plainview, N.Y.: JayJo Books, 2002).

William J. Knaus, *The Cognitive Behavioral Workbook for Depression: A Step-by-Step Program* (Oakland, Calif.: New Harbinger Publications, 2006).

Social Skills: Taking Perspective

Michelle Garcia Winner, *Thinking About You, Thinking About Me* (San Jose, Calif.: Think Social, 2007).

Kenneth W. Merrell, *Helping Students Overcome Depression and Anxiety: A Practical Guide* (New York: Guilford Press, 2008).

Jed Baker and Future Horizons Inc., *Social Skills Training & Frustration Management*, (Arlington, Tex.: Future Horizons Inc., 2007).

THE STUDENT WITH SEXUALIZED BEHAVIOR

Social Skills

Michelle Garcia Winner, *Think Social!* (San Jose, Calif.: Michelle Garcia Winner, 2005).

Michelle Garcia Winner, *Thinking About You, Thinking About Me* (San Jose, Calif.: Think Social, 2007).

Robert L. Leahy, *Cognitive Therapy Techniques: A Practitioner's Guide* (New York: Guilford Press, 2003).

Resiliency and Overcoming Trauma

Judith A. Cohen, Esther Deblinger, and Anthony P. Mannarino, *Treating Trauma and Traumatic Grief in Children and Adolescents* (New York: The Guilford Press, 2006).

Caron B. Goode, Tom Goode, and David Russell, Help Kids Cope with Stress & Trauma: Nurturing Peace and Balance (Fort Worth, TX: Inspired Living International, 2006).

Barbara Brooks and Paula M. Siegel, *The Scared Child: Helping Kids Overcome Traumatic Events* (New York: John Wiley & Sons, 1996).

Rules of Body Space

Michelle Garcia Winner, *Think social!* (San Jose, Calif.: Michelle Garcia Winner, 2005).

Julia Cook and Carrie Hartman, *Personal Space Camp Activity and Idea Book* (Chattanooga, Tenn.: National Center for Youth Issues, 2010).

Awareness of Whom the Student Can Touch

Marklyn P. Champagne and Leslie Walker-Hirsch, *Circles Curriculum* (Santa Barbara, Calif.: James Stanfield Company, 1993).

Robert D. Isett and Brian Isett, *Think Right, Feel Right: The Building Block Guide for Happiness and Emotional Well-Being* (Robert Isett, 2010).

Impulse Control

Lindy Petersen, "Stop, Think, Do," http://www.stopthinkdo.com/.

Tonia Caselman, *Stop and Think: Impulse Control* (Chapin, S.C.: YouthLight, 2005).

Lunch Buddies Permission Form

April 2012

To Whom It May Concern:

My name is _____. I am the _____ here at _____ school. Your child has been selected to join a friendship-building lunch group.

The goal of the group is to assist a particular student/s in building skills in the areas of social skills and friendship building. Since your child exemplifies good citizenship, kindness, and compassion, s/he has been nominated to be a role model for this group. Lunch buddies, as we will call it, will be held during lunch on Fridays. The group will consist of 3-4 fourth-graders and me in a separate room near the cafeteria.

The goal of the group will not be obviously stated to the students, in order to respect the dignity of the student/s for whom this group was developed; instead, we will emphasize our sameness, practice conversing, and have fun! We will play games and occasionally have surprise snacks or other foods.

If you have any questions about the group, please feel free to call me at 555-555-1234.

Thank you for your interest.

Sincerely,

_____

____ Yes, I would like my child _____ to be part of the lunch buddies group.

____ No, I would not like my child _____ to be part of the lunch buddies group.

Parent's or Guardian's signature

_____

Technology Resources

Technology can help many reluctant students who may reject paper-and-pencil work, and who may find online activities motivating and easier to understand. Many of these resources were compiled with the help of the following general Web pages: Jill Kuzma, "Jill Kuzma's Social & Emotional Skill Sharing Site," 2008, http://jillkuzma.wordpress.com/great-websites-and-resources; "Free Technology Toolkit for UDL in All Classrooms," http://udltechtoolkit.wikispaces.com; and Vicki Windman, "iPad Apps to Improve Your Executive Functioning Skills," http://www.techlearning.com/default.aspx?tabid=67&entryid=292. Mobile apps are compatible with most smartphones (such as the iPhone) and most tablets (such as the iPad).

SOCIAL SKILLS

These Web sites are good for students needing social skills instruction.

http://do2learn.com/games/learningames.htm: includes games about facial expressions and emotions.

http://jillkuzma.wordpress.com: includes links to YouTube videos about social skills and many other resources.

www.angelfire.com/pa5/as/socialskills.html: links to social skills printable material and other Web sites.

www.autism4teachers.com/autism4teachers_008.htm: includes links to social stories and social skills games.

www.cyke.com/depression.swf: four games about depression; helps kids learn what depression looks like, what causes it, and how to calm down.

www.jambav.com: game about following eye gaze. Click on "channel 9" for the game LukaHead, and then click on "play game." You can choose whether the child will be the follower (following Luka's gaze and clicking on the circle he's looking at) or whether the child will be the leader (clicking on the circle so Luka's head will look that way).

www.socialthinking.com: Michelle Garcia Winner's site; you can sign up for a free e-mail newsletter, too.

www.urbanext.uiuc.edu/conflict/guide/activities_perceptions.html: perspective-taking online exercise for younger children.

EMOTIONS

These Web sites are good for students needing instruction on reading emotions.

www.cyke.com/worryville.swf: includes games about worry and anxiety.

www.cyke.com/downloads/MonkeyExpress.mov: a short movie about anger.

www.btbetterworld.com/pg/developing_skills/free_resources/Making_Faces/home .ikml: drop-and-drag cartoon face activity designed for teaching emotions in schools.

www.thomasandfriends.com/usa/Thomas.mvc/Games/Home: two emotion games; one asks questions like "Which train is surprised?" and the other is a memory game.

www.symbolworld.org/Bits+bobs/games/faces/index.htm: emotions game where on some screens, you can roll your mouse over a face and see the same person change to a different expression.

www.do2learn.com/games/learninggames.htm: a simple "Feelings Game" with real faces; a "Facial Expressions" activity where you can manipulate a cyberface; and other simple learning games.

www.transporters.tv/watchep1.html: excellent online video with quiz, featuring Thomas-like vehicle characters with living human faces. Under "downloads," you'll find a character emotions pack "for classroom use."

www.senteacher.org/Print/?PHPSESSID=69c5ff8f5e8ebdaef bb26da60d1195a4: printables with neutral, happy, sad, angry, disgusted, and fearful expressions in male and female versions; can be printed as domino cards.

www.robotsandus.org/sensing/making_faces: interactive activity about facial expressions and recognition.

EMOTIONAL REGULATION

These Web sites are appropriate for students described in chapters 3 through 6 (students with anxious, oppositional, withdrawn, or sexualized behavior, respectively) and needing to learn how to regulate their emotions.

www.5pointscale.com: Web site for five-point scale resources, by Kari Dunn Buron and Mitzi Curtis.

www.goodcharacter.com/EStopics.html: great character education site with social skill topics such as dealing with anger, conflict resolution, saying no, and so forth.

http://pbskids.org/itsmylife/emotions/anger/index.html: activities related to dealing with anger.

www.e-learningforkids.org/courses.html#life: interactive learning tools and games to teach about bullying, communication, stress, depression and more.

www.embracethefuture.org.au/kids/index.htm?feelings2.asp: teaches students how to be more resilient when angry, depressed, sad, or anxious; includes games, including the resilient-thinking game.

MISPERCEIVED SOCIAL INTERACTION

Comic strips can be used to review a social interaction and teach how to gain perspective.

www.makebeliefscomix.com/Comix: interactive Web site where you can make your own comic strips, choosing from a menu of a variety of characters; you can insert talking and thinking bubbles and even change the facial expression and body language of the characters you choose.

www.bitstrips.com: another Web site to help you create your own comic strips.

PLAYING GAMES WITH PEERS

Games are particularly useful for students with oppositional behavior or any student having difficulty with play skills.

http://life.familyeducation.com/manners-and-values/parenting/34452.html: quiz about manners.

www.gameskidsplay.net: rules for common playground games, jump rope rhymes, and so forth.

www.lehman.cuny.edu/faculty/jfleitas/bandaides/tease.html: teaches about teasing.

http://urbanext.illinois.edu/conflict/index.html: interactive story about learning to get along.

www.kellymckinnonassociates.com/neurotypicaldevelopment.html: articles and video samples from Kelly McKinnon, an expert at social play skills.

AUDIO BOOKS AND E-BOOKS

Audio books and e-books are particularly useful for students with oppositional behavior if they refuse to read or any other student having difficulty or resistance to reading.

http://librivox.org: audio books read by volunteers and in the public domain.

www.gutenberg.org: text of books in the public domain, also available for mobile devices. Attach text-to-speech and can convert to MP3 format.

http://bookbuilder.cast.org: interactive book maker and reader.

www.bookshare.org: online digital library; a free subscription is provided with proof of a print disability.

www.60secondrecap.com: a sixty-second audio-video presentation of classic works of literature.

www.storylinemn.org: story read aloud over the phone each week.

www.onlineaudiostories.com: a collection of elementary audio books.

www.mothergooseclub.com/index.php: has a number of rhymes and songs that provide audio support for the text.

www.learnoutloud.com/Free-Audio-Video: over two thousand free audio and video titles, including books, lectures, speeches, and interviews.

www.readprint.com: free online book library with over eight thousand titles that can be read using any free text reader (tested with Natural Reader).

www.smories.com: a video site featuring kids reading kids' stories; many of the videos include captions.

www.raz-kids.com: online skill-leveled books library.

www.storylineonline.net: listen to stories read by Screen Actors Guild members; follow along with the text.

www.magickeys.com/books: illustrated stories for young children, older children, and young adults; some include audio.

http://staff.prairiesouth.ca/~cassidy.kathy/browserbooks/index.htm: allows beginning readers to read books on their Web browser.

http://tarheelreader.org: collection of easy-to-read books on a wide variety of topics, in multiple formats.

FREE LITERACY TOOLS

These tools are particularly useful for students with oppositional behavior if they are refusing to participate in phonics or reading instruction or for any student having difficulty or resistance to phonics or reading instruction.

www.starfall.com: pre-K through second-grade online activities that promote literacy.

http://literactive.com: interactive primary reading activities.

www.inklesstales.com/stories/index.shtml: listen to stories including Dolch words. (You can use the control and + keys to enlarge the font size if students are following along.)

http://reading.ecb.org: excellent reading comprehension resource for K–4, teaches about using prior knowledge, making connections, questioning, visualizing, inferring, summarizing, evaluating, and synthesizing.

www.kerpoof.com/#/activity/abc: excellent activity for building phonemic awareness, phonics, and spelling for early readers; lots of picture prompts.

http://bookbuilder.cast.org: free online tool for creating digital books with embedded prompts.

http://udleditions.cast.org: leveled support for seven texts geared for ages ten and up.

WRITING

These Web sites are particularly useful for students with oppositional behavior if they refuse to write or for any student having difficulty or resistance to writing.

www.learnalberta.ca/content/ssass/html/graphicorganizers.html: forty download-able graphic organizer templates to use in a word processing program; quick and easy.

https://bubbl.us: brainstorming and organizing tool, good for visual thinkers and learners, easy to use, very simple, customizable features, sharing capabilities.

www.storyjumper.com: story-building tool with scenes, props, and text with spell-check support; can add your own photos; also allows you to publish your work for a fee.

http://littlebirdtales.com: easy-to-use story-building tool; records audio and allows narration.

http://storybird.com: collaborative storytelling.

www.writingfun.com: interactive, structured writing tool to help elementary-age students write descriptions, narratives, poetry, explanations, procedures, and the like.

www.comicmaster.org.uk: create your own graphic novels.

http://comicstripcreator.org: a comic strip creator.

www.thestorystarter.com/jr.htm: sometimes, determining where to begin is the obstacle. This Web site provides first lines to begin story writing.

www.spellingcity.com: free to generate spelling lists; includes many games.

www.kerpoof.com: use for creating stories; very motivating.

www.carnegielibrary.org/kids/storymaker/storymaker.swf: another very motivating site for creating a story; we use these for creating fun social stories.

http://voicethread.com: a great alternative to a written assignment, VoiceThread is a collaborative, multimedia slide show that holds images, documents, and videos and allows people to navigate slides and leave comments.

Dragon Naturally Speaking: speech recognition software.

http://archives.nbclearn.com/portal/site/k-12: NBC News offers unique collections of video resources, primary sources, historic footage, images, minidocumen-taries, and text resources designed for use in the K–12 classroom.

www.apple.com/education/itunes-u: lectures, tours, audiobooks, and math lessons.

MATH

These Web sites are particularly useful for students with oppositional behavior if they are refusing to participate in math instruction or for any student having difficulty or resistance to math.

www.mathplayground.com: excellent site for math activities for K–8 students; make sure to explore the Mathcasts, which allow students to review math when they need to.

www.brainingcamp.com/resources/math: grade 6–9 animated lessons and interactive activities along with question sets to assess student understanding.

http://nlvm.usu.edu: a library of uniquely interactive, Web-based virtual manipulatives or concept tutorials, mostly in the form of Java applets, for mathematics instruction (K–12 emphasis).

www.glencoe.com/sites/common_assets/mathematics/ebook_assets/vmf/VMF-Interface.html: virtual manipulatives for K–8.

http://nrich.maths.org/public: online math games for many levels.

www.khanacademy.org: free webinar math lessons.

MOBILE DEVICE APPS FOR SELF-REGULATION, THOUGHT STOPPING, AND SELF-MONITORING

Sosh/Sosh lite: social skills assistance in five categories, relax, regulate, reason, recognize, and relate. The app includes a thought shredder that shreds negative thoughts, a way to track inappropriate behaviors, emotional thermometers, and calming activities such as deep breathing.

Voice Meter: shows the student how loud he or she is visually; scale gives in-the-moment feedback as to voice level (e.g., yellow too soft, orange just right, red too loud).

Symtrend: electronic emotional thermometer; can be created with link to strategies, and more.

BEHAVIOR REINFORCEMENT

Irewards: an electronic token chart to reinforce appropriate use of strategies.
www.oneplaceforspecialneeds.com/resources_online/resource_online_results.html?
    words=behavior+management+apps: list of behavior-tracking and behavior-
    reinforcing applications, including an electronic ABC sheet for the teacher.

EXECUTIVE FUNCTIONING

Time Timer: visual timer for students.
Evernote: for taking a picture or recording a sticky note electronically; for iPad.
Noteability: a note-taking iPad application that allows typing, recording the
    teacher, taking a picture
Nudge: reminder that you set will nudge you until you shut it off; for iPad.
CourseNotes: for color-coding notes and organizing class notes; for iPad.
www.oneplaceforspecialneeds.com/resources_online/resource_online_browse.html:
    Web site listing social skills applications.
www.happy-neuron.com/brain-games/executive-function: Web site for games that
    help students train and sharpen their executive functioning skills.

Calming Activities

	Putty	Squeeze the putty or find pennies or other small objects in it.
	Fidget tools	Fidget tools can be used during a break or to help attend to a lesson, as long as it is not distracting to you or others.
	Jumping jacks	Jumping in place or jumping jacks can be done throughout the day as needed. This should be followed by a quiet activity.
	Trampoline	Practice counting or singing when jumping on the trampoline. This should be followed by a quiet activity.

	Heavy work	Heavy work, such as moving desks, erasing the board, carrying books to the library, or holding the door open, can be calming.
	Bolster or Therapy ball	The teacher can roll the Bolster or therapy ball to you, and you can use two feet to push it back to your teacher.
	Scooter board	Use a scooter in a movement break.
	Weighted lap pillow	Placing a weighted lap pillow on student's lap in class or during a break.
	Beanbag chair	Sitting in a beanbag chair can provide deep pressure, which is calming.
	Music	Rhythmic music is organizing.

	Therapy ball	Lay on your stomach on, roll over ball, or have a teacher move a therapy ball over your back, legs, and arms.
	Headphones	Headphones can be used to screen out noise when you're in loud environments, such as the cafeteria or an assembly.
	Stretch	Stretching can help you get more energy or calm down.
	Yoga	Watch the yoga video or look at the yoga book and try some poses for calming.
	Chair pushups	You can sit in a chair with hands flat on the chair seat. Push so bottom is lifted off seat. You can hold this position, or do repetitions.

Source: Pics for PECS™ images are used and adapted with permission from Pyramid Educational Consultants, Inc. (www.pecs.com). Pyramid Educational Consultants, Inc. reserves all rights to the Pics for PECS™ images.

APPENDIX F

Self-Monitoring Sheet

DIRECTIONS FOR USING THE SELF-MONITORING SHEET:

1. The teacher will fill in the student's schedule in the Schedule column.
2. The teacher will fill in the strategies he or she wants the student to use in the Strategy box (no more than four), so the student knows what strategies to use to earn a bonus point.
3. The teacher will fill in the behaviors that the student is working on in the Expected Behavior boxes.
4. After every scheduled class period, the teacher will ask the student how his or her behavior was during the class.
5. The student will rate himself or herself by using the scale 1 = not demonstrated, 2 = somewhat demonstrated, 3 = consistently demonstrated, in each of the three Expected Behavior columns.
6. The teacher will support the student in remembering the details of the class period if needed.
7. The teacher will also rate the student's behavior, using the 1, 2, 3 scale.
8. The teacher and student will discuss these ratings as they fill in the form, especially if there is a discrepancy between the teacher's rating and the student's.
9. If the student uses a strategy written in the strategy box, he or she will earn a strategy point.
10. The strategy points can be totaled at the end of the day and be cashed in for a reward or praise.
11. The 1, 2, 3 rating numbers will not be added. They are simply for reflection and self-monitoring practice.

Name: _____   Date: _____

1	2	3
Not demonstrated	Somewhat demonstrated	Consistently demonstrated

Strategy:
(Use a strategy to earn a strategy point.)

• •

Schedule	Expected Behavior 1		Expected Behavior 2		Expected Behavior 3		Strategy point: "I used a strategy"
	Student	Teacher	Student	Teacher	Student	Teacher	
							Total strategy points:

EXAMPLE: SELF-MONITORING SHEET FOR SAM

Name: **Sam**   Date: **1/30/10**

1	2	3
Not demonstrated	Somewhat demonstrated	Consistently demonstrated

Strategy:
(Use a strategy to earn a strategy point.)

- **When I'm frustrated, I will ask for help or a break.**
- **When I'm frustrated, I will use my calming box.**

Schedule	Safe Behavior		Listen to Directions		Do My Work		Strategy point: "I used a strategy"
	Student	Teacher	Student	Teacher	Student	Teacher	
Morning meeting	2	2	3	3	3	2	
Math	3	3	3	3	3	3	
Reading group	2	1	2	2	2	2	1
Snack	1	1	2	2	1	1	
Recess	1	1	2	2	2	1	
Quiet reading	3	3	3	3	3	3	
Art	3	3	3	3	3	3	
Science	3	3	3	3	3	3	
Lunch	2	2	3	2	3	2	1
Social studies	3	3	3	3	3	3	
Writing	1	1	2	2	2	1	1
Dismissal	3	3	3	3	3	3	
						Total strategy points:	3

Taking Responsibility for Choices Worksheet

Student's Name: _____

First, ask yourself these questions:

1. What choice did I make?

2. What happens when this rule is broken?

3. Would I like to be treated the way I treated the person or people involved?
   Explain:

4. What was I trying to do or get when I chose to act inappropriately?
   Did my choice get me what I wanted?

5. How could I get what I wanted in a way that wouldn't hurt anyone or wouldn't
   get me in trouble?

Second, decide what to do now to make things better. Check one or two choices. Then *do* them!

☐ Apologize to _____

☐ Write a note to _____

☐ Do something nice for _____

☐ Make an appointment to talk with _____

☐ Do nothing right now, but remember to make the right choice from now on.

☐ Practice the right choice right now.

☐ Something else: _____

Sources: Adapted from *The Behavior Survival Guide for Kids: How to Make Good Choices and Stay Out of Trouble* by Tom McIntyre, PhD., © 2003. Adapted with permission of Free Spirit Publishing Inc., Minneapolis, MN 800-735-7323; www.freespirit.com. All rights reserved.

FAIR Plan Implementation Worksheet

Responsibility	Designated person
Calling the parent after an urgent incident	
Calling the parent to gather or relay information	
Calling and coordinating with outside professionals	
Explicit teaching of skill deficits (self-regulation, self-calming, flexible thinking, and social skills)	
Supervising breaks (list the recommended number of breaks): 1. First break (specify time) 2. Second break (specify time)	
Supervising rewards (e.g., computer, extra recess)	
Alternative lunch (facilitating and supervising)	
Alternative recess	
Alternative bathroom plan	

Notes

Introduction

1. Heather J. Walter, Karen Gouze, and Karen G. Lim, "Teachers' Beliefs About Mental Health Needs in Inner City Elementary Schools," *Journal of the American Academy of Child and Adolescent Psychiatry* 45, no. 1 (2006): 61–68.
2. Ibid.
3. John O. Cooper, Timothy E. Heron, and William L. Heward, *Applied Behavior Analysis* (Upper Saddle River, N.J.: Pearson/Merrill Prentice Hall, 2007).

Chapter 1

1. Robert Reid et al., "A Meta-Analysis of the Academic Status of Students with Emotional/Behavioral Disturbance," *Journal of Special Education* 38, no. 3 (2004); Kent McIntosh et al., "Reading Skills and Function of Problem Behavior in Typical School Settings," *Journal of Special Education* 42, no. 3 (2008).
2. G. Siperstein, A. Wiley, and S. Forness, "School Context and the Academic and Behavioral Progress of Students with Emotional Disturbance," *Behavioral Disorders* 36, no. 3 (2011).
3. Data Accountability Center, "Individuals with Disabilities Education Act (IDEA) Data," www.ideadata.org/PartBReport.asp; David Osher, Gale Morrison, and Wanda Bailey, "Exploring the Relationship Between Student Mobility and Dropout Among Students with Emotional and Behavioral Disorders," *Journal of Negro Education* 72, no. 1 (2003).
4. Data Accountability Center, "Individuals with Disabilities Education Act (IDEA) Data."
5. Osher, Morrison, and Bailey, "Student Mobility and Dropout."
6. Carl R. Smith, Antonis Katsiyannis, and Joseph B. Ryan, "Challenges of Serving Students with Emotional and Behavioral Disorders: Legal and Policy Considerations," *Behavioral Disorders* 36, no. 3 (2011).
7. Edward G. Carr and V. Mark Durand, "Reducing Behavior Problems Through Functional Communication Training," *Journal of Applied Behavior Analysis* 18, no. 2 (1985).
8. Nazanin Derakshan and Michael W. Eysenck, "Anxiety, Processing Efficiency, and Cognitive Performance: New Developments from Attentional Control Theory," *European Psychologist* 14, no. 2 (2009).

9. Marsha Mailick Seltzer et al., "Trajectory of Development in Adolescents and Adults with Autism," *Mental Retardation & Developmental Disabilities Research Reviews* 10, no. 4 (2004).

10. Ross W. Greene, *The Explosive Child: A New Approach for Understanding and Parenting Easily Frustrated, "Chronically Inflexible" Children* (New York: Harper Collins, 1998); Edward G. Carr and V. Mark Durand, "The Social-Communicative Basis of Severe Behavior Problems in Children," in *Theoretical Issues in Behavior Therapy*, ed. S. Reiss and R. Bootzin (New York: Academic Press, 1985); Robert E. O'Neill et al., *Functional Assessment and Program Development for Problem Behavior: A Practical Handbook* (Pacific Grove, Calif.: Brooks/Cole Pub., 1997); G. Roy Mayer, "Why Must Behavior Intervention Plans Be Based on Functional Assessments?" *California School Psychologist*, no. 1 (1995); G. Roy Mayer and Tom W. Butterworth, "A Preventive Approach to School Violence and Vandalism: An Experimental Study," *Personnel & Guidance Journal* 57, no. 9 (1979); Edward G. Carr et al., "Positive Behavior Support: Evolution of an Applied Science," *Journal of Positive Behavior Interventions* 4, no. 1 (2002).

11. Greene, *The Explosive Child.*

12. Bruce Perry eloquently describes the four parts of the brain that are organized in a hierarchal fashion: brainstem, diencephalons, limbic system, and cortex. The brainstem mediates core regulatory body temperature, heart rate, respiration, and blood pressure. The diencephalons and the limbic system manage emotional responses like fear, hatred, love, and joy. The cortex regulates the more complex functions such as speech, language, abstract thinking, planning, and deliberate decision making. Students with a trauma history can have a repeated activation of the stress response. This may have helped them cope with abuse, but in the long term, it can lead to anxiety, aggressive behavior, or inattention.

Bruce Duncan Perry and Maia Szalavitz, *The Boy Who Was Raised As a Dog: And Other Stories from a Child Psychiatrist's Notebook; What Traumatized Children Can Teach Us About Loss, Love, And Healing* (New York: Basic Books, 2006), 21–23.

13. Greene, *The Explosive Child.*

14. Vincent Mark Durand, *Severe Behavior Problems: A Functional Communication Training Approach* (New York: Guilford Press, 1990), 11–14.

15. J. Q. Bostic and P. K. Rauch, "The 3 R's of School Consultation," *Journal of the American Academy of Child & Adolescent Psychiatry* 38, no. 3 (1999).

16. Alan E. Kazdin and Carlo Rotella, *The Kazdin Method for Parenting the Defiant Child: With No Pills, No Therapy, No Contest of Wills* (Boston: Houghton Mifflin, 2008), 17.

17. Thomas E. Joiner, "The Price of Soliciting and Receiving Negative Feedback: Self-Verification Theory As a Vulnerability to Depression Theory," *Journal of Abnormal Psychology* 104, no. 2 (1995).

18. Brenda Smith Myles, *Asperger Syndrome and Sensory Issues* (Shawnee Mission, Kan.: Autism Asperger Publishing, 2005), 8, 17.

19. Carol Stock Kranowitz, *The Out-of-Sync Child: Recognizing and Coping with Sensory Integration Dysfunction* (New York: Perigee Book, 2005).

20. When an intervention is helping "a little" (e.g., a student goes from screaming ten times a day to screaming five times a day), this may be because the behavior has more than one function and the intervention is only addressing one part of the behavior. If the teacher stops giving the

screaming student attention but doesn't address the secondary function of escape (i.e., student is still able to escape a task by screaming), the behavior is only improved, not extinguished. For an intervention to work well, all intents of the behavior need to be addressed.

21. Robert G. Wahler and James J. Fox, "Setting Events in Applied Behavior Analysis: Toward a Conceptual and Methodological Expansion," *Journal of Applied Behavior Analysis* 14, no. 3 (1981); Mark Carter and Coralie Driscoll, "A Conceptual Examination of Setting Events," *Educational Psychology* 27, no. 5 (2007).
22. Durand, *Severe Behavior Problems*, 15.
23. G. Roy Mayer, "Preventing Antisocial Behavior in the Schools," *Journal of Applied Behavior Analysis* 28, no. 4 (1995).

Chapter 2

1. These five steps are from L. M. Bambara and T. P. Knoster, *Guidelines: Effective Behavioral Support* (Harrisburg: Pennsylvania Department of Education, 1995); Karen Topper et al., *A Positive Approach to Understanding and Addressing Challenging Behaviors: Supporting Educators and Families to Include Students with Emotional and Behavioral Disorders in Regular Education* (Burlington: University of Vermont, 1994); Diana Browning Wright, Harvey B. Gurman, and Southern California Positive Intervention Task Force California Association of School Psychologists/Diagnostic Center, *Positive Intervention for Serious Behavior Problems: Best Practices in Implementing the Hughes Bill (A.B. 2586) and the Positive Behavioral Intervention Regulations* (Sacramento: California Department of Education, 2001).
2. Robert E. O'Neill et al., *Functional Assessment and Program Development for Problem Behavior: A Practical Handbook* (Pacific Grove, Calif.: Brooks/Cole Pub., 1997), 74–76.
3. Kevin S. Sutherland et al., "Examining the Influence of Teacher Behavior and Classroom Context on the Behavioral and Academic Outcomes for Students with Emotional or Behavioral Disorders," *Journal of Special Education* 41, no. 4 (2008); Janine P. Stichter et al., "The Use of Structural Analysis to Develop Antecedent-Based Interventions for Students with Autism," *Journal of Autism & Developmental Disorders* 39, no. 6 (2009); G. M. Pace et al., "Antecedent Interventions in the Management of Maladaptive Behaviours in a Child with Brain Injury," *Brain Injury* 19, no. 5 (2005).
4. A behavior support plan (BSP) can be used as a "proactive action plan to address behavior(s) that are impeding learning of the student or others." If developed for a student with an IEP or a 504 plan, the BSP becomes a part of those documents. The plan includes "positive behavioral interventions, strategies and supports." BSPs should focus on understanding why the behavior occurred (i.e. the function, or communicative intent) and then should focus on teaching an alternative behavior that meets the student's need in a more acceptable way. This includes making instructional and environmental changes, providing reinforcement, reactive strategies, and effective communication. Definition adapted from Positive Environments, Networks of Trainers, "Behavior Support Plans," n.d., www.pent.ca.gov/beh/bsp/bsp.htm.
5. Sidney W. Bijou, Robert F. Peterson, and Marion H. Ault, "A Method to Integrate Descriptive and Experimental Field Studies at the Level of Data and Empirical Concepts," *Journal of Applied Behavior Analysis* 1, no. 2 (1968); Beth Sulzer-Azaroff and G. Roy Mayer, *Applying*

Behavior-Analysis Procedures with Children and Youth (New York: Holt, Rinehart and Winston, 1977), 48–77.

6. Unfortunately, in this litigious society, documentation of these incidents is vital to address questions and possible misconceptions. Parents can be upset and wonder if the teacher "picked on their kid," or they may blame the teacher for the student's behavior.

7. National Dissemination Center for Children with Disabilities, "Special Education: Adaptations and Modifications," September 2010, http://nichcy.org/schoolage/iep/iepcontents/specialeducation#mods.

8. Lynn Meltzer, *Executive Function in Education: From Theory to Practice* (New York: Guilford Press, 2007), 5–8.

9. Alex B. Morgan and Scott O. Lilienfeld, "A Meta-Analytic Review of the Relation Between Antisocial Behavior and Neuropsychological Measures of Executive Function," *Clinical Psychology Review* 20, no. 1 (2000).

10. Bonnie D. Singer and Anthony S. Bashir, "What Is EmPOWER?" Architects for Learning, 2009, www.architectsforlearning.com/empower.html.

11. Robert C. Pianta and Megan W. Stuhlman, "Teacher-Child Relationships and Children's Success in the First Years of School," *School Psychology Review* 33, no. 3 (2004).

12. Christopher Murray and Keith Zvoch, "Teacher-Student Relationships Among Behaviorally At-Risk African American Youth from Low-Income Backgrounds: Student Perceptions, Teacher Perceptions, and Socioemotional Adjustment Correlates," *Journal of Emotional & Behavioral Disorders* 19, no. 1 (2011).

13. Ibid.

14. Alan E. Kazdin and Carlo Rotella, *The Kazdin Method for Parenting the Defiant Child: With No Pills, No Therapy, No Contest of Wills* (Boston: Houghton Mifflin, 2008), 64.

Chapter 3

1. *Merriam-Webster*, s.v. "anxiety," www.merriam-webster.com/dictionary/anxiety; Douglas Davies, *Child Development: A Practitioner's Guide* (New York: Guilford Press).

2. Aureen Pinto Wagner, *Worried No More: Help and Hope for Anxious Children* (Rochester, N.Y.: Lighthouse Press, 2005), 31–34.

3. Kenneth W. Merrell, *Helping Students Overcome Depression and Anxiety: A Practical Guide* (New York: Guilford Press, 2008), 7.

4. Gail A. Bernstein and Ann E. Layne, "Separation Anxiety Disorder and Generalized Anxiety Disorder," in *Textbook of Child and Adolescent Psychiatry*, ed. Jerry M. Wiener and Mina K. Dulcan (Washington, D.C.: American Psychiatric Pub., 2004), 595.

5. E. Jane Costello et al., "The Great Smoky Mountains Study of Youth: Goals, Design, Methods, and the Prevalence of DSM-III-R Disorders," *Archives of General Psychiatry* 53, no. 12 (1996).

6. Bruce Black et al., "Specific Phobia, Panic Disorder, Social Phobia, and Selective Mutism, in *Textbook of Child and Adolescent Psychiatry*, ed. Jerry M. Wiener and Mina K. Dulcan (Washington, DC: American Psychiatric Pub., 2004), 595.

7. C. L. Donnelly and L. Amaya-Jackson, "Post-Traumatic Stress Disorder in Children and Adolescents: Epidemiology, Diagnosis and Treatment Options," *Pediatric Drugs* 4, no. 3 (2002).

8. Lenore Terr, *Too Scared to Cry: Psychic Trauma in Childhood* (New York: Harper & Row, 1990), 261–280.

9. Judith A. Cohen, Esther Deblinger, and Anthony P. Mannarino, *Treating Trauma and Traumatic Grief in Children and Adolescents* (New York: The Guilford Press, 2006), 21.

10. Ibid.

11. Costello et al., "Great Smoky Mountains Study of Youth."

12. Vivian Koda, Dennis S. Charney, and Daniel S. Pine, "Neurobiology of Early Onset Anxiety Disorders," in *Pediatric Psychopharmacology: Principles and Practice*, ed. Andres Martin, Lawrence Scahill, and Christopher Kratochvil (New York: Oxford University Press, 2011), 140.

13. Wiener and Dulcan, *Textbook of Child and Adolescent Psychiatry*, 575.

14. Tamar Ellsas Chansky, *Freeing Your Child from Obsessive-Compulsive Disorder: A Powerful, Practical Program for Parents of Children and Adolescents*, (New York: Crown Publishers, 2000).

15. Systemic interventions are the most effective way to prevent bullying in schools. Some examples are Open Circle (www.open-circle.org/), Steps to Respect (www.cfchildren.org/programs/str/overview/), Responsive Classroom (www.responsiveclassroom.org/), Second Step (www.cfchildren.org/programs/ssp/overview/), and the Olweus Bullying Prevention Program (www.olweus.org). See also Stan Davis, "Stop Bullying Now," n.d., www.stopbullyingnow.com/; and Stan Davis and Julia Davis, *Schools Where Everyone Belongs: Practical Strategies for Reducing Bullying* (Champaign, Ill.: Research Press, 2007).

Preventing bullying makes schools safer for all students, not just those with mental health disorders and social skill deficits. Gay, lesbian, bisexual, and transgender (GLBT) students are at particular risk of being bullied—one national study found that 84 percent of GLBT students reported being verbally harassed in school. See A. Melissa Crawford and Katharina Manassis, "Anxiety, Social Skills, Friendship Quality, and Peer Victimization: An Integrated Model," *Journal of Anxiety Disorders* 25, no. 7 (2011); Stan Davis and Julia Davis, *Schools Where Everyone Belongs: Practical Strategies for Reducing Bullying* (Champaign, Ill.: Research Press, 2007); Joseph G. Kosciw et al., *The 2009 National School Climate Survey* (New York: Gay, Lesbian, and Straight Education Network, 2010); Kate Sofronoff, Elizabeth Dark, and Valerie Stone, "Social Vulnerability and Bullying in Children with Asperger Syndrome," *Autism: The International Journal of Research & Practice* 15, no. 3 (2011).

16. For information on working with students with OCD, see Gail B. Adams, *Students with OCD: A Handbook for School Personnel* (Campton Hills, Ill.: Pherson Creek Press, 2011). For information on working with students with separation anxiety, see Andrew R. Eisen and Charles E. Schaefer, *Separation Anxiety in Children and Adolescents: An Individualized Approach to Assessment and Treatment* (New York: Guilford Press, 2005).

17. E. Jane Costello, Helen L. Egger, and Adrian Angold, "The Developmental Epidemiology of Anxiety Disorders: Phenomenology, Prevalence, and Comorbidity," *Child and Adolescent Psychiatric Clinics of North America* 14, no. 4 (2005).

18. Derek R. Hopko et al., "The Impact of Anxiety on Performance IQ," *Anxiety, Stress & Coping* 18, no. 1 (2005).

19. Matthew Owens et al., "Processing Efficiency Theory in Children: Working Memory As a Mediator Between Trait Anxiety and Academic Performance," *Anxiety, Stress & Coping* 21, no. 4 (2008).

20. N. Ialongo et al., "The Significance of Self-Reported Anxious Symptoms in First-Grade Children," *Journal of Abnormal Child Psychology* 22 (1994).

21. Matthew P. Mychailyszyn, Julia L. Mendez, and Philip C. Kendall, "School Functioning in Youth With and Without Anxiety Disorders: Comparisons by Diagnosis and Comorbidity," *School Psychology Review* 39, no. 1 (2010).

22. Suzanne Barrett and Bernd G. Heubeck, "Relationships Between School Hassles and Uplifts and Anxiety and Conduct Problems in Grades 3 and 4," *Journal of Applied Developmental Psychology* 21, no. 5 (2000); E. Jane Garland and Orion M. Garland, "Correlation Between Anxiety and Oppositionality in a Children's Mood and Anxiety Disorder Clinic," *Canadian Journal of Psychiatry* 46, no. 10 (2001).

23. Bruce Duncan Perry and Maia Szalavitz, *The Boy Who Was Raised As a Dog: And Other Stories from A Child Psychiatrist's Notebook; What Traumatized Children Can Teach Us About Loss, Love, and Healing* (New York: Basic Books, 2006), 24–25.

24. Crisis Prevention Institute Web page, www.crisisprevention.com/.

25. Negative reinforcement is when a behavior is reinforced by the removal of an unpleasant factor (e.g., canceling a test), rather than the addition of a positive one (e.g., giving a reward). In this example, the anxiety is removed when the student sits by himself. The avoidance behavior is reinforced and will probably continue.

26. Hill M. Walker, Geoffrey Colvin, and Elizabeth Ramsey, *Antisocial Behavior in School: Strategies and Best Practices* (Pacific Grove, Calif.: Brooks/Cole Pub. Co., 1995), 167.

27. Athena A. Drewes, *"Blending Play Therapy with Cognitive Behavioral Therapy: Evidence-Based and Other Effective Treatments and Techniques* (Hoboken, N.J.: John Wiley & Sons, 2009), 337.

28. John F. DeMartini, *From Stress to Success—in Just 31 Days!* (Carlsbad, Calif.: Hay House, 2009), 6.

29. Sarah Ward, "Practical Approaches to Remediate Executive Function Deficits," paper presented at Treating Students K–12: Clinicians and Educators Working Together, Harvard CME Course, Boston, 2009.

30. Time Timer Web page, www.timetimer.com.

31. Ward, "Practical Approaches to Remediate Executive Function Deficits."

32. Karen Janowski, "ReThinking: Assignment Notebooks," July 27, 2011, EdTech Solutions, http://teachingeverystudent.blogspot.com/2011/07/rethinking-assignment-notebooks.html.

33. Tony Attwood, "Should Children with Autistic Spectrum Disorders Be Exempted from Doing Homework?" n.d., Tony Attwood Web page, www.tonyattwood.com.au/index.php?option=com_content&view=article&id=76:should-children-with-autistic-spectrum-disorders-be-exempted-from-doing-homework&catid=45:archived-resource-papers&Itemid=181.

34. Vincent Mark Durand, *Severe Behavior Problems: A Functional Communication Training Approach* (New York: Guilford Press, 1990).

35. Mary Sue Williams and Sherry Shellenberger, *How Does Your Engine Run? A Leader's Guide to the Alert Program for Self-Regulation* (Albuquerque: TherapyWorks, Inc., 1996); Kari Dunn Buron, "The Incredible 5 Point Scale," n.d., www.5pointscale.com/; Philip C. Kendall, *Cognitive-Behavioral Therapy for Anxious Children: Therapist Manual* (Ardmore, Pa.: Workbook Pub., 2006); Kurt A. Freeman and Elizabeth T. Dexter-Mazza, "Using Self-Monitoring with an Adolescent with Disruptive Classroom Behavior," *Behavior Modification* 28, no. 3 (2004).

36. Buron, "The Incredible 5-Point Scale"; Kendall, *Cognitive-Behavioral Therapy for Anxious Children*; Williams and Shellenberger, *How Does Your Engine Run?*

37. Philip C. Kendall, *Coping Cat Workbook* (Ardmore, Pa.: Workbook Pub., 2006).

38. Douglas A. Bernstein, Thomas D. Borkovec, and Holly Hazlett-Stevens, *New Directions in Progressive Relaxation Training: A Guidebook for Helping Professionals* (Westport, Conn.: Praeger, 2000).

39. Alex Smith-Michaels, "Emotional Regulation," paper presented at the Asperger Syndrome: Connections Conference, Marlboro, Ma., 2010.

40. Kendall, *Cognitive-Behavioral Therapy for Anxious Children*, 32.

41. Drewes, *Blending Play Therapy with Cognitive Behavioral Therapy*.

42. Elisa Gagnon, *Power Cards: Using Special Interests to Motivate Children and Youth with Asperger Syndrome and Autism* (Shawnee Mission, Kan.: Autism Asperger Pub., 2002).

43. Madonna Tucker and Jeff Sigafoos, "Use of Noncontingent Reinforcement in the Treatment of Challenging Behavior," *Behavior Modification* 22, no. 4 (1998).

44. This is referred to as *behavior shaping*. For more information, see John O. Cooper, Timothy E. Heron, and William L. Heward, *Applied Behavior Analysis* (Upper Saddle River, N.J.: Pearson/Merrill Prentice Hall, 2007).

Chapter 4

1. Although whole-class rewards are a useful incentive for many students and cultivate a positive classroom environment, we have found that children with oppositional behavior who are held to the same standards as other students often fail. This can make the students become bitter and less invested in following rules because they perceive the teacher as unfair. The "Good Behavior Game" is an example of a whole-class preventive intervention (Sheppard G. Kellam, John Reid, and Robert L. Balster, "Effects of a Universal Classroom Behavior Program in First and Second Grades on Young Adult Problem Outcomes," *Drug and Alcohol Dependence* 95, Suppl. 1 [2008]).

2. Heather J. Walter, Karen Gouze, and Karen G. Lim, "Teachers' Beliefs About Mental Health Needs in Inner City Elementary Schools," *Journal of the American Academy of Child & Adolescent Psychiatry* 45, no. 1 (2006).

3. Ibid.

4. Minna Hämäläinen and Lea Pulkkinen, "Problem Behavior As a Precursor of Male Criminality," *Development and Psychopathology* 8, no. 2 (1996).

5. Lee Kern and Nathan H. Clemens, "Antecedent Strategies to Promote Appropriate Classroom Behavior," *Psychology in the Schools* 44, no. 1 (2007).

6. Kevin S. Sutherland et al., "Examining the Influence of Teacher Behavior and Classroom Context on the Behavioral and Academic Outcomes for Students with Emotional or Behavioral Disorders," *Journal of Special Education* 41, no. 4 (2008).

7. Raymond J. Waller, *Fostering Child and Adolescent Mental Health in the Classroom* (Thousand Oaks, Calif.: Sage Publications, 2006), 162.

8. Alan E. Kazdin and Carlo Rotella, *The Kazdin Method for Parenting the Defiant Child: With No Pills, No Therapy, No Contest of Wills* (Boston: Houghton Mifflin, 2008).

9. Adrian Angold and E. Jane Costello, "Toward Establishing an Empirical Basis for the Diagnosis of Oppositional Defiant Disorder," *Journal of the American Academy of Child & Adolescent*

Psychiatry 35, no. 9 (1996); Emily Simonoff et al., "The Virginia Twin Study of Adolescent Behavioral Development: Influences of Age, Sex, and Impairment on Rates of Disorder," *Archives of General Psychiatry* 54, no. 9 (1997).

10. Robert J. McMahon and Rex L. Forehand, *Helping the Noncompliant Child: Family-Based Treatment for Oppositional Behavior* (New York: Guilford Press, 2003), 1–3.
11. Larry M. Kalb and Rolf Loeber, "Child Disobedience and Noncompliance: A Review," *Pediatrics* 111, no. 3 (2003).
12. Hill M. Walker, Geoffrey Colvin, and Elizabeth Ramsey, *Antisocial Behavior in School: Strategies and Best Practices* (Pacific Grove, Calif.: Brooks/Cole, 1995), 13–14.
13. Ross W. Greene, *The Explosive Child: A New Approach for Understanding and Parenting Easily Frustrated, "Chronically Inflexible" Children* (New York: Harper Collins, 1998), 12.
14. Alan T. Sohn and Cathy Grayson, *Parenting Your Asperger Child: Individualized Solutions for Teaching Your Child Practical Skills* (New York: Perigee Book, 2005), 36.
15. Ross W. Greene and J. Stuart Ablon, *Treating Explosive Kids: The Collaborative Problem-Solving Book* (New York: Guilford Press, 2006), 214.
16. Marc S. Atkins et al., "Suspension and Detentions in an Urban, Low-Income School: Punishment or Reward?" *Journal of Abnormal Child Psychology* 30, no. 4 (2002).
17. Walker, Colvin, and Ramsey, *Antisocial Behavior in School*, 190.
18. Friedrich Losel and Andreas Beelmann, "Effects of Child Skills Training in Preventing Antisocial Behavior: A Systematic Review of Randomized Evaluations," *Annals of the American Academy of Political and Social Science* 587 (2003).
19. Walker, Colvin, and Ramsey, *Antisocial Behavior in School*, 219–224.
20. BrainPOP (www.brainpop.com/) is one Web site that has fun, animated educational videos.
21. Spencer J. Salend and Shawna Sylvestre, "Understanding and Addressing Oppositional and Defiant Classroom Behaviors," *Teaching Exceptional Children* 37, no. 6 (2005).
22. Kazdin and Rotella, *The Kazdin Method*, 45–46.
23. Walker, Colvin, and Ramsey, *Antisocial Behavior in School*, 231–235.
24. Robert C. Pianta and Megan W. Stuhlman, "Teacher-Child Relationships and Children's Success in the First Years of School," *School Psychology Review* 33, no. 3 (2004).
25. Robert C. Pianta, Michael S. Steinberg, and Kristin B. Rollins, "The First Two Years Of School: Teacher-Child Relationships and Deflections in Children's Classroom Adjustment," *Development and Psychopathology* 7, no. 2 (1995).
26. Sondra H. Birch and Gary W. Ladd, "Children's Interpersonal Behaviors and the Teacher-Child Relationship," *Developmental Psychology* 34, no. 5 (1998).
27. Walker, Colvin, and Ramsey, *Antisocial Behavior in School*, 117–119.
28. Charles D. Appelstein, *No Such Thing As a Bad Kid: Understanding and Responding to the Challenging Behavior of Troubled Children and Youth* (Weston, Mass.: Gifford School, 1998).
29. Charles D. Appelstein, *The Gus Chronicles: Reflections from an Abused Kid* (Salem, N.H.: Appelstein Professional Services, 1994), 12.
30. Pianta and Stuhlman, "Teacher-Child Relationships."
31. *Cambridge Dictionary Online*, s.v. "power struggle," http://dictionary.cambridge.org/dictionary/british/power-struggle.

32. Kristine Jolivette et al., "Naturally Occurring Opportunities for Preschool Children With or Without Disabilities to Make Choices," *Education & Treatment of Children (ETC)* 25, no. 4 (2002); Kristine Jolivette, Janine Peck Stichter, and Katherine M. McCormick, "Making Choices—Improving Behavior—Engaging in Learning," *Teaching Exceptional Children* 34, no. 3 (2002); Lee Kern et al., "Choice As an Intervention to Improve Behavior: A Review of the Literature," *Journal of Behavioral Education* 8, no. 2 (1998); Michelle L. Ramsey et al., "Using Choice to Increase Time On-Task, Task-Completion, and Accuracy for Students with Emotional/Behavior Disorders in a Residential Facility," *Education and Treatment of Children* 33, no. 1 (2010): 1–21; Katherine B. Green, Nicole M. Mays, and Kristine Jolivette, "Making Choices: A Proactive Way to Improve Behaviors for Young Children with Challenging Behaviors," *Beyond Behavior* 20, no. 1 (2011); Phillip S. Strain et al., "Keys to Being Successful When Confronted with Challenging Behaviors," in *Young Exceptional Children: Practical Ideas for Addressing Challenging Behaviors*, ed. Susan Sandall and Michaelene Ostrosky, Monograph series (Denver: Division for Early Childhood of the Council for Exceptional Children, 1999); Karrie A. Shogren et al., "The Effect of Choice-Making as an Intervention for Problem Behavior: A Meta-Analysis," *Journal of Positive Behavior Interventions* 6, no. 4 (2004).

33. Kazdin and Rotella, *The Kazdin Method*.

34. Sarah Ward, "Practical Approaches to Remediate Executive Function Deficits," paper presented at the Treating Students K–12: Clinicians and Educators Working Together, Harvard CME Course, Boston, 2009.

35. Steven E. Gutstein and Rachelle K. Sheely, *Relationship Development Intervention with Young Children: Social and Emotional Development Activities for Asperger Syndrome, Autism, PDD and NLD* (London: Jessica Kingsley, 2002), 41–51.

36. John O. Cooper, Timothy E. Heron, and William L. Heward, *Applied Behavior Analysis* (Upper Saddle River, N.J.: Pearson/Merrill Prentice Hall, 2007).

37. H. K. Reavis et al., *Utah's BEST Project: Behavioral and Educational Strategies for Teachers* (Salt Lake City: Utah State Office of Education, 1993).

38. Walker, Colvin, and Ramsey, *Antisocial Behavior in School*.

39. Walker, Colvin, and Ramsey, *Antisocial Behavior in School*, 65.

40. Cooper, Heron, and Heward, *Applied Behavior Analysis*, 276.

41. Allan Beane's "Good for You!" certificate provides an example of a concrete way to give students positive feedback for their behavior intermittently (Allan L. Beane, *The Bully Free Classroom: Over 100 Tips and Strategies for Teachers K–8* [Minneapolis: Free Spirit Pub., 2005], 68–69).

42. Madonna Tucker and Jeff Sigafoos, "Use of Noncontingent Reinforcement in the Treatment of Challenging Behavior," *Behavior Modification* 22, no. 4 (1998).

43. Crisis Prevention Institute, *Instructor Manual for the Nonviolent Crisis Intervention® Training Program* (Milwaukee: Crisis Prevention Institute, 2008).

44. Ibid.

45. Ibid.

46. Walker, Colvin, and Ramsey, *Antisocial Behavior in School*, 126.

47. Greene, *The Explosive Child*.

Chapter 5

1. Kenneth W. Merrell, *Helping Students Overcome Depression and Anxiety: A Practical Guide* (New York: Guilford Press, 2008); Barbara D. Ingersoll and Sam Goldstein, *Lonely, Sad, and Angry: A Parent's Guide to Depression in Children and Adolescents* (New York: Doubleday, 1995).

2. Shashi K. Bhatia and Subhash C. Bhatia, "Childhood and Adolescent Depression," *American Family Physician* 75, no. 1 (2007).

3. National Institute of Mental Health, "How Do Children and Adolescents Experience Depression?" in *Depression*, NIH Publication 08 3561, 2008 (Bethesda, Md.: National Institute of Health, 2007; revised 2008), http://wwwapps.nimh.nih.gov/health/publications/depression/nimhdepression.pdf, 9.

4. In a population-based study, 66 percent of depressed adolescents had not used any treatment services (J. M. Rey et al., "Depression among Australian adolescents," *Medical Journal of Australia* 175, no. 1 [2001]).

5. Brian L. Brooks et al., "Identifying Cognitive Problems in Children and Adolescents with Depression Using Computerized Neuropsychological Testing," *Applied Neuropsychology* 17, no. 1 (2010).

6. Joseph Rey and Boris Birmaher, *Treating Child and Adolescent Depression* (Philadelphia: Wolters Kluwer Health/Lippincott Williams & Wilkins, 2009), 19.

7. Nancy Rappaport et al., "Treating Pediatric Depression in Primary Care: Coping with the Patients' Blue Mood and the FDA's Black Box," *Journal of Pediatrics* 148, no. 5 (2006).

8. American Academy of Child and Adolescent Psychiatry, "Practice Parameter for the Assessment and Treatment of Children and Adolescents with Depressive Disorders," *Journal of the American Academy of Child & Adolescent Psychiatry* 46, no. 11 (2007).

9. This list includes some of the items in National Association of School Psychologists, "Times of Tragedy: Preventing Suicide in Troubled Children and Youth, Part I," 2001, www.nasponline.org/resources/crisis_safety/suicidept1_general.aspx.

10. Richard M. Glass, "Fluoxetine, Cognitive-Behavioral Therapy, and Their Combination for Adolescents with Depression: Treatment for Adolescents with Depression Study (TADS) Randomized Controlled Trial," *Journal of Pediatrics* 146, no. 1 (2005).

11. Philip C. Kendall, *Cognitive-Behavioral Therapy for Anxious Children: Therapist Manual* (Ardmore, Pa.: Workbook Pub., 2006), 32

12. Kenneth W. Merrell, *Helping Students Overcome Depression and Anxiety*, 116; David D Burns, *Feeling Good: The New Mood Therapy Revised and Updated* (New York: Avon, 1999).

13. John S. March and Karen Mulle, *OCD in Children and Adolescents: A Cognitive-Behavioral Treatment Manual* (New York: Guilford Press, 1998). Charlie Appelstein, "Cues to Use," Child Care Training, Consultation, and Publications, Web site, n.d., www.charliea.com/cuestouse.html, recommends using cues or "one-line raps" to help students create and practice coping thoughts—he suggests that the cues are more successful when they rhyme and are rhythmic, humorous, and repeated often. Some of his ideas follow. *Social cues:* "Take turns when you talk; if you don't the kids will walk." "Stop and listen, cause you don't know what you're missing." *Anti-anxiety rap:* "Don't be in a hurry to worry." *Encouragement and affirmations:* "I'm smart. It's in my heart." "I can make it if I choose. Only I can make me lose." *Anger control:* "NBD . . .

easy as 1-2-3! NBD . . . easier than 1-2-3! NO BIG DEAL!" "Stay in control, that's the goal. I can, I will, I gotta chill." *Organization and distractibility cues:* "Don't move all over the place; sit and learn with a happy face." "No need to groan; I can start [do it] on my own. Sit and relax, learn to the max!"

14. Elisa Gagnon, *Power Cards: Using Special Interests to Motivate Children and Youth with Asperger Syndrome and Autism* (Shawnee Mission, Kan.: Autism Asperger Pub., 2002).

15. James Hardy, "Speaking Clearly: A Critical Review of the Self-Talk Literature," *Psychology of Sport and Exercise* 7, no. 1 (2006): 81–97; The Free Dictionary, http://medical-dictionary.thefreedictionary.com/self-talk.

16. One tool that is available is SymTrend. See SymTrend home page, 2010, www.symtrend.com.

17. Sarah J. Jerstad et al., "Prospective Reciprocal Relations Between Physical Activity and Depression in Female Adolescents," *Journal of Consulting & Clinical Psychology* 78, no. 2 (2010); Catherine Rothon et al., "Physical Activity and Depressive Symptoms in Adolescents: A Prospective Study," *BMC Medicine* 8 (2010).

18. Robert C. Pianta, *Enhancing Relationships Between Children and Teachers* (Washington, DC: American Psychological Association, 2000).

19. James E. Carr, Jamie M. Severtson, and Tracy L. Lepper, "Noncontingent Reinforcement Is an Empirically Supported Treatment for Problem Behavior Exhibited by Individuals with Developmental Disabilities," *Research in Developmental Disabilities* 30, no. 1 (2009).

20. Doug Lemov, *Teach Like a Champion: 49 Techniques That Put Students on the Path to College* (San Francisco: Jossey-Bass, 2010).

21. Martin E. P. Seligman, *Helplessness: On Depression, Development, and Death* (New York: Freeman, 1996).

22. Sarah Ward, "Practical Approaches to Remediate Executive Function Deficits," paper presented at the Treating Students K–12: Clinicians and Educators Working Together, Harvard CME course, Boston, 2009.

23. Merrell, *Helping Students Overcome Depression and Anxiety,* 128–131.

24. Seligman, *Helplessness: on Depression, Development, and Death.*

25. A. VanDerHeyden et al., "Comparison of Within-Stimulus and Extra-Stimulus Prompts to Increase Targeted Play Behaviors in an Inclusive Early Intervention Program," *Behavior Analyst Today* 3, no. 2 (2002); M. Chesnut, P. N. Williamson, and J. E. Morrow, "The Use of Visual Cues to Teach Receptive Skills to Children with Severe Auditory Discrimination Deficits," *Behavior Analyst Today* 4, no. 2 (2003).

Chapter 6

1. Elkovitch and colleagues note that in community studies, parents reported that 3 percent or less of children exhibited behaviors that are considered "non-normative or problematic" and are "intrusive, aggressive, or more imitative of sexual behavior, such as attempted intercourse, oral-genital contact, masturbating with an object and inserting objects into the vagina" (Natasha Elkovitch et al., "Understanding Child Sexual Behavior Problems: A Developmental Psychopathology Framework," *Clinical Psychology Review* 29, no. 7 [2009]).

2. Ibid.

3. Mark Chaffin, "Our Minds Are Made Up—Don't Confuse Us with the Facts: Commentary on Policies Concerning Children with Sexual Behavior Problems and Juvenile Sex Offenders," *Child Maltreatment* 13, no. 2 (2008); Friedrich et al., "Sexual Behavior Problems in Preteen Children," *Annals of the New York Academy of Sciences* 989, no. 1 (2003).

4. Association for the Treatment of Sexual Abusers, "Report of the Task Force on Children with Sexual Behavior Problems," Beaverton, Ore., 2006.

5. Friedrich et al., "Sexual Behavior Problems in Preteen Children"; Toni Cavanagh Johnson, "Assessment of Sexual Behavior Problems in Preschool and Latency-Aged Children," in *Child and Adolescent Psychiatric Clinics of North America*, ed. A. Yates (Philadelphia: Saunders, 1993).

6. Douglas Davies, *Child Development: A Practitioner's Guide* (New York: Guilford Press); American Academy of Pediatrics, "Sexual Behaviors in Children," 2005, Web page, www.aap.org/pubserv/ PSVpreview/pages/behaviorchart.html; Johnson, "Sexual Behavior Problems in Preschool and Latency-Aged Children."

7. Teachers at a nursery school reported that only 5 percent of children were observed self-stimulating, whereas 43 percent of the parents reported that their children engaged in genital touching (F. Lopez Sanchez, A. Del Campo, and V. Guijo, "Pre-Pubertal Sexuality," *Sexologies* 11 (2002); IngBeth Larsson and Carl Goran Svedin, "Teachers' and Parents' Reports on 3- to 6-Year-Old Children's Sexual Behavior: A Comparison," *Child Abuse & Neglect* 26, no. 3 (2002).

8. William N. Friedrich, "Behavioral Manifestations of Child Sexual Abuse," *Child Abuse & Neglect* 22, no. 6 (1998).

9. Elkovitch et al., "Understanding Child Sexual Behavior Problems"; Friedrich et al., "Sexual Behavior Problems in Preteen Children."

10. In studies in Europe, parents reported that anywhere from 55 percent to 75 percent of their children engaged in "doctor games" (Larsson and Svedin, "Teachers' and Parents' Reports"; Lopez Sanchez, Del Campo, and Guijo, "Pre-Pubertal Sexuality."

11. Association for the Treatment of Sexual Abusers, "Report of the Task Force," 3.

12. Elkovitch et al., "Understanding Child Sexual Behavior Problems," found that 42 to 94 percent of adults recalled sexual experiences as a child when asked by researchers.

13. Association for the Treatment of Sexual Abusers, "Report of the Task Force," 3.

14. J. Silovsky and B. L. Bonner, "Sexual Behavior Problems," in *Encyclopedia of Clinical Child and Pediatric Psychology*, ed. T. H. Ollendick and C. S. Schroeder (New York: Kluwer Press, 2003).

15. Ibid.

16. Elkovitch et al., "Understanding Child Sexual Behavior Problems."

17. National Childhood Traumatic Stress Network, "Understanding and Coping with Sexual Behavior Problems in Children," April 2009, www.nctsnet.org/nctsn_assets/pdfs/caring/sexualbehaviorproblems.pdf ; Elkovitch et al., "Understanding Child Sexual Behavior Problems."

18. Barbara Geller et al., "Psychosocial Functioning in a Prepubertal and Early Adolescent Bipolar Disorder Phenotype," *Journal of the American Academy of Child & Adolescent Psychiatry* 39, no. 12 (2000).

19. Association for the Treatment of Sexual Abusers, "Report of the Task Force," 2.

20. Patricia Romanowski Bashe and Barbara L. Kirby, *The Oasis Guide to Asperger Syndrome: Advice, Support, Insight, and Inspiration* (New York: Crown Publishers, 2005), 413.

21. Pamela B. Tanguay, *Nonverbal Learning Disabilities at School : Educating Students with NLD, Asperger Syndrome and Related Conditions* (London: Jessica Kingsley, 2002).

22. Ibid.

23. Michelle Garcia Winner, *Thinking About You, Thinking About Me* (San Jose: Think Social, 2007), 152–172.

24. Karen Levine, Naomi Chedd, and Deborah Bauch, "The Social-Affective Diet: The Launch of a New Concept," *Autism Spectrum Quarterly* 2009.

25. Judith A. Cohen, conversation with authors, July 20, 2011.For further discussion, see Elkovitch et al., "Understanding Child Sexual Behavior Problems."

26. Johnson, "Sexual Behavior Problems in Preschool and Latency-Aged Children."

27. Judith A. Cohen, Esther Deblinger, and Anthony P. Mannarino, *Treating Trauma and Traumatic Grief in Children and Adolescents* (New York: Guilford Press, 2006), 214.

28. Silovsky and Bonner, "Sexual Behavior Problems."

29. Cohen, Deblinger, and Mannarino, *Trauma and Traumatic Grief*, 12.

30. Massachusetts Advocates for Children: Trauma and Learning Policy Initiative, "Helping Traumatized Children Learn," Boston, 2005. See also Cohen, Deblinger, and Mannarino, *Treating Trauma and Traumatic Grief*.

31. Carol Gray, *The New Social Story Book* (Arlington, Tex.: Future Horizons, 2010).

32. Adapted from Marklyn P. Champagne and Leslie Walker Hirsch, "Circles Curriculum," video program, n.d., James Stanfield Company, Santa Barbara, Calif.

33. Mary Sue Williams and Sherry Shellenberger, *How Does Your Engine Run? A Leader's Guide to the Alert Program for Self-Regulation* (Albuquerque: TherapyWorks, Inc., 1996)

34. Bruce D. Perry and Ronnie Pollard, "Homeostasis, Stress, Trauma, and Adaptation: A Neurodevelopmental View of Childhood Trauma," *Child and Adolescent Psychiatric Clinics of North America* 7, no. 1 (1998).

35. John O. Cooper, Timothy E. Heron, and William L. Heward, *Applied Behavior Analysis* (Upper Saddle River, N.J.: Pearson/Merrill Prentice Hall, 2007), 392–395.

36. Gray, *The New Social Story Book*.

Chapter 7

1. Suggestions in this list are adapted from Anne Brunette, "Self-Care for Teachers," Doll and Associates, Fond du Lac, Wis., 2005, www.dollandassociates.com/sft184/selfcareforteachers.pdf; John Norcross and Athena A. Drewes, "Self-Care for Child Therapists: Leaving It at the Office," in *Blending Play Therapy with Cognitive Behavioral Therapy: Evidence-Based and Other Effective Treatments and Techniques*, ed. Athena A. Drewes (Hoboken, N.J.: John Wiley & Sons, 2009).

2. Sara Lawrence-Lightfoot, *Worlds Apart: Relationships Between Families and Schools* (New York: Basic Books, 1978).

3. Gerald R. Patterson and Magda Stouthamer-Loeber, "The Correlation of Family Management Practices and Delinquency," *Child Development* 55, no. 4 (1984).

4. The suicide rate for children ages five to fourteen 2007 was 0.5 per 100,000, compared with an overall population rate of 11.5 per 100,000 (Amerian Foundation for Suicide Prevention, "Facts and Figures: By Age," www.afsp.org/index.cfm?fuseaction=home.viewPage& page_id=04EB7CD1-9EED-9712-89C9540AFCB44481).

Acknowledgments

To children who may struggle to show their potential; this is to acknowledge there is always help.

To teachers and all school-based professionals, whose dedicated caring, understanding, and commitment can turn the tide for struggling students.

To Nancy Walser, who had persistent optimism and could see the diamond in the rock before we could. Her editing and deep questions forced us to find clarity. To Sarah Reinfeld for her tireless effort and organizational abilities and skill. To Lila Flavin for taking the time to decipher what we were trying to say and using her keen mind to make this more coherent. To Andy Clark, with amazement that you found the time to give critical feedback with two toddler twins. To Amy Stein, thank you for your careful read under such a tight deadline. For Laura Gaugh, thank you for your meticulous editing and conceptual input. For Jeanne, a true comrade and colleague who gave so much time and insightful guidance.

To Linda Kelly, Peter Chubinsky, Nicole Johnson, Sandra DeJong, Ana Fonseca, Suzanne Vinnes, Jill Parkin, Patricia West, Susan Doherty, and Lois Flaherty for reviewing chapters and providing such helpful feedback. To Karen Levine, Maria Sauzier, and Judy Cohen for giving critical feedback on the chapter on sexualized behavior; we needed your expertise.

Nancy says: To the staffs of the Cambridge Public Schools and Cambridge Health Alliance and the students and families of Cambridge—this community sustains my effort. For Jay Burke, an amazing mentor. To my husband Colin, who has supported me, making me strong. For this, I am so grateful.

Jessica says: To my parents—I am eternally grateful for your unconditional love, support, and advice and for instilling in me the conviction of responsibility and concern for others. To my entire family—thank you. You are my favorite people and my closest friends. To Will and Brendan for being a source of joy and pride. To the Newton and Cambridge public school systems, whose teachers, special educators, assistants, behavior analysts, mental health professionals, parents, and students have all shared so much of themselves with me, patiently guiding me to grow and learn.

About the Authors

Jessica Minahan, MEd, BCBA, is a board-certified behavior analyst (BCBA) and special educator who is currently employed in the Newton, Massachusetts, public school system as a district-wide behavior analyst, where she does direct consulting for administrators, teachers, and support staff. She also consults to an in-house, forty-five-day stabilization program for Newton K–12 public school students who are in crisis. Jessica has more than ten years of experience with students exhibiting challenging behavior in both urban and suburban public school systems. She specializes in providing staff training and creating behavior intervention plans for students who demonstrate explosive and unsafe behavior, as well as for students with emotional and behavioral disabilities, high-functioning autism, and Asperger syndrome. She holds a BS in intensive special education from Boston University and a dual master's degree in special education and elementary education from Wheelock College. She has a certificate of graduate study (CGS) in teaching children with autism from University of Albany and received her BCBA training from Northeastern University. She has been an instructor for the Severe Disabilities Department at Lesley University and is a sought-after public speaker on subjects ranging from effective interventions for students with anxiety to supporting hard-to-reach students in full-inclusion public school settings. For more information about Jessica Minahan please visit http://jessica-minahan.com/.

Nancy Rappaport, MD, is the Director of School Programs at the Cambridge Health Alliance and an Assistant Professor of Psychiatry at Harvard Medical School. Dr. Rappaport has dedicated her career to improving the lives of children by constructing effective support for troubled youth who are in need of vital access to critical mental health services and who often have difficulty connecting with the services they require. She has created a case evaluation model for safety assessments of aggressive students. She oversees and coordinates mental health services at Cambridge Health Alliance's four school-based health centers in Cambridge, Somerville, and Everett, Massachusetts. A board-certified child and adolescent psychiatrist, Nancy also teaches undergraduates, medical students, and residents about child development and supervises child psychiatry fellows in local schools. In addition to publishing many journal articles, she is the award-winning author of *In Her Wake: A Child Psychiatrist Explores the Mystery of Her Mother's Suicide* (2009). In 2011, she received the Sidney Berman Award for School-Based Study and Intervention for Learning Disorders and Mental Health from the American Academy of Child and Adolescent Psychiatry. Dr. Rappaport is a graduate of Princeton University and Tufts University School of Medicine. For more information about Nancy Rappaport please visit http://nancyrappaport.com/.

Index

ABC (antecedent, behavior, consequence)
  charts, 32–35
  antecedents and consequences, 69, 137,
    175
  consequences, 98–99, 175
  sexualized behavior, 171–175
ABC data, 34–35
  anxiety, 52
  consequence patterns, 40
  inappropriate behavior, 66
  sample, 203–204
  third-grade student with anxiety, 67–68
  withdrawn behavior, 136
aberrant behavior and attention, 17
academic areas and anxiety, 76
acceptable behavior, 175
accommodations, 3–4, 35–37
  alerting strategies, 142, 144
  anxiety-related behavior, 69–82, 88–90
  curriculum, 36, 37, 73–76, 88, 103–104,
    123–124, 139–140, 153
  environment, 36, 69, 88–89, 123, 137–
    138, 153, 175–177, 188
  executive functioning, 36–37, 70–73, 88,
    103, 123, 138–139, 153
  gradual reduction, 35
  interaction strategies, 124–125, 189
  oppositional behavior, 100–105, 123–124
  proprioceptive exercises, 142, 144
  replacement behaviors, 88, 124, 154, 188

response strategies, 189
  self-monitoring, 89, 124, 141–142, 154,
    178–180, 188
  self-regulating, 89, 124, 141–142, 154,
    178–180, 188
  sexualized behavior, 175–180, 188
  skill development, 36–37
  underdeveloped skills, 77–82, 88–89,
    104–105, 123–124, 140–141, 154,
    177–178, 188
  withdrawn behavior, 137–144, 153–154
ADD (attention deficit disorder)
  oppositional behavior, 93–94
  sexualized behavior, 165
ADHD (attention deficit hyperactivity
  disorder), 93
adjustment disorder with depressed mood,
  131
administrators supporting teacher about
  challenging behavior, 193–194
aggressiveness, pattern of, 9
alerting strategies, 142, 144
Alert Program, 178, 180
all-or-nothing thinking, 95, 133
alternative lunch, 64–65
  depression, 138
  oppositional behavior, 101
alternative recess, 64–65
  oppositional behavior, 101
Amazon.com Web site, 81

American Psychiatric Association, 48, 93,
        130–131
"A Method to Integrate Descriptive
        and Experimental Field Studies at
        the Level of Data and Empirical
        Concepts," 33, 68, 99, 136, 173–174
antecedent, behavior, consequence format.
        See ABC (antecedent, behavior,
        consequence) format
antecedent analysis, 3–4, 32–35
    anxiety-related behavior, 66–69
    oppositional behavior, 97–100
    sexualized behavior, 171–175
    withdrawn behavior, 135–137
antecedents, 32–35
    ABC chart, 175
    accommodating, 28
    analyzing, 52
    anxiety, 69
    external triggers, 172
    managing, 28–29, 83
    minimizing, 28
    patterns, 23, 33, 35, 66, 98, 135, 172
anti-depressant, 132
anxiety
    ABC notes, 52
    academic performance, 48, 61, 62, 76
    antecedents, 52, 59
    anxiety-reducing breaks, 60–63, 62
    Asperger's syndrome, 47
    avoidance behaviors, 54–55
    behavior patterns, 52–54
    body reactions to feelings, 78
    calming box, 80
    chronically oppositional profiles, 49
    control and, 51, 54–55, 60
    coping, 59
    curriculum, 73–76
    definition of, 45, 51, 82
    depression, 47
    diagnoses, 48
    difficulty patterns, 50

early intervention, 51
escape motivation, 66
executive functioning deficits, 70–73
feelings of failure, 61
frustration tolerance, 49
GAD (generalized anxiety disorder), 48
gradually introducing demands, 60
hidden and breaking point, 44–45
highly disabling, 48–49
homework, 76
identifying, 50, 77
inconsistent behavior, 52, 66
increased rigidity, 54–55
inflexible thinking, 70
interacting one-on-one with students, 62
irrationality, 49
low self-esteem, 61
management, 30
managing emotions, 49
managing social demands, 64–65
nonverbal language disability, 47
no- or low-demand situations, 60
novel events or unexpected changes, 53
OCD (obsessive-compulsive disorder), 48
oppositional behavior, 92
organization, 72–73
overgeneralized, 169
panic disorder, 48
phobias, 48
physical reactions signaling, 78
power cards, 81–82
predictability and, 54–55
previewing, 76
PTSD (post-traumatic stress disorder), 48
reading room, 70
refusing to follow directions, 50
reintroducing demands, 59
relationships, 82
rewards, 61
SAD (separation anxiety disorder), 48
scheduled breaks, 69–70
self-consciousness, 82

self-defeating thoughts, 81
self-esteem building, 82–83
self-monitoring, 84
self-regulating, 59, 77
setting students up for success, 58–60
sexual abuse, 167, 169
sexualized behavior, 159
skewed sense of time passing, 71–72
social, 70
social deficits, 47
social interactions, 49
social phobia, 48
spelling, 74
stress, 49, 73–74
structure and, 53–54
students rating themselves, 80
sudden change in behavior, 51
supportive responses, 51
symptoms, 45
talking back, 50
thought-stopping instruction, 81
time management strategies, 71–72
timers, 71
transitions, 55–58
trauma, 131
tunnel vision, 70
underdeveloped skills, 77–82
unstructured times, 53, 60
verbal working memory, 48
visual schedules, 72
withdrawn behavior, 128
word processing, 74
anxiety disorders
    behavioral attributes, 49–50
    common features, 45
    GAD (generalized anxiety disorder), 45
    OCD (obsessive-compulsive disorder), 47
    panic disorder, 47
    PTSD (post-traumatic stress disorder),
        46–47
    separation anxiety disorder, 45–46
    social anxiety disorder, 46

anxiety-reducing breaks, 60–63, 65
anxiety-related behaviors, 3, 32, 41, 43–89
    accommodations, 69–82, 88–89
    antecedent analysis, 66–69
    attributes, 49–50
    avoidance behavior, 44
    behavior intervention plan, 87–90
    diagnosis of, 50
    executive functioning resources, 206
    FAIR Plan (functional hypothesis, ac-
        commodations, interaction strategies,
        and responses strategies), 65–84
    flexible thinking resources, 205
    functional hypothesis, 66–69, 87
    inappropriate behavior, 44
    interaction strategies, 82–83, 89
    intervention importance, 48–49
    negative thinking resources, 205–206
    outbursts, 44
    response strategies, 83–84, 89–90
    self-monitoring resources, 205–206
    self-regulating resources, 205–206
    social skills resources, 206
Appelstein, Charlie, 106
*Applying Behavior-Analysis Procedures
    with Children and Youth* (Sulzer-
    Azaroff and Mayer), 33, 99, 136, 173, 174
appropriate behavior
    choice, 109
    escaping demand or situation through, 77
    reinforcing, 23, 29, 111–113
    rewarding, 61
    rules about, 163–164
arguing
    with teachers, 95
    teaching student about, 118
Asperger's syndrome
    co-occurring anxiety, 47
    counterintuitive behavior, 9–10
    humor, 113
    social deficits, 162
assessment of behavior, 12

attention, 16–19
   oppositional behavior, 96, 98, 111–112
   predictable, 181
   reinforcing behavior, 23
   sexualized behavior, 159, 167
   successful ways of getting, 164
attention deficit disorder. *See* ADD
   (attention deficit disorder)
attention deficit hyperactivity disorder. *See*
   ADHD (attention deficit hyperactivity
   disorder)
attention-motivated behaviors, 16–19, 125
   abnormal or problematic, 17
   oppositional behavior, 118
   replacement behaviors, 88
   response strategies, 118
attention span and depression, 138
audio books and e-books Web sites,
   215–216
Ault, Marion H., 33, 68, 99, 136, 173, 174
authority, difficulty with, 108
autism and sensory behavior, 21
autism spectrum disorder and social
   deficits, 162
avoidance behaviors, 50
   anxiety, 54–55
   anxiety-related behavior, 44
   PTSD (post-traumatic stress disorder), 46
   sexual abuse, 167
avoider trap, 81
awareness, 209–210

Baker, Jed, 207, 209
banking time, 145
Bashe, Patricia Romanowski, 78
bathrooms and anxiety, 177
behavioral problems and mental health
   evaluation, 4
behavior incidents
   documenting, 32–35
   duration and frequency reduction, 66

behavior intervention plan, 24
   anxiety-related behavior, 87–90
   oppositional behavior, 122–125
   sexualized behavior, 187–189
   withdrawn behavior, 152–155
behavior management plans, 24–25
behavior modification strategies, 2–3
behavior reinforcement Web sites,
   218–219
behaviors, 7–24, 32–35
   ability to change, 24–25
   antecedent analysis, 52
   anxiety-related, 3, 32, 41, 43–89
   appropriate, 18
   attention function, 16–19
   bookends, 23
   changes in, 51
   communication and, 15–16
   concepts, 13–25
   counterintuitive, 9
   depression, 129
   determining intent or function of, 23
   environments and, 22
   escape-motivated, 19
   failure and, 1
   functional hypothesis, 32–35
   functions, 16–20
   inconsistent patterns, 50, 52
   incremental change, 25
   intent of, 12
   internal or external triggers, 52
   interpreting, 9
   intervention, 10
   key to breaking, 23
   message conveyed by, 15
   motivation behind, 9, 16
   multiple functions simultaneously, 21–22
   oppositional, 3, 32, 41, 91–125
   patterns, 9, 22–24, 32
   positive opposites, 105
   preventing escalation, 58
   problematic, 16

purposeful actions, 15
quickly showing change, 25
recognizing changes in, 51
reinforcing, 23, 29
repetitive, 8, 16, 21
replacement strategy, 10, 12
sensory function, 20–21
sexualized, 3, 32
sudden changes in, 50–51, 82
support for, 4
tangible function, 19
teacher's responses to, 33–34
unclear intent of, 8
underlying causes of misbehavior, 3,
    13–15
withdrawn, 3, 32, 41
Bijou, Sidney W., 33, 68, 99, 136, 173, 174
bipolar depression, 131
bipolar disorder
    hypersexuality, 161
    sexualized comments, 166
Birch, Sondra, 106
*Blending Play Therapy with Cognitive
    Behavioral Therapy: Evidence-Based
    and Other Effective Treatments and
    Techniques* (Drewes), 78
blind spots, 176
bookends of behavior, 23
brain wiring, 13–14
Brantley, Jeffrey, 205
breaks, 100–101
    anxiety-reducing, 65
    classroom space, 69–70
    demand-free, 117
    earning, 117–118
    escape-motivated behavior, 62
    outside classroom, 70
    reinforcing activity, 117
    sexualized behavior, 178
Brooks, Barbara, 210
bullying, 95
Buron, Kari Dunn, 206

calming activities, 220–222
calming box, 80
    oppositional behavior, 102
calm space
    breaks and, 101
    withdrawn behavior, 137–138
Cambridge Dictionary, 108
Cardon, Teresa A., 208
Caselman, Tonia, 207, 210
catastrophizing, 133
"caught being good" certificates, 112
CBT (cognitive behavioral therapy), 78,
    132–134, 138
    thinking traps, 81
challenging behaviors, 8–10
    demonstrating behavioral progress, 192
    emotional and behavioral diagnoses
        criteria, 199
    extra responsibilities with, 193
    family involvement, 196–197
    hope for, 201
    hurting peers, 197–198
    reasons for, 8–12
    stress, 193
    teachers maintaining stamina, 191–193
challenging repetitive questions, 114–115
Champagne, Marklyn P., 210
checklist for students, 74–75
children and mental health problems, 1
Circles Curriculum (Champagne and
    Walker-Hirsch), 210
Circles of Intimacy Curriculum, 177–178
classroom and oppositional students, 92
clinical depression, 129
cliques, 64
cognitive behavioral strategies and
    withdrawn behavior, 133–134
cognitive behavioral therapy. *See* CBT
    (cognitive behavioral therapy)
*Cognitive-Behavioral Therapy for Anxious
    Children: Therapist Manual* (Kendall),
    81

The Cognitive Behavioral Workbook for Anxiety: A Step-by-Step Program (Knaus), 205, 208
"Cognitive Connections" Web site, 206
cognitively inflexible, 94–95
cognitive shifting, 37
Cognitive Therapy Techniques: A Practitioner's Guide (Leahy), 209
Cohen, Judith A., 168, 209
Comic Strip Conversations: Colorful, Illustrated Interactions with Students with Autism and Related Disorders (Gray), 207
communication, behavior form of, 15–16
communication notebook, 196
compulsions, 47
concise language, 82
conduct disorder, 93
conflict relationships with teachers, 38
consequences, 32–35
    ABC chart, 175
    oppositional behavior, 115
    patterns, 33, 135, 172
continuous reinforcement, 112
control
    desire for, 50
    need for, 94
    oppositional behavior, 108
Cook, Julia, 210
Copeland, Mary Ellen, 208
Coping Cat Workbook (Kendall), 205
Coucouvanis, Judith, 208
countdown approach to transitions, 56
counterintuitive behavior, 9–10
criminal sexual offenders, 158
curriculum
    accommodations, 36–37, 73–76, 88, 103–104, 123–124, 139–140, 153
    anxiety, 73–76
    creative and project-based, 140
    delivery, 37
    oppositional behavior, 103–104, 123

supplemental activities, 37
technology and, 104
withdrawn behavior, 139–140, 153

Davies, Amelia, 207
Dawson, P., 206
dealing with anger resources and oppositional behavior, 207–208
Deblinger, Esther, 209
declarative language, 109, 111
delayed gratification, 20
demand-free breaks and noncompliance, 117
depression
    See also withdrawn behavior
    adjustment disorder, 131
    alternative lunch plan, 138
    anti-depressant, 132
    attention span, 138
    behaviors, 129
    biological causes, 130
    bipolar depression, 131
    blaming others pattern, 134
    catastrophizing, 133
    causes, 130–131
    CBT (cognitive behavioral therapy), 132–133
    clinical, 129
    comprehensive evaluation, 132
    co-occurring anxiety, 47
    decreased interests and motivation, 139
    dysthymic disorder, 131
    environmental stressors, 130–131
    exaggerating negative, 146–147
    extra time for assignments, 140
    hidden disability, 128
    humor, 145
    identifying student interests, 139–140
    incapacitating, 130
    initiative, 138
    irritability, 129
    isolating themselves, 144

magnifying negative aspects of situation, 133

negative behavior responses, 150

negative thoughts, 133–134

nonspecific physical ailments, 129

organization, 138

overlooking positive experiences, 146–147

physical exercise, 142

play therapy, 132

positive self-talk, 134

power cards, 134

praise responses, 146

recognizing, 128–134

recurring episodes, 130

relationship building, 144–145

role-playing, 134

seeing things as all-or-nothing, 133

self-critical tendencies, 146

self-fulfilling rejection cycle, 144

showing how they feel, 129

signs, 130

social, 138

social skills, 134

subtypes, 131

suicide risk, 132

therapy, 132

thinking traps, 133, 134

thought stopping, 134

trauma, 131

underdeveloped skills, 140–141

unrecognized and untreated, 129

withdrawn behavior, 128–134

The Depression Workbook (Copeland and McKay), 208

desired behavior, reinforcing, 29

Diagnostic and Statistical Manual of Mental Disorders, 4th ed. (American Psychiatric Association), 48, 93, 130, 131

The Dialectical Behavior Therapy Skills Workbook: Practical DBT Exercises for Learning Mindfulness, Interpersonal Effectiveness, Emotional Regulation & Distress Tolerance (McKay, Wood, and Brantley), 205

disruptive behaviors, 92

  academic demands, 2

  attention, 17

  early intervention, 3, 92

  elementary teachers, 3

  empathy, 15

  managing, 24

  medication, 2

  problems dealing with, 2

  sexualized behavior, 160

distress and sexual abuse, 167

doubting, 47

downtime, 102

Doyle, Conan, 35

Drewes, Athena A., 78

Durand, Mark, 16

Durand, Vincent Mark, 22

dysthymic disorder, 131

Easy Activities for Building Social Skills (Leber), 206

E/BD (emotional and behavioral disturbance), 7

Education & Treatment of Children. See ETC (Education & Treatment of Children)

elementary teachers and disruptive students, 3

emotional and behavioral disability, 13

emotional and behavioral disturbance. *See* E/BD (emotional and behavioral disturbance)

emotional numbing and PTSD (post-traumatic stress disorder), 46

emotional regulation Web sites, 214

emotions, 78

empathy, 15

empowering statements, 82

environment
  accommodations, 36, 69, 88–89, 123,
    137–138, 153, 175–177, 188
  oppositional behavior, 100–102, 123
  scanning and observing, 70
  sexualized behavior, 175–177, 188
  withdrawn behavior, 137–138, 153
environmental triggers, 168–169
escape, 19
  inappropriate behavior, 77
  oppositional behavior, 96, 98
escape-motivated behavior, 19, 125
  anxiety-reducing breaks, 62
  difficulty identifying, 19
  oppositional behavior, 118
  response strategies, 83, 89, 118
  school discipline procedures reinforcing,
    19
  technology, 104
ETC (Education & Treatment of Children),
  110
evidence to dispute negative perceptions,
  148–149
executive functioning
  accommodations, 36–37, 70–73, 88, 103,
    123, 138–139, 153
  anxiety-related behavior resources, 206
  deficits and anxiety, 70–73
  oppositional behavior, 103, 123
  withdrawn behavior, 138–139, 153
executive functioning Web sites, 219
Executive Skills in Children and Adolescents:
  A Practical Guide to Assessment and
  Intervention (Dawson and Guare), 206
expected behavior, 115–116
explosive behavior, 78
The Explosive Child (Greene), 94
external triggers, 168–169, 172

failure and behavioral challenges, 1
fairness, best way to deal with, 198

FAIR Plan (functional hypothesis,
    accommodations, interaction
    strategies, and responses strategies),
    3–5, 27
  accommodations, 35–37
  antecedent analysis, 32–35
  antecedent management, 28–29, 69, 83
  anxiety-related behaviors, 65–84
  changing inappropriate behavior to
    appropriate behavior, 28
  empowering teachers, 40–41
  fairness, 198
  flexible teachers, 28
  functional hypothesis, 32–35
  implementation of, 228
  inappropriate behavior responses, 30–31
  interaction strategies, 38–40
  modifying, 41
  oppositional behavior, 92, 97–119
  practicing, 31–41
  preemptive strategies, 27
  reaction strategy, 27
  reinforcing desired behavior, 29
  replacement behavior, 29
  response strategies, 40–41
  rewarding students, 27
  selecting, 41–42
  self-monitoring sheet, 223–225
  sexualized behavior, 171–183
  time-consuming, 194–195
  underdeveloped skills, 30, 77
  withdrawn behavior, 134
family involvement, 196–197
family violence, 93
Fersch, Ellsworth A., 207
fight-or-flight response, 14
FlagHouse Web site, 81
flexibility, defining, 118
flexible thinking resources and anxiety-
    related behavior, 205
foster care, 93
free literacy tools Web sites, 216

frequent moves, 93

friendship group, 141

frustration, expressing with sexualized behavior, 164

Functional Assessment and Program Development for Problem Behavior: A Practical handbook (O'Neill et al.), 31

functional behavior assessment, 34

functional hypothesis, 3–4
  anxiety-related behavior, 66–69, 87
  behavior, 32–35
  oppositional behavior, 97–100, 122
  sexualized behavior, 171–175, 187
  withdrawn behavior, 135–137, 152

functional hypothesis, accommodations, interaction strategies, and responses strategies. *See* FAIR Plan (functional hypothesis, accommodations, interaction strategies, and responses strategies)

function-matched responses, 40

Fureman, Sasha, 144

Future Horizons Inc., 207, 209

future planning skills, 36–37

GAD (generalized anxiety disorder), 45, 48
  perfectionists, 71

Gagnon, Elisa, 208

Gardner, Luci, 208

generalized anxiety disorder. *See* GAD (generalized anxiety disorder)

Giler, Janet Z., 206

giving demands strategies, 108–111, 125

Goode, Caron B., 209

Goode, Tom, 209

grade school and normative sexual behavior, 159

Gray, Carol, 207

Greene, Ross, 94

Guare, R., 206

habituation, 60

Hamilton-Wenham Regional High School, 207

harassment with sexualized comments or acts, 160

hard-to-reach students behavior, 12

harsh and inconsistent discipline, 93

Hartman, Carrie, 210

Helping Students Overcome Depression and Anxiety: A Practical Guide (Merrell), 79, 81, 208

"Helping Traumatized Children Learn" report, 171

Help Kids Cope with Stress & Trauma: Nurturing Peace and Balance (Goode, Goode, and Russell), 209

The Hidden Curriculum: Practical Solutions for Understanding Unstated Rules in Social Situations (Myles, Trautman, and Schelvan), 206

homework and anxiety, 76

hospitalized students, helping return to school, 200–201

How Does Your Engine Run? A Leader's Guide to the Alert Program for Self-Regulation (Williams and Shellenberger), 206, 207

How to Take the Grrr out of Anger (Verdick and Lisovskis), 207

hugging, 180–181

humor
  Asperger's syndrome, 113
  depression, 145
  oppositional behavior, 113
  withdrawn behavior, 145

hyperarousal, 47

hypersensitivity, 21

hypersexuality, 161

hypervigilance and trauma, 175

hyposensitive, 21

IEPs (individual education programs), 2, 7

IEP teams, 5
imitation and sexualized behavior, 159
"The Importance of Sensory Processing"
    Web page, 144
impulse control
    limited, 11
    sexualized behavior resources, 210
impulsiveness, 95, 158
    blurting out inappropriate things, 165
    inability to control, 166
    interventions, 166
    masturbating, 165
    negative attention, 171
    response strategies, 182–183
    sexualized behavior, 160, 165–167, 182–183
    unstructured time supervision, 166–167
inappropriate behavior
    antecedents, 28–29
    anxiety-related behavior, 44
    attention, 17
    changing to appropriate behavior, 28
    consistent, 17
    escape, 77
    executive functioning deficit, 36
    function of, 32
    instant assessment of, 8–9
    intense dramatic responses, 18
    managing, 25
    patterns, 66
    predictable, 17
    preventing, 31
    recording, 66
    reducing or changing, 25
    regressing to, 30
    removing attention from, 115
    replacement behavior, 30
    responding to, 16, 30–31, 83
    rewards, 20, 61
    underdeveloped skills, 37
incompatible behaviors, 184
inconsistent behavior and anxiety, 52
"The Incredible 5 Point Scale" Web site, 206

individual education programs. *See* IEPs
    (individual education programs)
infants and behavior, 15
inflexible thinking, 94
information seeking repetitive questions,
    114
initiating task, 102
initiative and depression, 138
instruction, child-centered approach to, 37
interaction strategies, 3–4, 38–40
    accommodations, 124–125, 189
    anxiety-related behaviors, 82–83, 89
    concise language, 82
    critical junctures for adding, 38–39
    empowering statements, 82
    evidence disputing negative perceptions,
        148–149
    giving demands strategies, 108–111
    leadership opportunities, 83, 146
    in the moment, 39
    narrating student's experience, 146–147
    noncontingent reinforcement, 82–83
    oppositional behavior, 105–113, 124–125
    positive feedback, 145–146
    promoting cooperation and reducing
        stress, 39
    punishment, 9
    reframing, 148
    reinforcing appropriate behavior,
        111–113
    relationship building, 105–106, 144–145
    self-esteem building, 82–83
    sexualized behavior, 180–181
    strictness, 39
    withdrawn behavior, 144–149, 154–155
intermittent reinforcement, 112
internal triggers, 168–169
interpreting behaviors, 9
interventions
    anxiety-related behaviors, 48–49
    choosing, 32
    early, 51

exposure, 60
impulsive students, 166
long-term effects, 35
low or no demands, 60
unsuccessful, 11
when to discontinue, 35
in-the-moment interaction strategies, 39
intimidation and sexualized comments or
    acts, 160
irritability, 129
Isett, Brian, 210
Isett, Robert D., 210

Jaffe, Amy V., 208
Johnson, David W., 207
Johnson, Roger T., 207
Jolivette, Kristine, 110
Jones, Alanna, 208
Journal of Applied Behavior Analysis, 33,
    68, 99, 136, 173, 174

Kazdin, Alan, 105
Kendall, Philip C., 81, 205
kindergarten teachers, 106
Kirby, Barbara L., 78
Knaus, William J., 205, 208
Korb-Khalsa, Kathy L., 208
Kranowitz, Carol Stock, 22

lack of understanding, 162–164
Ladd, Gary, 106
lateness as source of stress, 73
leadership opportunities and withdrawn
    behavior, 146
Leahy, Robert L., 209
learned helplessness, 149
Leber, Nancy, 206
*Let's Talk Emotions: Helping Children with
    Social Cognitive Deficits, Including AS,*

*HFA, and NVLD, Learn to Understand
    and Express Empathy and Emotions*
    (Cardon), 208
limited impulse control, 11
Lisovskis, Marjorie, 207
Logan, Gaea, 205, 206
low self-esteem, 18
lunch
    alternative, 64–65
    social anxiety, 70
    social demands, 64–65
    social exclusion, 64
    supervision during, 176
lunch buddies permission form, 211
lunch groups, 64–65, 70

MAC (Massachusetts Advocates for Chil-
    dren), 171
major depressive disorder, 131
maladaptive behaviors and
    underdeveloped skill, 13
managing antecedents, 28–29
mania and hypersexuality, 161
Mannarino, Anthony P., 209
Massachusetts Advocates for Children. *See*
    MAC (Massachusetts Advocates for
    Children)
masturbation, 165, 184–185
math Web sites, 218
Mayer, G. Roy, 33, 68, 99, 136, 173, 174
McAfee, Jeanette L., 207
McKay, Matthew, 205, 208
medication and disruptive students, 2
mental health
    children, 1
    evaluation for behavioral problems, 4
Merrell, Kenneth W., 79, 81, 208
misbehavior as symptom of underlying
    cause, 13–15
misperceived social interaction Web sites,
    214

mobile device applications for self-regulation, thought stopping, and self-monitoring, 218
mobile devices, 142
modifications, 35–36
    sexualized behavior, 175–180
multisensory lessons, 140
My Book Full of Feelings: How to Control and React to the Size of Your Emotions (Jaffe and Gardner), 208
Myles, Brenda Smith, 206

narrating student's experience, 146–147
"Naturally Occurring Opportunities for Preschool Children With or Without Disabilities to Make Choices," 110
Navigating the Social World (McAfee, Davies, and Future Horizons Inc.), 207
negative attention, 17–18, 113, 164, 181
    desirability, 18–19
    impulsiveness, 171
    low self-esteem, 18
    negative behavior, 181
    obviousness, 18
    oppositional behavior, 96, 111, 115–116
    reasons for, 17
    repetition prevention, 17
    response strategies, 115–116, 150
    sexualized behavior, 172
    social deficits, 18, 171
    withdrawn behavior, 150
negative behavior
    negative attention, 181
    reducing, 148
negative response and social interaction, 164
negative statements, 148–149
negative thoughts, 133–134, 205–206
The New Social Story Book (Gray), 207
noncompliance, 116–118
    frequent or severe, 94
    traditional ways teachers interact with, 38

noncontingent reinforcement, 82–83, 112–113, 145
non preferred subject, embedding reinforcing activity within, 100
nonverbal attention, 17
nonverbal language disability and anxiety, 47
nonverbal learning disorder. *See* NVLD (nonverbal learning disorder)
normative childhood sexualized behavior, 158–159
No Such Thing As a Bad Kid (Appelstein), 106
NVLD (nonverbal learning disorder), 162
    anxiety and, 47

The Oasis Guide to Asperger's Syndrome: Advice, Support, Insight, and Inspiration (Bashe and Kirby), 78
obsessions, 47
OCD (obsessive-compulsive disorder), 47–48
    perfectionists, 71
104 Activities That Build: Self-Esteem, Teamwork, Communication, Anger Management, Self-Discovery, and Coping Skills (Jones), 208
oppositional behavior, 3, 32, 41, 91–125
    ABC format, 97
    academic expectations, 103
    accommodations, 100–105, 123–124
    accurately monitoring, 104
    ADD (attention deficit disorder), 93–94
    ADHD (attention deficit hyperactivity disorder), 93
    aggression, 95
    all-or-nothing thinking, 95
    alternating nonpreferred and preferred activities, 100
    alternative lunch or recess, 101
    anger resources, 207–208

antecedent analysis, 97–100
anxiety, 92
arguing with teachers, 95
attempting to escape teachers' demands, 96
attention, 96, 98, 111–112, 118, 125
attributes of student with, 94–95
authority and, 108
behaviors, 97
blaming others, 105
breaks, 100–101
bullying, 95
calming box, 102
causes, 92–94
challenging questions, 114–115
choice, 109
chronically oppositional profiles, 49
cognitively inflexible, 94–95
complying with authority, 100
consequences, 115
control, 94–95, 108
curriculum, 103–104, 123–124
declarative language, 109, 111
definition of, 92
delayed gratification, 102
desirable behaviors, 95
difficulty playing games, 105
disorders associated with, 93
distractions, 102
environment, 100–102, 123
escalating, 95
escape, 96, 98, 118, 125
evaluation, 93
executive functioning, 103, 123
explosive and aggressive, 97
extended time to comply, 111
FAIR Plan (functional hypothesis, ac-
    commodations, interaction strategies,
    and responses strategies), 92, 97–119
family violence, 93
flexibility, 100, 118
foster care, 93
frequent moves, 93

functional hypothesis, 97–100, 122
functions of, 95–96
giving demands strategies, 108–111, 125
hands-on projects, 103
humor, 113
impulsiveness, 95
inconsistent or harsh discipline, 93, 95
indifference to consequences, 95
inflexible thinking, 94, 102
information seeking questions, 114
initiating task, 102
interaction strategies, 105–113, 124–125
intermittent reinforcement, 112
interpreting social information, 95
intervention plan, 122–125
less preferred activities, 100
low frustration tolerance, 49
negative attention, 96, 111, 115–116
noncompliance, 94, 116–118
noncontingent reinforcement, 112–113
one-on-one relationship-building
    activities, 106–108
open-ended demands, 103–104
oppositional defiant disorder, 93
organized safety plan, 97
patterns, 97
peer conflict, 95
perceptions, 106
positive attention, 106, 112
power struggle, 108
preventing, 92
processing behavior incident, 105
reinforcing appropriate behavior, 111–113
relationship building, 105–106
reminding of rules and expectations,
    110–111
replacement behaviors, 124
response strategies, 114–119, 125
responsibility for behavior, 104–105
rewards, 115
schools reactive to, 105
self-monitoring, 124

oppositional behavior, *continued*
  self-monitoring resources, 206–207
  self-regulating, 104, 124
  self-regulation resources, 206–207
  self-talk, 103
  setting events, 97
  setting limits, 114–115
  social skills, 94–95, 101, 105
  social skills resources, 207
  structured and predictable environment,
    100
  tangible motivation, 96, 98
  tangible-reward-motivated behavior, 118,
    125
  targeted behaviors, 122
  transitions, 102
  underdeveloped skills, 104–105, 123–124
  unproductive patterns, 92
  unstructured time, 101–102
  visual schedules, 103
  waiting, 102
  warning signs, 96–97
oppositional defiant disorder, 93
organization
  anxiety, 72–73
  depression, 138
outbursts and anxiety-related behavior, 44
*The Out-of-Sync Child: Recognizing and
    Coping with Sensory Integration
    Dysfunction* (Kranowitz), 22
overactive fight-or-flight response, 14
overgeneralized anxiety, 169

panic disorder, 47–48
parents. *See* families
patterns, 22–24, 32
  antecedents, 23, 33, 35, 66, 98, 135, 172
  consequences, 33, 135, 172
  inappropriate behavior, 66
  oppositional behavior, 97
  responses, 23

peers
  aggressive behavior with, 106
  interactions, 9
  personal space, 183–184
  suicide, 200
perfectionists, 50, 71, 74
personalized handshake, 180–181
personal space, 176, 183–184
*Personal Space Camp Activity and Idea
    Book* (Cook and Hartman), 210
Peterson, Robert F., 33, 68, 99, 136, 173,
    174
phobias, 48, 52–53
physical exercise and depression, 142
Pianta, Robert, 145
playing games with peers Web sites,
    214–215
play therapy, 132
positive attention, 17, 112–113, 164
positive feedback, 146
positive opposites, 105
positive reinforcement, 82–83
  withdrawn behavior, 145
positive relationships, 38
positive self-talk, 134–135
positive self-talk resources, 208
positive social interactions, 149
positive thinking and withdrawn behavior,
    140
post-traumatic stress disorder. *See* PTSD
    (post-traumatic stress disorder)
*Power Cards: Using Special Interests to
    Motivate Children and Youth with
    Asperger Syndrome and Autism*
    (Gagnon), 208
power cards and depression, 134
power struggle, 108
praising, 112
  withdrawn behavior, 145
predictability, 50
predictable behavior patterns and anxiety,
    52–54

preemptive strategies, 27
preschooler normative sexual behaviors, 158–159
previewing and anxiety, 76
privileges, 182
problematic behavior, 16
Project Adventure (Fersch, Smith, and Hamilton-Wenham Regional High School), 207
prompting student effectively, 149
proprioceptive exercises, 142
    withdrawn behavior, 144
proprioceptive input-seeking behaviors, 21
proprioceptive sense, 21
prosocial behavior, 106
psychiatric disorders
    depressive or withdrawn behavior, 129
    treatable, 93
PTSD (post-traumatic stress disorder), 46–48, 52
Pudney, Warwick, 207
purposeful actions, 15
Pyramid Educational Consultants, Inc., 75, 79, 139

quiet space, 199

random acts of kindness, 112–113, 145
reaction strategy, 27
reading emotions Web sites, 213
Reavis, H. K., 112
recess
    alternative, 64–65
    blind spots, 176
recognizing depression, 128–134
record setting events and withdrawn behavior, 135
reflection sheet, 142, 143
reframing withdrawn behavior, 148
reinforcing appropriate behavior, 23, 29

oppositional behavior, 111–113
relationship building, 38–39
    activities, 113
    family, 197
    indirect way of, 144–145
    interaction strategies, 105–106, 144–145
    narrating during, 145
    oppositional behavior, 105–106
    withdrawn behavior, 144–145
relationships, positive, 38
relationship sabotage, 39
repetitive behavior, 16, 21
repetitive questions, 114–115
replacement behaviors, 12, 83
    accommodations, 88, 124, 154, 188
    attention-motivated behaviors, 88
    desired outcome efficiency, 29–30
    eliminating inappropriate behavior, 30
    escape-motivated behavior, 77
    oppositional behavior, 124
    sexualized behavior, 188
    withdrawn behavior, 154
resiliency resources and sexualized behavior, 209–210
responses
    breaking cycle with, 40
    escape-motivated behavior, 83
    inappropriate behavior, 30–31, 83
    matching function of behavior, 40
    minimizing, 182
    patterns, 23
response strategies, 3–4, 40–41
    accommodations, 189
    anxiety-related behavior, 83–84, 89
    attention-motivated behavior, 118
    escape-motivated behavior, 89–90, 118
    impulsiveness, 182–183
    negative-attention-seeking behavior, 115–116, 150
    noncompliance, 116–118
    oppositional behavior, 114–119, 125
    sexualized behavior, 182–183, 189

response strategies, *continued*
  social deficits, 182–183
  social misperception, 150
  tangible-reward-motivated behavior, 118
  touching adults inappropriately, 182–185
  withdrawn behavior, 150, 155
rewards
  oppositional behavior, 115
  self-calming strategies, 83–84
role-playing, 112, 141
  depression, 134
Room 14: A Social Language Program (Wilson), 207
rule-breaking behavior, 181
rules of body space resources and sexualized behavior, 210
Russell, David, 209

SAD (separation anxiety disorder), 45–46, 48
safe space, 78
  best use of, 199
  sexualized behavior, 177
Sahd, Tiffany, 144
sample ABC (antecedent, behavior, and consequence) data sheet, 203–204
sarcasm, 113
Saunders, D., 144
The Scared Child: Helping Kids Overcome Traumatic Events (Brooks and Siegel), 210
Schelvan, Ronda L., 206
school counselor, 5
school mental health clinician, 5, 132
School Outfitters Web site, 81
schools
  anxiety and behavioral attributes, 55
  disruptive behavior, 92
  oppositional behavior, 105
  physical contact between teachers and students, 180

punishing undesired behavior, 17
  social workers, 5
  trauma-sensitive environments, 171
self-advocacy and withdrawn behavior, 140
self-calming, 14
  positive practice of, 78
  sexualized behavior, 178
  teaching, 80
self-calming strategies, 78
  rewards, 83–84
self-concept, 18
self-defeating thoughts, 81
self-esteem building, 82–83
self-monitoring
  accommodations, 89, 124, 141–142, 154, 178–180, 188
  masturbation, 185
  mobile devices, 142, 218
  oppositional behavior, 124
  reflection sheet, 142, 143
  sexualized behavior, 178–180, 188
  withdrawn behavior, 141–142, 154
self-monitoring resources, 205–206
  oppositional behavior, 206–207
self-monitoring sheet, 178, 223–225
self-regulating, 14
  accommodations, 89, 124, 141–142, 154, 178–180, 188
  anxiety, 77
  mobile device applications, 218
  mobile devices, 142
  oppositional behavior, 124, 206–207
  resources, 205–206
  sexual abuse, 169
  sexualized behavior, 178–180, 188
  skills, 30
  transitions, 56
  withdrawn behavior, 141–142, 154
Self-Regulation for Kids K-12: Strategies for Calming Minds and Behavior (Tollison, Synatschk, and Logan), 205, 206

self-regulation strategies
    multiple, 199
    oppositional behavior, 104
    reinforcing, 115
self-soothing and sexualized behavior, 159
self-talk and oppositional behavior, 103
self-worth, 145
sensory function, 20–21
sensory input, 21
sensory-seeking behavior, 21
separation anxiety, 47
separation anxiety disorder. *See* SAD
    (separation anxiety disorder)
setting events, 23–24, 35
    oppositional behavior, 97
    recording, 66
    sexualized behavior, 172
Severe Behavior Problems: A Functional
    Communication Training Approach
    (Durand), 16, 22
sexual abuse, 160–161, 167–170
sexual attention, 167
sexual comments, 163
sexualized behavior, 3, 32, 157–185
    ABC format, 171–175
    acceptable behavior, 175
    accommodations, 175–180, 188
    ADD (attention deficit disorder), 165
    adult sexual behavior, 159–160
    Alert Program, 178, 180
    antecedent analysis, 171–175
    anxiety, 159
    appropriate behavior, 162–164
    attention-seeking, 159, 183
    awareness of others resources, 209
    awareness of whom the student can
        touch resources, 210
    bathroom supervision, 176–177
    behavior intervention plan, 187–189
    body space, 177–178
    boys versus girls, 160
    breaks, 178
    causes of, 159–171
    coaching other students about, 166
    cognitive behavior therapy strategies, 178
    craving contact, 180
    criminal sexual offenders, 158
    defining, 157–158
    disruptive behavior, 160
    dysregulated, 180
    emotional response to, 164, 170
    emotional thermometer, 178
    environment, 175–177, 188
    expressing frustration, 164
    FAIR Plan (functional hypothesis, ac-
        commodations, interaction strategies,
        and responses strategies), 171–183
    family adversity, 159
    functional hypothesis, 171–175, 187
    hugging, 180–181
    imitation, 159
    impulse control resources, 210
    impulsiveness, 158, 160, 165–167,
        182–183
    increased supervision for, 176–177
    interaction strategies, 180–181, 189
    interventions, 161
    lack of understanding, 162–164
    life changes, 172
    masturbation, 184–185
    minimizing attention, 175
    modifications, 175–180
    negative attention, 172
    negative emotional impact, 162–164
    normative childhood, 158–159
    other students' reactions, 177
    out-of-district placement, 158
    overstimulation, 159–160
    personalized handshake, 180–181
    personal space, 167, 176, 183–184
    reasons for, 158
    recess, 176
    replacement behaviors, 188
    resiliency resources, 209–210

sexualized behavior, *continued*
  response strategies, 182–183, 189
  rules of body space resources, 210
  safe place, 177
  safety reflexes, 167–168
  self-calming, 178
  self-contained classroom, 158
  self-monitoring, 178–180, 188
  self-regulating, 178–180, 188
  self-soothing, 159
  separating students with, 175
  setting events, 172
  sexual abuse, 159–161
  sexualized statements, 182
  social deficits, 158, 162–164, 182–183
  social interaction resources, 209
  social skill deficits, 160
  taking another person's perspective
    resources, 209
  targeted behaviors, 178, 187
  touching adults inappropriately, 182–185
  trauma, 158, 160, 167–171
  triggers, 168–169
  underdeveloped skills, 177–178, 188
  zero-tolerance policy, 171
sexual language, 164, 182
Shellenberger, Sherry, 206, 207
should-be trap, 81
shutdown behavior, 24
Siegel, Paula M., 210
skills, 10
  accommodations, 36, 37
  reinforcing, 115
  self-calming, 14
  self-regulating, 14, 30
  underdeveloped, 30, 35, 37
Smith, Mary, 207
social anxiety and alternative lunch, 70
social anxiety disorder, 46
Social Behavior Mapping (Winner), 207
social deficits
  anxiety, 47

appropriate behavior, 163
Asperger's syndrome, 162
autism spectrum disorder, 162
diagnosis of, 50
inappropriate comments, 163
negative attention, 18, 171
nonverbal language disabilities, 162
response strategies, 182–183
sexual comments, 163
sexualized behavior, 158, 162–164,
  182–183
social cues, 162–163
social interactions rules, 162
social demands, 64–65
social exclusion, 64
social interactions, 164
  positive, 149
  resources and sexualized behavior, 209
*Socially ADDept: Teaching Social Skills
  to Children with ADHD, LD, and
  Asperger's* (Giler), 206
social misperception, 150
social phobia, 46, 48
social skills
  acceptable personal space, 177
  deficits and sexualized behavior, 160
  depression, 134
  friendship group, 141
  lacking basic, 14
  oppositional behavior, 95, 105
  role-playing, 141
*Social Skills Picture Book: Teaching
  Communication, Play and Emotion*
  (Baker), 207
social skills resources
  anxiety-related behavior, 206
  oppositional behavior, 207
  withdrawn behavior, 208–209
*Social Skills Training & Frustration
  Management* (Baker and Future
  Horizons Inc.), 209
social skills Web sites, 212–213

special education and disruptive behavior, 92

spelling, 74

staff
  awareness of students' triggers, 169
  responses reinforcing escape, 66
  supporting teacher with challenging student, 194

"Stop, Think, Do" Web site, 210

Stop and Think: Impulse Control (Caselman), 210

"Strategies for Sensory Success," 144

stress
  challenging behaviors, 193
  overreactive response to, 49
  oversensitivity to, 14
  writing and, 73–74

strictness, 39

structured breaks, 101

structured tasks, 57–58

students
  accommodations, 35–37
  anxiety-related behavior, 43–89
  control of, 24
  current internal state, 10
  detecting teachers' negative feelings, 106
  disruptive, 92
  E/BD (emotional and behavioral disturbance), 7
  emotional and behavioral disability, 13
  environmental events or conditions, 23–24
  inappropriate behavior, 8, 10
  known trauma history, 183–185
  low expectations, 38
  not trusting teacher, 38
  oppositional behavior, 91–125
  relationship building with, 38–39
  replacement behavior, 12
  setting up for success, 58–60
  sexualized behavior, 157–185
  special treatment, 198

suicide, 199–200
  touching adults inappropriately, 183–185
  withdrawn behavior, 127–155

Study in Scarlet (Doyle), 35

suicide, 133, 199–200

Sulzer-Azaroff, Beth, 33, 68, 99, 136, 173, 174

Super Skills: A Social Skills Group Program for Children with Asperger Syndrome, High-Functioning Autism and Related Challenges (Coucouvanis), 208

symmetry urges, 47

Synatschk, Katherine O., 205, 206

tactile hypersensitivity, 21

taking another person's perspective resources and sexualized behavior, 209

Taking Depression to School (Korb-Khalsa), 208

Taking Responsibility for Choices Worksheet, 226–227

talking back and anxiety, 50

tangible function, 19

tangible motivation and oppositional behavior, 96, 98, 118

tangibly motivated behavior, 19–20, 118, 125

targeted behaviors, 32
  oppositional behavior, 122
  sexualized behavior, 187
  withdrawn behavior, 152

Task Force on Children with Sexual Behavior Problems, 159

teachers
  ABC data, 32–35
  administrative support, 193–194
  behavioral strategies and, 63
  caring for themselves during school year, 191
  challenging behaviors and, 2, 191–193
  changing dynamic with student, 24

teachers, *continued*
conflict relationships with, 38
controlling their own behaviors, 24
disruptive students, 194
empowering, 24, 40–41
exercise, 193
explosive incidents, 195–196
fairness and, 198
flexible, 28
giving demands strategies, 108–111
healthy boundaries, 192
helping hospitalized student return to
school, 200–201
inappropriate behavior, 40
interactions, 114
interpreting students' behavior, 12
interventions, 11
listening and validating concerns, 197–198
noncompliant students, 38
pessimistic attitude, 192
pressures faced by, 2, 194
preventative strategies, 63
random acts of kindness by, 83
rating student's behavior, 84
replacement behaviors, 10
reporting to parents, 197–198
responses, 40, 66
scheduling breaks, 193
self-care tips, 192–193
staff and, 193
stress, 193
suicide, 199–200
teaching
self-calming strategies, 78
underdeveloped skills, 30, 83, 88–89
*Teaching Children Empathy: The Social
Emotion: Lessons, Activities and
Reproducible Worksheets (K-6) That
Teach How to "Step into Other's Shoes"*
(Caselman), 207
Teaching Students to be Peacemakers
(Johnson and Johnson), 207

teams, 5
technology and escape-motivated
behavior, 104
technology support
audio books and e-books Web sites,
215–216
behavior reinforcement Web sites, 218–219
emotional regulation Web sites, 214
executive functioning Web sites, 219
free literacy tools Web sites, 216
math Web sites, 218
misperceived social interaction Web
sites, 214
mobile device applications for self-
regulation, thought stopping, and self-
monitoring, 218
playing games with peers Web sites,
214–215
reading emotions Web sites, 213
social skills Web sites, 212–213
writing Web sites, 216–217
Thinking About You, Thinking About Me
(Winner), 206, 208, 209
thinking on the downside, 133
thinking traps, 81, 133–134
thinking traps resources and withdrawn
behavior, 208
*Think Right, Feel Right: The Building Block
Guide for Happiness and Emotional
Well-Being* (Isett and Isett), 210
*Think Social! A Social Thinking Cur-
riculum for School-Age Students: For
Teaching Social Thinking and Related
Social Skills to Students with High
Functioning Autism, Asperger Syndrome, PDD-NOS, ADHD, Nonverbal
Learning Disability and for All Others
in the Murky Gray Area of Social
Thinking* (Winner), 205, 206, 209, 210
thought stopping, 134
instruction, 81
mobile device applications, 218

thought-stopping resources and withdrawn behavior, 208
time-out room, 78
timers, 71, 181
Time Timers, 71
token board, 181
Tollison, Patricia K., 205, 206
touching themselves, 165
traditional interactions with noncompliant students, 38
transitions and anxiety, 55–58
trauma
 emotional response to students, 170
 extra personal space, 181
 hypervigilance, 175
 inappropriate close relationships, 168
 sexual abuse, 167
 sexualized behavior, 158, 160, 167–171
 shame associated with, 181
 triggers, 168–169
trauma-sensitive school environments, 171
traumatic play, 46
Trautman, Melissa, 206
treatable psychiatric disorders, 93
Treating Trauma and Traumatic Grief in Children and Adolescents (Cohen, Deblinger, and Mannarino), 209
trigger-free environment, 168
triggers, 168–169, 177

underdeveloped skills, 13, 35, 77–82, 104–105
 accommodations, 123–124, 140–141, 154, 177–178
 identifying, 94
 inappropriate behavior, 37
 oppositional behavior, 123–124
 sexualized behavior, 177–178
 social skills, 94
 teaching, 30, 83, 88–89, 154, 188
 training, 77–82, 104–105, 140–141

withdrawn behavior, 140–141, 154
unstructured times, 53
unsuccessful intervention, 11
unwanted behavior, 23
 secret signals about, 184–185

verbal attention, 17
Verdick, Elizabeth, 207
vestibular sense, 21
visible disability, 13
visual schedules
 anxiety, 72
 oppositional behavior, 103
visual timers, 71
A Volcano in My Tummy: Helping Children to Handle Anger; A Resource Book for Parents, Caregivers and Teachers (Pudney and Whitehouse), 207

Walker-Hirsch, Leslie, 210
walking-with-blinders trap, 81
Washington Parent, 144
Web sites
 audio books and e-books, 215–216
 behavior reinforcement, 218–219
 emotional regulation, 214
 executive functioning, 219
 free literacy tools, 216
 math, 218
 misperceived social interaction, 214
 playing games with peers, 214–215
 reading emotions, 213
 social skills, 212–213
 writing, 216–217
"what's the use" syndrome, 149
Whitehouse, Elaine, 207
Williams, Mary Sue, 206, 207
Wilson, Carolyn C., 207
Winner, Michelle Garcia, 205, 206, 207, 208, 209, 210

withdrawn behavior, 3, 32, 41, 127–155
   See also depression
   ABC data sheet, 135–136
   accommodations, 137–144, 153–154
   alerting strategies, 142, 144
   antecedent analysis, 135–137
   antecedents, 135
   anxiety, 128
   behavior intervention plan, 152–155
   buddy system, 138
   calm space, 137–138
   cognitive behavioral strategies, 133–134
   cognitive flexibility, 141
   communication, 132
   consequences, 135
   curriculum, 139–140, 153
   depression and, 128–134
   distracting other students, 128
   environment, 137–138, 153
   executive functioning, 138–139, 141, 153
   FAIR Plan (functional hypothesis, ac-
     commodations, interaction strategies,
     and responses strategies), 134
   functional hypothesis, 135–137, 152
   humor, 145
   interaction strategies, 144–149, 154–155
   leadership opportunities, 146
   major life change, 128
   multisensory lessons, 140
   narrating student's experience, 146–147
   negative attention, 150
   negative perceptions, 148–149
   positive feedback, 146
   positive reinforcement, 145
   positive self-talk resources, 208
   positive thinking, 140
   praising, 145
   prompting student, 149
   proprioceptive exercises, 142, 144
   record setting events, 135
   reframing, 148
   relationship building, 144–145
   replacement behaviors, 154
   response strategies, 150, 155
   self-advocacy, 140
   self-monitoring, 141–142, 154
   self-regulating, 141–142, 154
   social misperception, 150
   social skills, 141
   social skills resources, 208–209
   targeted behaviors, 152
   teacher and counselor collaboration, 132
   technology and, 140
   thinking traps resources, 208
   thought-stopping resources, 208
   trauma, 128, 131
   underdeveloped skills, 140–141, 154
Wood, Jeffrey C., 205
word processing, 74
writing, 73–75
writing Web sites, 216–217